★ ★ ★ ★ ★

FIVE STARS FOR
FIVE LEAGUE TITLES AND A PACKET OF CRISPS

'A great read from a great player.
Some of the stories are hilarious.'

'Took this book away on a two-week holiday. Couldn't put it
down and ended up finishing it after two days. Great insight
into an LFC legend in the 80s and 90s.'

'This is one of the best autobiographies I've read in a long
time and I thoroughly recommend it. Enjoy!'

'A must-buy for any Liverpool fan who saw the great teams
of the Eighties. Go and buy this book and enjoy the days
when footballers were normal people.'

'I've read a lot of autobiographies by ex-Liverpool players
and *5 League Titles and a Packet of Crisps: My Autobiography* is the
funniest of them all. Not only was Steve Nicol a brilliant
footballer, the antics he got up to are almost unbelievable.'

'Superb book, great stories, excellently written.
Stevie's character shines through.'

'Brilliant nostalgic read. Thanks Nico. Carefully put together
and very easy to read. I was there in all the pages in my head.'

STEVIE
NICOL
MY AUTOBIOGRAPHY

5 League titles and a Packet of crisps

Sport Media Ⓢ

To Eleanor, Michael and Katy.

Sport Media

Written with Mark Donaldson.

Paperback published in Great Britain and Ireland in 2017 by
Trinity Mirror Sport Media, PO Box 48, Old Hall Street, Liverpool, L69 3EB.

www.tmsportmedia.com
@SportMediaTM

Trinity Mirror Sport Media is a part of Trinity Mirror plc.
One Canada Square, Canary Wharf, London, E15 5AP.

1

Hardback ISBN: 978-1-910335-32-1
Trade paperback ISBN 978-1-910335-65-9
eBook ISBN 978-1-908319-66-1

Photographic acknowledgements:
Front cover image: Colorsport/REX/Shutterstock
Other images: Trinity Mirror, PA Photos, SNS (Ayr United),
Steve Nicol personal collection.

Book editing: Paul Dove
Production: Michael McGuinness, Chris McLoughlin
Cover design: Rick Cooke

Printed and bound by CPI Group (UK) Ltd, Croydon, CR0 4YY.

Contents

CONTENTS

Foreword

By Alan Hansen

Steve Nicol was a fantastic footballer. I knew he was good, but it wasn't until I first played alongside him at centre-back that I realised just how good he was. You can tell within five minutes if somebody can play there or not and he was absolutely seamless. When I got injured, he replaced me in the centre of defence and was named Footballer of the Year in 1989 – a tremendous accolade.

And what about his versatility? Phenomenal. I think left-back was his best position, he was really comfortable there. But in my opinion he was the best right-back that Liverpool had. Some people might argue with that because Phil Neal was a phenomenal player, and I don't want to decry Phil, but I think Nico just shaded him as Liverpool's best right-back. I once said on Match of the Day that the best left-back and right-back of the season was Denis Irwin, and you could describe Nico like that as well. The best left-back and right-back was the same player.

I used to love playing at left centre-back when Nico was at left-back, he just instinctively knew what to do. That really speaks volumes because going from right to left is not easy – some people think it is but it's not. Going from left to right centre-back is hard enough, but going from right-back to left-báck and then maybe to right-midfield – it's not easy at all. But he always made it look easy.

When you look closely at Liverpool and their success in the Eighties, I actually think Nico was a bit unlucky because of his versatility. He played right-back, left-back, right-midfield, left-midfield and he scored goals – including that hat-trick at

Newcastle – but if he had only played one position throughout his career then I'm sure he would have been rated even higher than he is.

He played a tremendous part in the vast majority of our successes at Liverpool, and being able to do that as a utility player is, in my opinion, an even bigger accomplishment. His consistency was exceptional season after season and if you've got the ability to play four or five positions as well as anybody else then you're a special type of player. Nico really was a special player.

'Bumper' was also a great teammate and so much fun in the dressing room. He was a character and used to mimic people all the time, and he never stopped laughing.

Nico was hammered early on in his Liverpool career, we used to constantly take the mick, but then he sort of caught on a bit and started to join in. He was such fun, great to be around, but when the serious stuff came he was right at it. You were allowed to have a laugh and a joke at Liverpool but when it was time to knuckle down, if you weren't producing then basically you didn't last long. It was as simple as that. Nico was there constantly, one of the first names on the teamsheet, and he was invaluable. He was a great addition on every level to Liverpool Football Club.

Stevie's a bit of a scatterbrain but that only added to his persona. His wife Ellie had to organise him, do this and that for him, and he was always getting things wrong and saying the wrong things. He'd only been at the club for nine months when Bob Paisley came in to the dressing room one day with brown envelopes containing tax demands. We told Nico it was something else – so he went to see Bob effectively demanding a tax demand. You couldn't make it up. To be fair to him, year after year he got sharper and sharper, although I'm still not sure that's much of a compliment!

He also used to forget things. After we won the European Cup in Rome we went to Swaziland (back in the days when your entire reservation was a paper ticket) and at the end of the trip the whole squad was gathered at the airport ready to fly home. The travel agent passed around all the tickets then said 'Steve Nicol, you've got your own because you came out separately from the rest of the boys.' His response of 'what do you mean, I threw it away after I got here' – absolutely phenomenal. The boys were in stitches.

The fancy dress contest on a Norwegian cruise we were on in 1983 was his finest moment. The ship's director of entertainment came to me and asked if I would judge a competition they were having. I said I didn't fancy it, but I told him I knew just the person who would. After going to see Nico the guy came back to me twenty minutes later and he was really excited… "Not only is Steve going to judge it but he's going to dress up as well."

Nico obviously got dressed up thinking it was a competition for adults and he would get in the swing of things. He walked in and there were seats for three judges – two of them were occupied, one by a guy in his mid-eighties and the other by a woman in her mid-eighties. The third seat was for him, a 21-year-old who was more than sixty years younger than his judging colleagues.

The boy gave him the grand announcement – 'Steve Nicol, Liverpool legend, you'll see him now but you'll never see him like this again.' Ellie was sitting with us. I asked her what was wrong – she said 'wait til you see him when he comes out.'

He'd dressed up as a woman and he came in to the room wearing a pale green dress and carrying a bottle of Budweiser. It was only then – when he saw the room full of kids – that he realised it was a children's fancy dress competition he was judging. The director of entertainment hadn't told him so he never knew. I have never seen anyone so dejected in his life. It was unreal. He was gutted. When I think about it now it's one of the funniest things I've ever seen. Absolutely sensational – just the best – if only I had it on video! That's just one of so many stories about Nico and I look forward to reading his version of the rest of them in this book.

When I told the boys I was taking over from Kenny as manager in 1991, and said to Nico that I wanted him to be my captain, I'm sure he'll try to say in this book that he knew it was a prank. But he didn't know. None of them knew. I had to put a stop to the wind-up when I saw two Irish kids, a couple of the lads on the groundstaff, running past me in the corridor on their way to the players' lounge to use the one public phone we had at the club. They were talking about calling home to Dublin and telling family and friends to 'get as much money as you possibly can' on Alan Hansen to be the next manager of Liverpool Football Club! None of the players knew it was a prank – even if Nico claims he did – and it was one of the finest wind-ups. It was my parting gift to my teammates and I announced my retirement at a press conference a few hours later.

I don't think in the ten years we were together at Liverpool there was one person who ever said a bad word about Nico. Every day when we got on the bus to go to Melwood – we would always sit in the same seats – I would get him going and then he'd give a rendition of an irate Scottish football supporter, and he was sensational by the way: 'Ball up the park Scotland!' or 'that's rubbish Scotland!' – he was absolutely brilliant at it and he used to have the bus in hysterics.

The team spirit at Liverpool was always fantastic and people genuinely liked Nico. He never failed to make us laugh. Human nature may dictate that not everyone is going to like each other but I can't ever remember one person saying a bad word about him. They used to say he was daft, but it was always said in a nice way.

Steve Nicol was one of the best players that ever pulled on the red jersey of Liverpool Football Club.

Alan Hansen,
May 2016

Acknowledgements

A few thank yous…

To Alan Hansen for agreeing to write the foreword.

To Mark Donaldson, my ESPN colleague, fellow Scot and ghostwriter, for all of his hard work. Mark has done a fantastic job over the past two years or so, listening to my stories and putting it all together in this book.

To all my teammates, particularly those at Ayr United and Liverpool, and the boys in the bootroom at Anfield. And to Gerry Marsden for singing You'll Never Walk Alone at my testimonial – that was special.

Thanks also to Paul Dove and the rest of the team at the publishers, Trinity Mirror Sport Media.

And lastly to Kenny, Big Al and Souey – thanks for taking the piss.

Steve Nicol

Prologue:
I'll Never Walk Alone

When you walk through a storm
Hold your head up high
And don't be afraid of the dark...

That song. Those lyrics. The history. From the time it starts to the moment it ends all you think about is Liverpool Football Club and what it means to everybody.

Every time I hear it I get goose pimples and a lump in my throat. It's our song. It belongs at Liverpool because − and this probably sounds daft − there's no way it could possibly have the same meaning or impact at any other club. It's Liverpool Football Club in a nutshell.

What does 'You'll Never Walk Alone' mean to me? Well, it makes me think of Hillsborough. All the sad things that happened, but the positive things as well. Like being able to help those affected. Eleanor and me − we can't listen to it without getting emotional. Just too many memories come flooding back. It's a sentimental anthem. It's also a poignant anthem.

When a choral arrangement of the song was played at the first Hillsborough Memorial Service at Liverpool's Anglican Cathedral two weeks after the tragedy there wasn't a dry eye in the church. It was already our anthem but from that day forward it would also be forever associated with the healing process. "We've always sung it but it's more meaningful now," said Margaret Aspinall, the chair of the Hillsborough Family Support Group. "We've never walked alone, we have had support from everywhere."

That will always be the case, Margaret.

It also takes me back to when I was younger, watching black and white footage of the Liverpool greats of years gone by. Ron Yeats, the Saint, Tommy Smith, Chris Lawler. And Gerry Byrne playing in the Cup Final with a broken collarbone. Then watching Toshack and Keegan in colour. Alec Lindsay, Terry Mac, Steve Heighway and Ray between the sticks. Alan Kennedy and Jimmy Case. Those European Cups.

Joining the club in 1981 and wondering what part, if any, I'd be able to play. Would I be a help or a hindrance? Kenny, Big Al, Souey, Thommo, Sammy, Lawro, Rushy, Ronnie Whelan, Bruce and Phil Neal, who just never gave the ball away, plus all the others. Then the Barnes era with Beardsley, Aldridge and Houghton followed by the emergence of the young guns – Fowler, McManaman, Gerrard and Carragher.

No matter who or when – every Liverpool player over the last fifty years will have his own story, his own description of what 'You'll Never Walk Alone' means to him.

The routine was always the same for home games. Down the steps, touch the sign – 'THIS IS ANFIELD' – and then, once everyone was on the pitch, match announcer George Sephton would start the song. It gave us all a huge lift, it is the club anthem after all, but I honestly think you can only properly appreciate 'You'll Never Walk Alone' when you're not playing. It's much easier to take everything in – the emotion and the passion – if you're a substitute and sat on the bench or in the stands and not actually part of the action.

In those two minutes and thirty-eight seconds of the song you're taken from the Shankly era to modern day Liverpool Football Club. It pulls at you all the way through. It's amazing. Then at the end of the song – every time, without fail – I think 'wow, I was part of that.' I mean how many people in their life get to experience something like that first hand? Not many. I'm very lucky to have had the chance to play such a small part in the club's history.

Up until I joined ESPN as an analyst, I was still in the mindset of the football industry – what happened in the building stayed in the building. It wasn't until three or fours years after being here at ESPN HQ in Bristol, Connecticut when that mindset changed. My job is about opening up, being honest and talking about why things happened – providing an insight – and after being guarded with my comments for so many years, thankfully I became much more comfortable opening up. I've always said I would never write a book but that changed with my new mindset.

A lot of this book, I hope, is humorous – I'm happy to tell all the tales when I ended up being the victim of the many pranks – but it's also provided me with a platform to discuss what happened both at Hillsborough and in the years after.

As I explain in the pages that follow, the players never received counselling but were expected to provide it to the families – so being able to finally write down my thoughts after 27 years has been extremely cathartic.

Don't get me wrong it's been hard, really hard, to open up about something I had never really discussed before but I felt it was a hurdle that I needed to jump. It's been a release for me and also for Eleanor, my wife, and a big weight has been lifted off my shoulders. The Hillsborough verdict came just before publication so I was able to give my reaction to that. Knowing the families finally got justice with the verdict they craved gives me as much satisfaction as anything I achieved in football.

On the whole it's been a really enjoyable process doing this book, remembering all the fun we had at Liverpool as well as the successes. I still laugh at some of the stories even though I was usually the butt of the jokes. I hope you get the same pleasure and enjoyment from reading it as Mark and I got from putting it together over the last couple of years.

Having been away from the club for more than twenty years now the song 'You'll Never Walk Alone' actually means even more to me now than it did then. I may live more than three thousand miles away but every time I watch Liverpool on television and hear it being sung before a game at Anfield I still get shivers.

Absence does indeed make the heart grow fonder.

Steve Nicol,
Connecticut, USA,
May 2016

It's been great fun putting this book together with my ESPN colleague and fellow Scotsman, one of the nicest and most genuine people I've ever met. I'm just glad these stories actually happened because there's no way you could make some of them up!

I asked Stevie not long after he started at ESPN if he thought he'd ever do a book. I'd written a couple of others and wanted to offer my services. 'No chance' was the response. Imagine my surprise when he showed up at my desk at ESPN HQ a few years later, in February 2015, and asked if I wanted to write his autobiography. I said yes straightaway and the whole process has been thoroughly enjoyable. A labour of love.

We first worked together in 2011 commentating on Champions League matches, and always got on well after that, but it wasn't until I went round to his house on a weekly basis to put this book together that I really got to know Steve Nicol the person. I've yet to hear anyone say a bad word about him.

The whole process of putting this book together has been remarkably trouble-free, but that doesn't mean it's not been emotional. Once I knew I was writing it with Stevie I spent several days wondering how best to approach the topic of Hillsborough, something he'd hardly spoken about in public since 1989. As it turned out HE brought up the subject, completely unprompted, during our first meeting at his home. He spoke for 35 minutes. There were tears. I typed for 35 minutes. There were tears. I didn't interrupt him once. I just listened to the outpouring. And typed. I didn't ask any questions. Putting together that Hillsborough chapter? That was hard. Really hard.

Tears have been a regular occurrence over the last eighteen months when we've met in his kitchen, but thankfully the majority of them were tears of laughter because of the stories of pranks and anecdotes that Stevie told.

It's been a real honour to be asked and a privilege to help him put this book together. I hope you enjoy it.

Mark Donaldson,
May 2016

1

The Biggest Feet
In Football

'There are, funnily enough, one or two differences
between the dressing rooms at the Stadio Olimpico in
Rome and Somerset Park in Ayr. But on this occasion
my surroundings didn't matter. I wasn't along just
for the ride. I was there to play my part for Liverpool
in a European Cup final'

My shoe size? I wear a UK 11. The myth that I had unnaturally huge feet began after I started wearing size 12s at Ayr United. The leather in new boots used to be unforgiving and would destroy my feet so I tried going up a size.

'The biggest feet in football' was the headline that accompanied the picture used by one newspaper when I signed for Liverpool in October 1981 – it didn't help that the photo showed my feet virtually touching the camera lens, making my size 11s look gigantic.

Footballers receive letters all the time. Dalglish, Souness, Rush and Hansen used to get regular requests from fans asking for autographs or signed photos. I would receive letters as well, except they were from parents…

'Dear Steve – I need your help. My son has size 13 feet and I can't get shoes to fit him. What do you recommend?'

The older pros at Liverpool used to give the apprentices their new boots to wear in. Billy Stewart, a young goalkeeper at the club, was the same shoe size as me so I used to give him my boots if they felt tight. Billy would always return them the following day, minus the tissue paper from the toe area of course, and they felt great. This routine would carry on every time I got new boots. He never said a word. I was none the wiser.

Two days before the European Cup final in 1984 I received a parcel. Puma had sent me some new boots to wear in Rome. Just before training at Melwood I tried them on. Once again my toes felt crushed.

"I can't believe my fucking luck," I said to Alan Hansen. "New boots from Puma and they've sent me the wrong size." Big Al gave me one of his looks and asked: "Have you taken the paper out?"

Our last training session on English soil before the final was lively. One last opportunity for fringe players to force their way into manager Joe Fagan's thoughts for Rome.

As we were finishing up, the boss suggested having a penalty shoot-out. No pressure, just a light-hearted way to end training while also giving us some practice in the unlikely event that a European Cup final, for the first time ever, was decided by spot kicks. We knew that if the game against Roma did go to penalties, the occasion would take care of itself. It's impossible to replicate the pressure situation of any penalty shoot-out on any training field.

Joe picked five young reserve players at random to go up against the first team. Then he asked us who wanted to take a spot kick. Phil Neal was always going to be one of the five. He was the best at the club and our designated penalty taker. I volunteered to take one of the others.

Goals flew in...and all of them past Bruce Grobbelaar. The kids couldn't miss and Bruce failed to save a single one of their penalties. Unfortunately it wasn't the same story for the senior players. Nineteen year-old goalkeeper Billy Stewart was in inspired form and only conceded once.

Who scored against him? Yours truly. I put it to his right and he went the other way. What did I have to worry about?

With the league title wrapped up, we had travelled to Israel ahead of the European Cup final for a change of scene. Our usual routine was brunch at the hotel, followed by a short stroll to the beach nearby to spend a few hours lazing on the sand with beer in hand and plenty more cans chilling in a giant bin we'd filled with ice.

On one occasion, we packed up a little early so we could go back to the hotel and get changed before going to a local pub to watch the 1984 FA Cup final – Everton against Watford. About an hour after the game, we left the bar. When Bruce saw a local in the street pushing a bicycle, he went over and started a bizarre conversation.

"Can I borrow your bike?" Somehow, with the help of a few hand gestures, the guy understood what he was trying to say and was kind enough to hand it over. Our keeper simply couldn't be arsed walking back to the hotel and wanted to ride instead. He promised the owner his bike would be left at the front of the hotel for him to pick up. Surprise, surprise – when the Israeli arrived at our hotel later that night it was nowhere to be seen and Bruce had no recollection of what he'd done with it. The guy was compensated for the cost of his bike, taking a fair bit extra in local currency for his troubles.

It was that kind of trip. I suppose it was no surprise when things got out of hand one night. We were in a big group enjoying a drink when someone accidentally pushed Rushy in the back, causing him to fall over.

"Who did that?" said David Hodgson before getting involved in a scrap with Ronnie Whelan. Then everyone else got involved. Alan Kennedy tried to break things up, moving in to prevent John McGregor from hitting Rushy, but he got caught with a punch himself and ended up with a black eye.

Word had reached Liverpool Football Club director Syd Moss back at the hotel that there was trouble in the square and it wasn't long before he arrived to see for himself exactly what was going on. He rounded us all up and told us it would probably be best if we made our way back immediately – not so much a suggestion as a club order.

Back at the hotel, Big Al went straight to Kenny and Graeme's room and banged on the door, claiming all hell was breaking loose. That was maybe a slight exaggeration, but the pair of them came out to see what all the fuss was about. Al was the only player in sight – the rest of us were stuck in the lift.

It had stopped working because of the excess weight after all of us piled in at once. So while Al, Kenny and Graeme informed reception what had happened with the elevator we decided to have a drunken singsong, starting with the theme from M*A*S*H – Suicide Is Painless.

Halfway through our version of a second song, the lift doors opened and someone, I can't remember who, landed face down on the landing. Everyone else piled on top of him for a laugh.

I hate to imagine how this must have looked to the hotel staff. The English champions, preparing to play in one of the biggest games of their lives, lying in a drunken heap on the hotel floor? It shouldn't have happened but there was no lasting damage and nobody was seriously hurt.

So far, our little trip to the Middle East had seen Alan Kennedy end up with a black eye; Italian journalists watching us get pissed every night and the team's usual wind-up victim – me – being tricked into thinking that Kenny Dalglish was seriously unwell!

Rome is a busy and noisy city at the best of times. Throw in the staging of a European Cup final featuring the home town team and the place was bedlam. Excited locals everywhere. From the moment we landed, every Italian I saw was wearing Roma colours – and most of them had a smile on their face, all utterly convinced their team was going to win. At home, in their own stadium – what could possibly go wrong?

Knowing this would be the case, the club booked us into a hotel perched up in the hills, about a thirty-minute bus ride from the stadium. Well away from all the madness. A swanky place with great views overlooking the Eternal City. Peace and quiet to prepare for such a huge occasion with no disruptions. That was the plan, anyway.

I slept well the night before the game. I always did. Nerves? Not really. Certainly not enough to prevent me sleeping properly. I'm such a heavy sleeper that I couldn't tell you if

Bruce, my roommate, slept well or not. Dalglish and Souness weren't so lucky, however. "We were up until the early hours, couldn't sleep – fella next door to us had the radio on really loud," Kenny told us at breakfast the next morning.

They had banged on the wall but couldn't stop the noise. Eventually a phone call to reception did the trick and it was switched off. The culprit? Joe Fagan. The boss had only fallen asleep with the radio on.

A little later on, Joe stood up in the hotel dining room after the pre-match meal and mumbled a few words. "They're good, but we are better," he said. "Get an early goal to quieten the home crowd," and "get some rest in the afternoon." Oh, and "make sure you're not late for the bus." That was about it. We didn't need someone to give us a lengthy ra-ra speech. Liverpool was all about responsibility. We knew what we were doing. Players knew their jobs and what was expected. None of the managers I played for at Anfield ever gave a pep talk that made a slight bit of difference to how I played. Watching Braveheart is fantastic, but if it's not inside you, then it's not coming out.

The journey to the stadium got a bit hairy as we approached the Stadio Olimpico. A handful of Roma fans tried to throw stones at our bus, but we had armed security guards accompanying us and things never really got out of hand. I was actually surprised at how few people there were milling around outside on such a big night.

The reason soon became clear when we went inside. Ninety minutes before kick-off and the stadium was already two-thirds full. The atmosphere was fantastic. Liverpool fans were doing their best to try and be heard away to our left as we came out for our first look at the pitch. But the majority of the noise was coming from the Roma supporters occupying the rest of the terracing and the main stand. That noise level increased substantially when they spotted us wandering down the steps from the dressing room. The baddies had arrived, led by tormentor-in-chief Graeme Souness.

Now if there was one person you would want leading you into battle it would be him. Charlie (short for Champagne Charlie after he amassed a rather large drinks bill at the Holiday Inn when he signed for Liverpool) had this look on his face from the moment we arrived at the stadium. He was relishing what lay ahead. Couldn't wait.

Charlie gave the impression that he enjoyed walking into a stadium full of people that hated him. It seemed he got more pleasure turning over opponents that didn't like him. You can imagine what that did for someone like me. I'm looking at our captain and he's got that 'I can't wait for this' look on his face. It fills you up. You know you're going to be okay. The thought of defeat never crosses your mind. Losing was not something that we ever contemplated, even for a second.

After we had acknowledged our families and the Liverpool fans, Charlie beckoned us to follow him as he led us on a walk round the perimeter of the pitch towards the famous Curva Sud, home of the fearsome Roma Ultras.

He wanted to show their supporters that we weren't fazed by the occasion. Like a red rag to a bull. I've never heard noise like it. Gutsy? Yes. Crazy? Of course. But his actions summed him up perfectly. Fearless. I wish I could say the same about me as I attempted to dodge missiles being thrown at us from the terracing.

We headed back inside. Joe named the team about an hour

before kick-off. I was among the substitutes which wasn't a surprise. Of course I would have loved to be in the team but I had only started one game in the previous three and a half months – a two-nil defeat at Southampton in mid-March – and that was only because Souness was unavailable for selection following the death of his mother. I also twisted my ankle in that game at The Dell and was out for nearly a month. During that time the team remained unbeaten, and had also beaten Dinamo Bucharest home and away in the European Cup semi-final, so there was no way the boss was going to change a winning side.

With the European Cup final less than 45 minutes away, most of us were pretty relaxed.

None more so than Big Al who was sitting in his suit reading a newspaper. It wasn't until Joe came over and asked: "Any danger of you lot getting changed?" that we realised the time. Al talks now of how nervous he used to get before games. He could have fooled us. We all thought he was the coolest man on the planet. The big man deserves as Oscar for those performances!

After the warm-up and a few pre-match words from Joe, we arrived in the tunnel before the Roma team. As we stood there, from out of nowhere we heard Sammy Lee burst into the first line of a song: *'Could it be just that I'm crazy?'*

We recognised it straight away. Our trip to Israel to 'prepare' for the European Cup final was when the players had first adopted this obscure tune by Chris Rea called I Don't Know What It Is But I Love It. It became our anthem.

Craig Johnston was usually in charge of the music on the team bus and he knew about Chris Rea from his time at Middlesbrough.

28

The rest of us joined in and it wasn't long before the Roma players made their way down the tunnel and were met by sixteen nutters singing loudly while marching up and down with big daft smiles on our faces. I glanced over at them. They looked confused. We just continued with our song:

'Could it be the way I feel this time of year
When a certain situation seems to bring the best out of me
I don't care...'

2

Twelve Yards

*'We were on the bus going back to the hotel when I
felt a hand on my left shoulder. Big Al was sitting
behind me. 'What the fuck was that?' he said.
'You missed it by miles!'*

As I walk from the halfway line to take the first penalty, I'm
completely in command of my senses. In my head I'm telling
myself the same thing over and over again – 'I'm going to
score.' That's all I'm thinking. I'm on autopilot. My mind isn't
cluttered. It's as clear as a bell.

Then I reach the box and things begin to change. Reality
starts to set in. My head has so far been clear but now I'm
thinking about the situation I find myself in.

> *I'm only 22...I'm about to take the first penalty in a
> European Cup final shoot-out...*

Silly thoughts, I know. For the first time I start to doubt myself.

I rub the ball, an Adidas Tango, on my shirt before putting it
down on the spot.

I deliberately take an extra couple of seconds to ensure that it's sitting up and in exactly the right place on the grass. Seven, maybe eight paces back. Near-perfect preparation so far.

Then I turn around. I take an initial glance towards goal. That's the moment everything changes. For the first and only time in my career I don't feel in full control.

Roma goalkeeper Franco Tancredi is talking with the referee on the goal line. I just stand there, hands on hips, waiting for him to finish. Pure gamesmanship, of course, on his part but the delay doesn't make me feel any different, doesn't change my plans.

As I wait, I think about my penalty at Melwood against young Billy. It had plenty of power, about three feet off the ground and I put it just inside the post. If you can hit a penalty right in the corner with power then 99 times out of 100 the goalkeeper is not saving it, even if he goes the right way. I start my run-up. Then, midway through, I lift my head and look where I want to put the ball. A classic mistake. The ball soars over the bar. I've missed.

I haven't missed the penalty because of all those photographers behind the goal with their flashbulbs going off. I haven't missed the penalty because the ball boys on each side of the goal – all wearing Roma tracksuits – were trying to put me off. I haven't missed the penalty because a klaxon had sounded just before I took the spot kick. I was oblivious to all those things. I missed simply because I lifted my head.

Throughout my playing days I was always aware of everything around me. You can throw anything at me about my career and I'll be able to tell you exactly what was going on in my head at that specific moment.

Except for that time in Rome.

The walk back felt like a lifetime. From the moment I missed that penalty to reaching the lads in the centre circle – I don't remember anything. It was just a blur. It's only through watching old footage of the game all these years later that I can fill in the blanks of my blackout.

As I walked back, I started to grab at my throat with my left hand. I've got no idea why. I had never done such a thing before and I've not done it since. It was a gesture that I would be reminded of time and time again. Back at Melwood, whenever I had a shocker in training, Kenny Dalglish would pull at his throat and mimic my gesture, taking the piss. He knew it wouldn't wind me up but he still found it funny.

Bruce walked past me as I was heading back to the halfway line. He was on his way to face the first Roma penalty. There was no physical contact between us but I did turn my head slightly to the left and muttered something towards him. I honestly can't remember what I said – there's no way he would have heard me anyway.

At least I had the presence of mind to realise there were a lot more penalties still to be taken. If every Roma player scored his penalty then I would forever be the answer to a football trivia question. But I kept telling myself there were plenty of players who still had to try and handle the pressure of taking a penalty. I knew it wasn't over. It wasn't as if I had missed the spot kick that handed Roma the trophy.

When I got back to the centre circle I intentionally stood off to one side. I didn't want to be a distraction. I wasn't looking for a hug and I wasn't looking for players or coaches to come and console me.

A few of the boys came up to me and tried to be sympathetic. Then Lawro appeared with perfect comic timing.

"Unlucky Nico…you dickhead."

It took a second or so for it to sink in. Then the mayhem started. There's no hard and fast rule – no textbook – that says once you win the European Cup then this is what you must do and this is where you should go.

But I knew exactly where I was going: straight for the man who, ultimately, had got me out of a big hole. Alan Kennedy, aka Barney Rubble. The man whose cool, side-footed penalty secured our fourth European Cup after Bruno Conti and Francesco Graziani had missed from the spot. Craig Johnston got to Barney first, then Rushy followed by me and Lawro. Other players went to hug the staff.

My overriding emotion was that of relief. Barney had saved me but that's what Liverpool Football Club was all about. If something went wrong there was always someone there to cover your back. That's how it was. All in it together. The Liverpool Way.

To be honest, we had absolutely no idea what Barney was going to do. He had missed in the shootout against Hamburg in a pre-season tournament in Rotterdam the previous August. Then, two days later, he failed to even hit the target against Feyenoord when the second game was also decided by spot kicks.

When you consider that Barney also failed to find the back of the net at training two days before the final then you can understand why most of the boys were not exactly confident. When he stepped up and went left it was the opposite way to his penalty at Melwood…but it worked!

Talk about mixed emotions. It turned out to be the greatest day of my life – a European Cup winner at the age of just 22 – but when I missed that first penalty in the shoot-out I felt like I may have cost Liverpool Football Club the chance of winning the greatest club prize in football.

When Joe had gathered us all together with the scores locked at 1-1 after extra time, I had no hesitation putting myself forward for a penalty. "Who wants to take one?" he asked. The squad was split in two: those who were keen to volunteer for duty and those who were doing their best not to make eye contact with the boss.

Straight away I put my hand up. Why not? I was only 22 years old but I was fearless. Maybe because I didn't know any better. Looking back I had absolutely no idea of the magnitude of the occasion. That was a good thing.

There had been a debate about who would go first. Nealy was our best penalty taker, but the discussion about whether he would take one of the first spot kicks or the last ones went on for longer than it should have. In the end I simply said, 'I'll go first.' I picked up the ball and off I went. I may have missed but I wasn't unhappy with how I hit my penalty. I knew what I was trying to do and it had lots of power behind it. But I lifted my head.

We talk about inexperience and that was a great example. I hit a clean penalty, but I was leaning back and it went over because I was anxious to see it hitting the back of the net. Psychologists talk now about visualising what you're going to do before going ahead and doing it. Well, either I was ahead of my time or they are talking bollocks.

We didn't hang about the stadium for too long after the game.

All we wanted to do was get back to the hotel so we could celebrate with our families. Big Al's witty remark on the bus about my penalty certainly raised a smile but, although said in jest, his words got me thinking how different it might have been. Instead of heading back to a party at the hotel I could just as easily have been the guy who couldn't even hit the target from twelve yards and cost Liverpool the European Cup. Cancel the disco pronto if that had been the case. People always talk about ups and downs in football. If there was ever an example of the fine margins that separate victory and defeat – being top of the tree or down the drain – this was it.

So many thoughts went through my head during that 30-minute bus journey back to the hotel – what we had achieved as a team, how it so nearly went wrong, what I'd do differently if I was to take the penalty again. Positive thoughts mixed with contemplation of 'What if…'

I also thought about how quickly things could change. The realisation of that was just as important to me going forward. Don't get too carried away or complacent with what's been achieved. All you've done is set the bar. Just like if we had lost it would have been a huge disappointment but it wouldn't have been the end of the world.

Bob Paisley once said he thought I had the perfect temperament for a football player. I'm sure that was one of the reasons why Joe, Roy and Ronnie agreed to let me take a penalty in Rome when I put my hand up. Yes I was daft as a brush at times, and common sense was clearly lacking on many occasions off the pitch, but when it came to football I had a grown-up thought process from an early age and was able to balance my emotions. It's one of the traits I'm most proud of.

In the weeks that followed in the summer of 1984 I lost count of the number of the people passing on their well wishes and congratulations. It was all very humbling. And what I found especially interesting was when many of them spoke in a positive way about my penalty. I found that a little strange to begin with. I thought it would have been the other way around.

Instead of 'sorry you missed that penalty, lad' which I expected, they would instead praise me for having the balls to take it. I turned that into a positive and it gave me strength going forward.

I was getting patted on the back for volunteering to take a penalty kick in a European Cup final at a young age and also being praised for the way I reacted to the disappointment of missing it.

Would they still have done that if we had lost on penalties in Rome? Thankfully, I never had to find out.

3

Blackcurrant and Lemonade

'We were boxing in the kitchen, just dicking around, and I had my hands behind my back while trying to avoid her punches. She tried to hit me so I swung my head out of the way but I only succeeded in whacking it against the wall. I collapsed like a sack of spuds. To this day, my twin sister Susan claimed she knocked me out but it's not true!'

The only thing I wanted as a wee boy every Christmas was a new football. I used to spend hours knocking a ball against the wall of the Co-op just across the road from our house in Muirhead, Troon. I lived there with Mum Helen, Dad Jim, twin brothers Kim and Ken, twin sister Susan and two older sisters Sandra and Helen.

The neighbours always used to complain about the noise – 'thump, thump, thump' every single night.

One day that 'thump' was replaced by the 'crack' of shattering glass when the ball went through the Co-op window. As soon as I saw it happen I ran home as quick as I could, hoping no-one saw me.

Then I remembered the flaw in my escape plan – my name was written in big bold letters on the ball…Muirhead wasn't a big place so when it came to finding the culprit, it wasn't a hard case to solve. As it happens, no-one did knock on my mum and dad's door. But I never wrote STEPHEN NICOL on any other ball I owned from that day forward.

Most kids go to primary school to receive an education. I was different from most kids. All I was interested in was the time between classes when I got to play football in the playground during breaks and also at lunchtime. That lack of focus might not have helped improve my education but it did improve my game. In fact, I was the youngest kid ever to play for the school team at Muirhead Primary. They first asked me when I was just ten years old – most of the other kids selected were a couple of years older than me.

"Are you ready for the kicks you'll get?" asked Craig Fraser, one of the 'big' twelve year-olds in the team before he booted me in the shin.

It hurt like hell. But I pretended I hardly felt it. He was satisfied I was hard enough to take any future on-field punishment. If only he knew…

My football career actually started at local juvenile side Troon Thistle when I was nine and playing for the under 11s. It's hard to believe but I began as a left-winger before eventually being moved into the centre of the park a few years later. In the beginning I used to take all the corners. Not due to the fact that

I was better at doing that than my teammates, simply because I was the only one who could kick it as far as the goalmouth area on those ridiculously huge pitches that young kids used to play games on. Tactics – what tactics?!

When I turned 12, things changed, and not for the better.

My secondary school, Marr College in Troon, was a rugby school. We didn't get the chance to play football until fourth year so in those first three years we played rugby in the winter and took part in athletics and cricket in the summer. No organised football whatsoever other than our kickabouts during breaks or at lunchtime in the playground.

So, on Saturdays between the ages of twelve and fifteen, I played rugby for the school in the morning and football for Troon Thistle in the afternoon. Then, in 1976, a man who also worked in a bakery during the week offered me my first big break. Willie Blair was a scout at weekends and he'd been watching me play for Troon for some time before eventually asking if I wanted to join Ayr United Boys Club, the youth set-up for the professional club. I had a choice to make – school rugby or football.

It took very little time to make a decision. I told the school I didn't want to play rugby anymore because it would clash with this new footballing opportunity. That didn't go down well with head of PE, Keir Hardie, and a couple of his teaching colleagues Alan Gilbert and John Sharkey. So I got the rarest of things, an invite into the staffroom – their sanctuary. They must have been serious. The crux of their argument for me to give up football was that it would be easier for me to get a proper job if I played rugby. A job? They clearly didn't view my report cards or research any of my grades from the rest of my classes!

The famous Scotland rugby player Gordon Brown – Broon Fae Troon, who was actually a friend of the family – was used by the teachers as an example of an ex-Marr College pupil I could follow in the footsteps of if I chose the oval ball: "He's someone who's gone on to do well in life and has an excellent job with the bank, all with his rugby background as a base," I was told.

It fell on deaf ears. At no stage of their verbal propaganda did I ever think about giving up football. I subsequently accepted Willie Blair's offer and joined Ayr United Boys Club in 1976. From that point onwards I knew I was where I wanted to be and doing what I wanted to do.

I felt like a proper grown-up football player for the first time in 1977, preparing properly for games and travelling throughout the west of Scotland playing teams of the calibre of Celtic Boys Club in Glasgow and various other top juvenile sides. This was a big step up from Troon Thistle and all of a sudden, for the first time in my life, I had teammates who were as good as or better than me. Up until I joined my new club I had always been head and shoulders above anybody else.

I started in central midfield with Ayr United BC before being moved to a wider position – actually the opposite of what happened to me at Troon Thistle. Initially I wasn't pleased to move out wide because I didn't feel as though I'd be as involved in the action. But it was actually a bit of a wake up call for me. It made me think that maybe I wasn't quite as good as I thought I was. That was enough to give me a different attitude. It made me work harder and, ultimately, was probably the reason I was eventually offered the chance to turn professional, a process which began at the age of sixteen when I was offered an 'S' form by Ayr United. That particular type of youth contract gave them first dibs on signing me once I was eligible to turn pro a couple of years later.

While things were going well on the pitch the same couldn't be said about my education. I left Marr College with absolutely no qualifications – I'm not ashamed to say that because I didn't give a monkey's – but I was unemployed. My first job application was sent to KP Electrics in Troon and, remarkably, they somehow decided to employ me. Less than six months later and I was out the door. Cutbacks they said. The fact I still can't wire a plug forty years on suggests that might not have been the only reason for my removal.

Back on the scrapheap again and looking for employment while signing on the dole in return for £10.60 a week. I got another job, courtesy of a pal, washing the walls of a factory in Irvine (needs must!) You won't be surprised to learn that I didn't last too long as a factory wall washer either. My next job was washing dishes at my sister's boyfriend's hotel. That lasted one night. Sacked by my own family. This working lark just wasn't for me. I had other things on my mind. Well, only one other thing. Football.

I continued to make steady progress through the ranks at Ayr United. After the under 16s came the under 18s before I was offered professional terms with the club. For the princely sum of ten pounds, sixty pence less than I pocketed each week on the dole. But who was I to argue at the measly weekly wage when it gave me the opportunity to potentially fulfil my ambition.

A Scotland under-18 trial game was taking place at Somerset Park in Ayr on the same night that I signed professional terms with Ayr United. Manager Willie McLean had obviously mentioned me to one of the Scotland coaches so just after I had signed the contract Willie told me to go home and get my boots so that I could take part in the game. I actually played right-back that night for the first time in my life. I thought I did okay but in the end wasn't picked.

I did learn one thing from the experience. I had never worn shin guards previously and one of the coaches enquired in the changing room prior to the trial where mine were. I didn't even own a pair so he told me in no uncertain terms that if I wasn't prepared to wear them then I wouldn't be playing. I managed to borrow a tatty old pair that must have belonged to one of the Ayr United first team players and I'm thankful I did. During the game one of the opposition players lunged in with a nasty tackle and it was my borrowed right shin guard that protected me from what could have been a serious leg injury. From that point on I understood their importance and never once played another game without them.

I was 17 when I played my first game for the reserves under the floodlights at Somerset Park. I started at centre-back with my good friend Billy Hendry, who I'd played alongside at Ayr United Boys Club. I thought this was the big time, even though the only people who were at the game were coaches or family members.

I played for the reserves at centre-back for about six months and did well enough on a consistent basis that I was called up to the first team squad. I made my debut for Ayr United as a substitute at Arbroath in December 1979, eleven days after my eighteenth birthday. To say it was cold up there at Gayfield, right on the coast and just a few hundred metres from the North

Sea, is an understatement. In all my years playing football, I think those were the coldest conditions I ever experienced. It was hard to know if you touched the ball because you couldn't even feel your feet.

After playing a couple of games as sub for the Ayr United first team I was summoned for a chat with a club official. They realised that having an unemployed player on the books wasn't good for either of us going forward. This was a part-time set-up and everyone else had other jobs in addition to playing football. One of the gentlemen associated with the club was a director of local firm Paton the Builders and he did his best to try and help me find a job.

"Where do you see your future, son?

"I just want to play football."

"Look, the chances of you making a career of that are pretty small. Would you consider an apprenticeship in bricklaying or joinery?"

"To be honest I'm not really interested in either of them."

I can still see the look on his face as I turned my nose up at being a bricklayer or a joiner. The main reason was the fact that apprenticeships would have taken three or four years and I didn't plan on hanging around that long. In the end, he made a couple of calls and found me a labourer's role with Paton the Builders.

"You start on Monday. Don't be late."

I must have been the worst labourer they'd ever had. I was lazy as well as being absolutely useless. To me this job was simply a stopgap. Big Wattie, my first foreman, detested me from the get-go because of my complete lack of enthusiasm. He knew I was crap at the job and used to scowl at me all the time.

The boys on the building site told me he fancied himself as a footballer when he was younger, so the chances of us getting on were slim to none. His dislike of me was particularly clear every time we played five-a-side during dinner breaks. There were no football boots on the building site, all the boys just played in their steel-toecaps, and I'm convinced Big Wattie rigged the team selection so he was always in opposition to me. Thankfully I was as fit as a fiddle and usually kept out of harm's way, despite his best intentions.

Fortunately for me, one of the days Big Wattie was off-site coincided with a little 'accident' I had with a dumper truck. One of my other colleagues tried to teach me how to operate the thing but at the time I had no licence to drive a car. This was all new to me. He spent half an hour explaining to me how things worked, then told me to go and fill it full of bricks. That part I managed. My next job was to drive it round the outside of the foundations, which were approximately six feet deep, and to drop the bricks into the founds [the base]. So I filled up the dumper truck with bricks and drove it round the foundations towards the edge. Then my bottle went, I shit myself and completely forgot what he had told me about how to stop the vehicle.

As the big dumper truck, and me, made our way towards the founds I panicked and bailed as we got closer to the edge, jumping to safety and wanting no part of the upcoming chaos. Everything – dumper truck, bricks and all – disappeared into the foundations followed by a mighty thud. I had some explaining to do. A call was made to the main office and a rescue truck was sent to pull the truck out. That was the first time I'd had anything to do with a dumper truck. It was also the last. I still shudder when I think what might have been if Big Wattie had been working that day.

Things in general weren't going well for me on the building site. I'd been late for work a couple of times and it was made clear to me that if it happened again I was on the way out. After another heavy Sunday night on the beers I fell asleep on the bus taking me to site the following morning. Not for the first time, the driver had to wake me up at the bus terminal and I had to get a taxi to take me to work. Late again. Three strikes and you're out, I'd been told, so I figured I would lose my job. Amazingly that wasn't the case. I couldn't believe my luck when, instead of Big Wattie, another foreman was deputising. He was much more understanding when I told him my dad had fallen that morning and I had to drive him to the hospital. A pack of lies, of course. I couldn't even drive…

The writing had been on the wall for a while so it was no surprise when I was finally let go. Belt-tightening, they said, with costs having to be cut across the company. I knew I was shit at my job, so was fine with their decision. I didn't want special treatment because one of the company directors had got me the job in the first place and I would have hated one of the other labourers who were reliant on the employment to have been let go instead. Back on the dole I went.

Being unemployed again meant I had time on my hands once more. I spent most nights of the week at the pub – except Tuesdays and Thursdays when I was training with the reserves. My local was the South Beach Hotel in Troon where, one Saturday night, things took a turn for the worse. I was in the pub with Gordon Jackson, who went to school with my older twin brothers Kim and Ken, and at closing time Gordon asked if I wanted to go back to his for a few more beers. The flat was probably less than a mile from the pub and we must have spent another couple of hours just drinking, smoking and talking about football. Eventually he went to bed and I went to sleep on the couch in the living room after I finished my cigarette – or at least I thought I had finished it…

In the middle of the night I woke and saw flames shooting from the back of the sofa. The room quickly filled with smoke. I couldn't see properly but, somehow, I crouched down and eventually found the back window. One hit on the window and it smashed. I crawled out and immediately wondered where Gordon was. Once outside I saw another window, which I figured was his bedroom. I tried to do the same thing and smash the window but it just wouldn't break. It wasn't long before the neighbours appeared and then a fire engine. I told them I thought Gordon was still inside. Thankfully, it turns out he had escaped but unfortunately Gordon's dog – a boxer – had not been so lucky and suffocated because of the smoke.

I was taken straight to hospital and it wasn't until I got there that I realised my feet were bleeding. I had no socks or shoes on and there were cuts all over my hands and feet from climbing out of the window. We were sitting in the emergency room and Gordon asked if I had any idea what had happened. I said no, but told him when I woke up there were flames coming out from the back of the sofa. I remember having a quick smoke just before going to sleep and I desperately hoped I hadn't fallen asleep with a cigarette in my hand. Gordon couldn't have been more understanding. "We're both alright and that's all that matters," he told me.

A couple of weeks later, I went back to the house with him and some fire officers who told us they thought the inferno had started because of an electrical fault. That actually makes sense to me because if I had fallen asleep with a lit cigarette then I don't think the flames would have been coming from the back of the sofa. In any case it was a huge relief to hear that they didn't think I started the fire. It was one of the scariest experiences of my life.

When I think about it now, the presence of mind and the calmness I showed when I first saw the flames – and the way I reacted – well it's something that's always been there both on and off the field. It's a trait I definitely got from my dad. We would both get irate about the silliest of things, but when something serious happened Dad was the one to take charge and was always very rational and calm about the whole thing. Not a bad trait to have in any walk of life.

A few substitute appearances for the first team – that was the sum total of my Ayr United career up until April 1980. After making my debut as a sub in December 1979 at freezing cold Arbroath, I had to wait another four months for my first start. Arbroath provided the opposition once more but thankfully this time the game was at Somerset Park in Ayr and it was a fair bit warmer than Gayfield had been.

Regular first choice centre-back Ian McAllister had been hurt in a motorcycle accident during the week and I was told at training on the Thursday night – remember we were part-time – that I would be making my first start. I was apprehensive but it helped knowing that I would be playing in central defence alongside Jim Fleeting, who I used to travel to training with and knew well.

We won 5-0. I didn't make any mistakes, won my challenges and generally was safe and sound.

I was feeling pretty optimistic about the future. I'd had a taste of the first team – and hadn't let anybody down – and was enjoying my life. But although I didn't realise it at the time, there was something stopping me from making a step-up – I liked a drink or two. If I didn't make the first team squad I would play for Ayr United reserves on the Saturday then spend the rest of the day in the pub. Then, on Sunday, it was back to the South Beach Hotel for another session after I'd watched my pals play for the pub team in the morning. This routine actually started when I was sixteen, except I used to play for the pub team on the Sunday even if I had played for the reserves the day before. I soon figured out playing twice at the weekend wasn't the best idea if I was serious about having a football career. However, it never dawned on me that my drinking was also an issue until I received a call one day from Ayr United assistant manager George Caldwell asking me to come in early for training to see him.

"I've been told that you've been spending a lot of time in the pub," he told me. He said an anonymous person had been in touch with the club to say I was drinking a lot.

After hearing those words the penny finally dropped. I had no idea at the time who had made the call but it got me thinking. A couple of weeks before, there was a guy in the pub I hadn't seen before and he had started asking me about Ayr United. In my confused mind I thought he had some sort of link to the club and was monitoring my behaviour and drinking habits. Of course that was complete nonsense. I played for Ayr United but in my brain I was thinking I had hit the big time and that the club had spies all over town making sure none of their players were getting up to no good. This was Ayr United, not Manchester United. From that meeting with George onwards I made a conscious decision that I would only drink on a Saturday night after a game. I would still go to watch the pub team on a Sunday and hang out at the South Beach but my regular heavy drinking sessions were a thing of the past from that point onwards.

With this fresh outlook ahead of the 1980-81 season, I was picked to start the first league game against Motherwell at Somerset Park. I played left-back that day because Willie Kelly, who normally played the position, was a correctional officer and couldn't get the afternoon off work. The joys of trying to put together a part-time team in lower league football! We won 5-0 – just like we'd done against Arbroath back in April in my first start for the club – and I was soon playing for the first team on a regular basis.

Things didn't always go according to plan. I remember playing in a game at Dumbarton in October 1980 and I came forward with the ball, got over the halfway line and everything just opened up. I remember thinking 'what the fuck do I do now?' I tripped, gave the ball away and the crowd laughed.

After losing only one of our opening nine league games at the beginning of season 1980-81, manager Willie McLean felt the team might have a chance of getting promotion so he wanted us all to sign new contracts to help ensure none of us left.

We were all offered 25 quid per week. I had been on 16 pounds per week – a six-pound increase from my initial wage when I first signed – so accepting another increase was a no-brainer for me. However, two of my teammates, Billy Hendry who wasn't even in the first team, and Gerry Phillips, who was our best player, refused to put pen to paper. Billy's dad was a union man and told him not to sign while Gerry believed we were getting short-changed and could maybe get more out of the club if we got promotion. Every single player apart from me had a full-time job away from football so this was just extra pocket money for them, but Gerry also had a family and thought by holding out he could get us all more money. Eventually Billy and Gerry were persuaded that 25 quid per week wasn't too bad a deal after all for part-time football so we put pen to paper. Imagine that scenario these days – every player on the same basic wage at any club – it just wouldn't happen.

So with my weekly windfall now a colossal 25 pounds, minus the fiver I had to give my mum for keep, I was doing alright for myself. And more often than not I'd get the fiver back from Mum as well.

The frequent visits to the South Beach pub continued but while the rest of the locals were enjoying their beer I was content with three or four pints of blackcurrant and lemonade. This change in habit, without question, helped considerably. I was fitter, stronger and healthier. It opened my eyes as to what I was capable of. My chat with George Caldwell and cutting out the alcohol at Ayr United was a huge turning point in my career, as was meeting Eleanor, my future wife, in February 1981.

I eventually found out who it was that called the club about my drinking habits. As it turns out, it wasn't the guy from the pub. It was a friend of mine called Alan Taylor who was simply concerned about how much I was drinking. I will forever be grateful to him. My change in lifestyle certainly made a huge difference and was one of the main reasons why I would go on to sign for one of the biggest teams in the world.

4

Next Stop Anfield

"That's it,' said SwallowMeKnob, 'I'm not driving this thing anymore.' Ronnie Moran, as quick as Ronnie could move, left his seat and got off the bus as well. But instead of politely trying to persuade our driver to reconsider his actions Ronnie simply demanded that he 'get back on the fucking bus.' The daily journey to Melwood for training was never dull'

'Don't worry about St Mirren. You've got bigger things ahead of you.' Ayr United assistant boss George Caldwell clearly knew more about my future than I did. The first time I found out there was interest in me from other clubs was at the start of the 1981-82 season. I was sitting in the house reading the Sunday Post the day after we lost 4-3 at home to League Cup holders Dundee United.

'ST MIRREN TO SIGN AYR KID'... At first it didn't even register that the headline related to me. St Mirren were in the top flight at the time – why would they be interested? On the way back from our League Cup tie at Motherwell a few days later I asked George if there was any truth in the story in the Sunday Post. That's when he told me he thought bigger things lay ahead.

Up until then, the biggest headline I had read involving Ayr United was when we lined up against a certain George Best, who was enjoying his infamous spell at Hibs in the twilight of his career.

I was looking forward to coming up against him when Hibs drew Ayr in the Scottish Cup in February 1980. As it happened, I got injured and wasn't named in the squad, so I ended up knocking back a few in the South Beach in Troon. Turns out George had the same idea, going on a marathon Saturday night drinking session in Edinburgh with Debbie Harry and French rugby legend Jean-Pierre Rives. Neither of us made the game – for very different reasons!

I did get to share a pitch with Best a few months later, on a Wednesday night in October 1980. It was a League Cup quarter-final first leg tie in front of nearly five thousand fans, more than double our average attendance. George was lucky if he touched the ball on five occasions during the game but every time he was in possession the crowd just melted. Oohs and ahhs from the terraces. I was in awe, too. The fact he was on the same pitch as me was fantastic, especially since I used to wear the same tatty pair of George Best football boots in every game I played for Muirhead Primary School.

Anyway, it wasn't long before articles were regularly appearing in newspapers linking me with various clubs, including English sides Sunderland and Crystal Palace. During all the speculation I was lucky enough to be surrounded by a great group of older professionals – Jim Fleeting and Jim McSherry in particular.

They told me to forget about what may happen in the future, just keep playing well and if I did that then things would work out. And they certainly did.

It was when my Ayr United teammate Davie Armour told me that Rangers also wanted me that I really started to think seriously about what may lie ahead. Davie had played for the Ibrox club and still had connections there. He said Rangers chief scout Dave McParland had watched me play for Ayr on a few occasions and they were very keen. Being a Rangers supporter, this was music to my ears. What I didn't know at the time was that Rangers had already made a bid for me and the board of Ayr United had turned it down.

Although there was plenty of speculation about my future, one club that was never mentioned by the newspapers was Liverpool. They went about their business differently. Out of sight, out of mind. Not once did the club apply for a complimentary ticket for their chief scout, Geoff Twentyman. He came to plenty of games at Somerset Park but always played the incognito card. Geoff would pay at the turnstiles and stand in a different spot on the terraces each time. Subtle enquiries were made to Ayr fans in close proximity about 'the lad Nicol' but he would also ask about other players as well so as not to give the game away.

Liverpool's interest in me began during the second half of the 1980-81 season, soon after I'd become a regular in the first team, and they decided to make a move after a couple of months of the new 1981-82 season. All along, Geoff had been keeping Bob Paisley updated on my progress. He later told me that he had said to Bob that the kid he was watching from Ayr United would go on to play for Scotland. Incidentally, when I

WAS playing for Scotland – at the World Cup in 1986 – Alex Ferguson mentioned that he also came to see me and that Aberdeen were close to making a bid. But he didn't take his interest any further after deciding he wanted a left-back who was predominantly left-footed.

My final game for Ayr United, although I wasn't to know that at the time, was the 5-1 victory over East Stirlingshire at Somerset Park on Saturday, October 17, 1981. Going out on a high. Two days later, on the Monday, Ayr received an offer from Liverpool and a board meeting was hastily arranged for later that evening to discuss the bid. In the early Eighties, there weren't many six-figure sums offered for teenagers so I can't imagine the meeting lasted too long before the whisky was removed from the boardroom cabinet!

It began as just another normal Tuesday. It ended with my life about to change forever. After getting the bus into training – we started at seven o'clock but had to be there by six-thirty – assistant boss George Caldwell was there waiting for me.

"Follow me to the manager's office."

Something wasn't right but I just couldn't figure out what it was. I'd practically given up the drink, no more dumper trucks had been harmed that I was aware of and I'd been on my best behaviour.

"Sit down over there."

George then sat in the boss's chair and told me we were waiting for Willie McLean, the manager, but he refused to elaborate why. I asked if he wanted me to go and get changed for training while we waited for Willie.

"Don't worry about training – just wait here," said George.

Baffled and confused. A few minutes later Willie entered the room. I didn't even have time to ask why I was in his office – he just got straight to the point:

"The club has accepted an offer from Liverpool and you're being sold."

So many things I could have said in response, so many emotions available to me at this life-changing moment – instead I just lifted my head slightly and mumbled a single solitary word…

"Awrite."

A look of incredulity on Willie's face – his eyes wide open, like billiard balls.

"AWRITE? FUCKING AWRITE? Is that all you've got to say?"

So matter-of-fact, so nonchalant but that was me in a nutshell. I wasn't intentionally downplaying what had happened. I was just in shock and had absolutely no idea of the enormity of what was to come. But my emotion, my reaction wouldn't have changed even if I had been able to take it all in. Just the way I was. Just the way I am.

Willie then explained what would happen next. I grabbed my boots – no training session that evening, or ever again with Ayr United – and he drove me home so I could tell my folks and pack an overnight bag. I might not have shown much emotion when I found out but the same can't be said about my parents, especially Mum. She turned into a nervous wreck the minute I told her, so there was no way she would be travelling south with me the next day. It would be just Willie and me. Mum and Dad trusted him so that was good enough for me.

I packed an overnight bag with enough clothes for a couple of days then stayed at his house on the Tuesday night. It enabled us to get on the road south quickly in the morning – it also meant he didn't have to worry about the whereabouts of someone who was now a prized possession for Ayr United. Incidentally, I had no idea at the time the transfer fee was £300,000. Didn't even ask. It made no difference to me.

We travelled down to Manchester on the Wednesday morning. Liverpool were in Holland for a European Cup second round tie against AZ '67 Alkmaar that night, hence why the signing wasn't taking place until the Thursday, but Willie wanted us down there early to get away from the press in Scotland. That was his story anyway. (Of course, it had nothing to do with him arranging for us to go to Old Trafford on the Wednesday night to watch Manchester United play Middlesbrough). That was fun but it was also a surreal experience. I'd only ever previously seen Old Trafford on television yet here I was sitting in a stadium that one day I might be playing in for Liverpool. In actual fact, in a strange quirk of fate, I found myself running out of the Old Trafford tunnel and playing on that very same pitch just three days later.

I didn't have a say in the contract negotiations. Didn't want one. I trusted Willie but more importantly my mum and dad trusted Willie, and they were happy for him to negotiate with Liverpool chief executive Peter Robinson on my behalf. While Peter and Willie were going about their business inside the office at Anfield I sat outside the room like a kid at school waiting to be called in to see the career advisor to find out what kind of future lay ahead.

"You'll be getting 250 pounds per week and it's a three-year deal," said Willie as he poked his head round the door. A slight improvement on the twenty-five quid I was getting for part-time football with Ayr United, although I should point out there was also a £15,000 signing-on fee. "Now get your arse in here and sign the contract!"

Straight after signing Willie got in his car and went back up the road. His job was done. Mine was just beginning. I was escorted up to the Main Stand at Anfield to get my photo taken. No press conference, just a couple of local photographers invited by the club to take some pictures of me with a Liverpool scarf raised above my head.

I was then introduced to Tom Saunders. Tom was the Youth Development Officer at Liverpool, the first one of its kind in England and a role he'd held since 1968 when appointed by Bill Shankly. Tom explained I would be staying in digs and told me to follow him to my new abode. We got to the car park outside the Main Stand and I wondered which car was his but he kept walking, past all of the vehicles. Less than sixty seconds later, he proclaimed that we had arrived at my accommodation, an end terrace house at 156 Anfield Road. It was owned by a wonderful couple – Bunty and Ed – and I spent the first six months of my Liverpool career living there along with Tim Bredbury, another youngster at the club, before moving into a flat of my own with girlfriend [and future wife] Eleanor.

"Help yourself," they said. "Whichever ones you want."

Although my top, shorts, socks and jumper were all laid out at Anfield, I had to pick out a jockstrap or a pair of pants from the pile on the table in the middle of the dressing room. Day one as a Liverpool player – the reigning European Cup holders don't forget – and it was every man for himself when it came to the team underwear.

I picked out a pair of undies but didn't know if they would be mine from that point forward. I was too scared to ask. It was my first day after all. After training I waited to see the routine of the other players before I undressed and got in the bath. They took off their pants and jockstraps and – as I feared – threw them into the middle of the floor. The apprentices then picked them up and took them to get washed. No chance of getting the same pair of pants and same jockstrap the following day then! I soon got used to it, though, and realised that it was all part of the Liverpool way of doing things. It didn't matter who you were or what you had achieved in football, everyone was treated the same. I liked that.

The routine after home games was similar to training. No matter if you'd been playing for the reserves or the first team, you would come in, take off your gear and throw it into the middle of the dressing room. But there were rules. Sleeves had to be pulled out properly and socks had to be unrolled and not crumpled or there were consequences. "Hold on a minute, are you big time or something?" It didn't matter who you were or what you'd won, the rules were the same for everyone. Nobody was better than anybody else. We were all equals. All for one and one for all.

Hangers-on were never tolerated at Liverpool. The only people with us were those who had to be there. If that meant players and coaches having to do mundane chores then so be it. Anyone acting like 'Billy Big Time' would quickly be cut down to size. The younger players – even those who were named in the team and playing – would help carry the kit hampers from the bus into the dressing room. Then, afterwards, Ronnie Moran and Roy Evans would make sure everything was put away properly, they'd clean up all the used tape and even sweep the dressing room (both home and away) ensuring it was always left the way they found it.

Our routine for away games was slightly different. I remember one particular club when they played at Anfield in the Eighties had a member of their staff who was solely responsible for cooking meals for the players using the microwave on board their 'fully-equipped' team bus. Not us. On the bus heading from the hotel to the stadium Ronnie Moran used to go round with a bit of paper and a pen and ask each player what they wanted from the chip shop for the return journey back to Anfield. Always three choices: pie and chips, fish and chips or chicken and chips. Healthy eating this was not. Any alternative request was met by a quizzical look from Ronnie and a straight-to-the-point reply: "That's all there is. Who the fuck do you think you are?"

Although I didn't make my full competitive debut for Liverpool for another ten months I was still considered a member of the first team squad from the day I arrived at the club. And that meant being allowed to use the first team dressing room at Anfield. I suppose it also meant I could have chosen to sit with the big boys on my first bus ride to training.

Being the new guy, of course, I didn't feel comfortable doing that. I felt I needed to prove myself first. So I sat with some of the reserves. The bus ride from Anfield to Melwood took about twenty minutes, but each day it was twenty minutes of noise, patter, piss-taking and sheer pandemonium. It was like being back at school again and going on a day trip.

First team players would sit up at the back of the bus, the

reserves in the middle and the kids were at the front, allowing them a prime position to terrorise our driver, SwallowMeKnob – a nickname given to him because that was his stock answer to the kids each time one of them slapped the back of his head. I never did find out his real name.

I thought the laughing and joking would stop once we got to Melwood. Not the case. There was usually around half an hour between arriving and the start of training, plenty of time to get ready and exchange stories from the night before. We would always start the day with a brisk walk. The first team pros and the reserves would then join up for stretches before we'd split into our respective groups. Only then did it start to get serious. We were split into three groups: 1. The first team squad, 2. The reserves, 3. The kids and apprentices. And the routine was usually something like this:

Monday – more of a casual day if there was no midweek game. Get the legs going, get the heart pumping, nothing too rigorous. Two pitches were set up across the width of the 'B Team' field – the pitch the reserves trained on – and the coaching staff would pick four teams made up of first team players and reserves for a round-robin tournament. This gave the reserves and guys on the fringe the chance to play together with the first team. A way of integrating everybody. Meanwhile, the kids and apprentices would train on a pitch we used to call 'Wembley' in as much as it was so bad that it bore absolutely no resemblance to the actual pitch at Wembley. Any player who was making a comeback from injury, regardless of who they were or their status at the club, would play on the staff team against the apprentices on the 'Wembley' pitch. The whole purpose of these exercises on a Monday was to integrate all the pros and give the coaching staff a chance to see how the young apprentices were progressing. Of course the first team was the priority, but Bob and Joe and Ronnie and Roy never forgot about the kids.

Tuesday – a normal training session at Melwood unless there was a game on a Wednesday.

Wednesday – ABG, anything but golf. If the coaching staff found out we'd been golfing then we were in deep shit. 'We don't give you a day off to go walking five miles on a golf course with a heavy bag of clubs on your backs.' Definitely not worth the risk.

Thursday – the day when the majority of our preparation took place for the game at the weekend. It was always the most intense training session and was usually pretty lively. If we'd had a midweek fixture on a Wednesday then we would go in at 1pm for a bath to help ease the aches and pains from the game the night before. Getting us in at one o'clock stopped us from doing anything substantial the day after a match. And players with pre-school children were encouraged to bring the kids in to play in the bath as well. The coaching staff at Liverpool were content because they knew exactly what their players were up to and the wives were happy because Dad was taking the children to work (we never did tell them just how filthy the water was…) Even though she was only about five years old at the time, my daughter Katy can still remember jumping in the bath with all the other kids because John Barnes was in there. She still talks about it now.

Friday – training would consist of a light warm-up and maybe a 20-minute five-a-side match. Not much more than that. Friday sessions were always low-key and we never worked on shape or tactics. It wasn't until Kenny took over that we practised set pieces on a Friday. Didn't happen before then. And Friday was also the day when Kenny would bring in two packets of digestive biscuits to go with our morning cups of tea – training wouldn't start until the biscuits were eaten!

I trained with the reserves on the Friday morning, the day after I'd signed. We were getting ready for the Central League fixture against Manchester United on the Saturday and my quick-fire return to Old Trafford. Just a couple of days earlier I was sat in the main stand with Willie McLean watching United take on Middlesbrough and now I was just 24 hours away from taking the field there and pulling on a Liverpool jersey for the first time.

It may have been a reserve game but it could easily have passed for a first team fixture such was the talent on show. United's reserves featured the likes of Mark Hughes, my future Liverpool teammate Peter Beardsley and Paul McGrath. We had Steve Ogrizovic between the sticks, Alan Kennedy in defence, Craig Johnston and Kevin Sheedy in midfield and Ian Rush alongside David Fairclough up front. I played right-back in a 3-2 win and despite the whirlwind of a week I'd had I was able to remain focussed and actually played quite well.

The crowd at Old Trafford was sparse – no surprise as Liverpool were taking on Manchester United at Anfield in a First Division match at the same time – but that didn't matter to me. My Liverpool career was now officially up and running.

The first time I trained with the first team was in November 1981, just after Liverpool had beaten Middlesbrough 4-1 in a midweek League Cup third round tie at Anfield. I'd been at the club for less than a month but with a Friday night friendly upcoming against an Irish International XI at Tolka Park in Dublin, and with Phil Neal away on England duty, Bob Paisley saw this as a perfect opportunity to see me in action as a right-back.

The supporting cast read like a who's who of Liverpool greats: Grobbelaar; Nicol, A.Kennedy, Hansen, Lawrenson; Johnston, Souness, Whelan, Sheedy; Johnson, Dalglish.

I kept things simple, thought I did pretty well when I had to mark Frank Stapleton and can best describe my performance as steady. The main thing was not appearing out of my depth and sticking out like a sore thumb. Mission accomplished.

Only once more that season was I included in a first team squad – as an unused sub in Bulgaria in a European Cup tie against CSKA Sofia – but even that small taste of the big time made me want more. I just had to do my best in training every day and hope my hard work would somehow get me noticed.

I didn't have to wait long for my competitive debut. My chance came against Birmingham City on Tuesday, August 31, 1982. It was one of only two league games I started under the manager who signed me.

There were only one or two subtle differences between Bob Paisley, Joe Fagan and Kenny Dalglish as managers. The main one was that Kenny would wait until an hour before kick-off on the Saturday before announcing the team. I think he thought if he said who was playing on a Friday then those who weren't involved would maybe act unprofessionally. Bob and Joe used to name the team on a Friday morning but we still didn't work on shape or tactics or setpieces even though we knew who was playing the following day. That only changed when Kenny came in.

Bob announced the line-up for the Birmingham game just before a light training session on the Monday. Mark Lawrenson was injured so Phil Neal was moving across to centre-back alongside Phil Thompson and I was playing at right-back. After hearing my name, and not being previously aware that I was even in contention to start, I heard very little else. It was like being a kid at the dentist waiting to get a tooth taken out. They'd give you gas and while it didn't knock you out all you could hear was lots of voices. I could hear him talking but nothing was clear. After the meeting I approached Joe Fagan outside the dressing room and asked him for confirmation of what the gaffer had said.

"Doesn't matter. Just go and play, son."

I was to learn later the 'just go and play' philosophy was their way of giving a player confidence that what he had was what they wanted. Liverpool's way of playing wasn't complicated. They wanted what you had for their particular system, that's why they brought you to the club. That's why they played you. They were only looking for what you could specifically offer to the team. Simple as that.

Once things had settled down and I began to come to terms with the fact that I would be part of the Liverpool team to face Birmingham I started to have negative thoughts. Nerves didn't really play a part but negativity did. 'Am I going to fuck this up?' and 'Will I make the team worse?' Six months previously this same group of players were European champions so how on earth was a 20 year-old from Ayr in Scotland going to step into their shoes? How on earth could I be an adequate replacement at right-back for Phil Neal who had played what seemed like three million games for Liverpool and never appeared to give the ball away, never made mistakes and always made good decisions? Stupid, really, but I suppose it's understandable.

As I've said, I remember most things about my career but strangely I don't remember a single thing about how I played in my debut. I'm told I kept it simple, didn't try anything fancy and made very few mistakes. That was good enough for me. After the goalless draw I received compliments from the coaching staff and my teammates and a couple even said it looked like I had been playing in the first team for years. But I still didn't feel truly worthy of wearing that same Liverpool jersey as those players who had worn it with such distinction before me. I felt like I had done a job. Nothing more than that. At that time, there were certain things expected of you if you played for Bob Paisley's first team. You had to win and you had to do your job. Anything else was a bonus. There was no a parade or cheering from the rafters after a win – that was what we were expected to do.

I was only nineteen when I moved to Anfield and didn't really have a proper appreciation of what Bob Paisley was all about. I soon learned. Bob was a man of very few words but when you walked through that front door at Anfield it soon became clear who was in charge. When he spoke it was worth listening to.

Opportunities were few and far between for me during season 1982-83 but that was expected. Liverpool won the league by eleven points and the line-up picked itself when everybody was fit. Why change a winning team?

Bruce Grobbelaar, Kenny Dalglish, Phil Neal and Alan Kennedy played in every league game; Graeme Souness missed one while Sammy Lee and Mark Lawrenson were only absent twice. Throw in Alan Hansen, Ian Rush and Craig Johnston only missing a handful and Ronnie Whelan, David Hodgson and Phil Thompson playing in more than half the fixtures and that only left scraps left to go around. David Fairclough, Terry McDermott and myself were the only others who managed any game time in the league that season with Bob using only sixteen players as Liverpool cantered to the title.

My only other start for Bob was in another goalless draw, this time at Sunderland three days after Christmas and I played in midfield. A couple of end of season substitute appearances – at the City Ground in Nottingham and at Vicarage Road in Watford – completed my first team action that season.

I still felt I made a contribution to the 1982-83 season, one of five league titles that we would win during my time in the first team squad. I featured in four games, I was on the bench for another four and travelled to many more without being used. But I didn't receive a medal and didn't expect one. I was under no illusions. I still had to play in a competitive match for the first team at Anfield and was yet to establish myself at Liverpool Football Club more than eighteen months after joining from Ayr United.

Plenty for me to ponder over the summer holidays.

5

Teddy Bear's Picnic

'He sat there and munched his way through fourteen packets of crisps without taking a break. I'd never seen anything like it in my life. A horrendous diet, yet he was still one of the fittest guys at training the next day. Truly staggering'

Don't laugh but my main mode of transport in the early stages of my Liverpool career – and the final few months at Ayr United – was Eleanor's white 50cc Honda moped complete with a very feminine storage basket between the handlebars.

Obviously the butt of many jokes, it was thankfully retired to scooter heaven when I purchased my first ever car, from a certain Mr A. Hansen of Liverpool. Eleven hundred pounds in cash was handed over to this dark-haired mystery man with a distinctive Scottish brogue in return for his 'good-as-new' red Datsun Sunny. Good as new my arse. He should have been wearing a black and white striped jersey and a robber mask.

In June 1983, Eleanor and me were travelling down the motorway towards Tilbury Docks ahead of a cruise with Alan and his family on the MS Mikhail Lermontov (before it sank!) when our newly purchased car started to shudder. The vibrating got progressively worse until it was the equivalent of a hydraulic drill going full pelt.

As a mechanical expert (not!), I kept telling Eleanor there was nothing seriously wrong with the vehicle, that everything would be fine and the shuddering would soon stop but people in other cars kept pointing at the back rear tire on the driver's side. I eventually pulled over after Eleanor told me to do so for the umpteenth time. We'd had a blowout following a puncture and the tire was shredded to bits. I put the spare on but it was practically flat. With no other option we started driving again, slowly of course, to the next exit. Fellow motorists were once again pointing at the back rear tire on the driver's side.

Thankfully it wasn't long before we found a garage. We had four remoulds on the car. Oh, and the spare was a remould as well! New tires required as soon as possible. The vehicle was not road-worthy. And this was before we had even started our holiday, which was free in return for a couple of personal appearances on the boat. Just as well the cruise didn't cost us anything because the new tires certainly did.

When we eventually met up with Alan and his wife Janet at Tilbury Docks I was furious and demanded answers. "You sold me a shitheap of a car with fucking remoulds for tires?"

"Well, what do you expect for eleven hundred pounds," he replied, very matter-of-factly. The robbing bastard.

It was impossible to stay mad at Big Al for too long and the cruise up to the Norwegian fjords was mostly enjoyable. I say mostly because the big bugger had one other trick up his sleeve. Al and his wife Janet were travelling with their son, Adam, and Janet's younger brother, Neil, so understandably they wanted to explore different places when the ship docked. Lerwick in the Shetland Islands was our first port of call. An early morning arrival meant they got off the boat sharpish to go and do touristy things while Eleanor and me spent the morning in bed. When I eventually dragged my saggy carcass out of my pit – around lunchtime – we decided to walk into town to get some supplies for the rest of the journey. As we were getting off the boat Big Al and his family were getting back on. I asked if there was anything worth seeing and he told us there was a great indoor bowling alley they'd been to.

Now remember this was 1983 in Lerwick. Of course there were no indoor bowling alleys on the island. In fact, I believe there's only one now! But this gullible pair sauntered off anyway in search of the mecca of indoor bowling that Al had recommended. I remember asking three different people for the location but each time a stare coupled with a blank look was offered in return. We were not daft enough to ask a fourth time.

It wasn't long before we found a newsagent and topped up on our usual healthy snacks – packets of crisps and cans of Coca Cola – then we went next door to the chemist to purchase some aspirin to help ease the alcohol-induced headache caused by excess drinking the night before. While Eleanor was at the checkout I decided, for a laugh, to weigh myself on one of those machines that at the time was standard in every pharmacy.

I put down the bags carrying the snacks, inserted the ten pence in the slot and stepped on to the scales. THIRTEEN STONES. How on earth had I managed to put on a full stone in the space of a couple of days? I was twelve-stones even when I weighed myself before we headed down to Tilbury. Something wasn't right.

"Eleanor, ELEANOR – come and see this," I yelled. "I can't believe I've put on so much weight."

Without moving from the checkout she simply turned her head, took one look at me and shouted back: "Stephen, you've got the shopping bags in your hands."

I'd only gone and picked them up again before standing on the scales to weigh myself!

No, I didn't tell Hansen what had happened when we got back on the boat. Unfortunately Eleanor did.

Six games in twelve days in four different countries. Pre-season in August 1983 was hectic to say the least. Manchester United provided the opposition at Windsor Park in Belfast for Irish FA secretary Billy Drennan's testimonial then it was on to Rotterdam to face Hamburg and Feyenoord followed by a trip to Morocco for yet another testimonial before ending with games against Atletico Madrid and Dinamo Bucharest in southern Spain. As English champions Liverpool were very much in demand.

Results in the Rotterdam tournament might not have been good – we lost on penalties in both the semi-final and the third place match – but our performances against Hamburg then hosts Feyenoord, who included Johan Cruyff in their line-up, were decent. Especially the way we played against the Germans, who were the reigning European Cup holders don't forget.

It was all the more remarkable when you consider the very different ways the two teams prepared for the match. The day before the game, and because of the extreme daytime heat, the Hamburg players trained at 7am, went back to bed for a few hours then trained again at 6pm when the temperature had dropped. Meanwhile, we trained for an hour at noon, allowing our milk-bottle coloured skin maximum exposure to the heat of the midday sun, and that was it. We'd be at dinner when the Hamburg squad was heading back out on the training field.

The following day we played them off the park but somehow couldn't find a way to score. In the hotel bar that night we noticed their legendary manager Ernst Happel sitting with his coaching staff and they were all shaking their heads and smiling when they looked over at us. All the preparation they'd put in ahead of the game yet we still managed to outplay them with our unscientific basic routine. We were just as strong, just as physical as them and I don't think they were able to work out how this was possible. But we were fit, we were a unit, we played as a team and more often than not we did the right things at the right time. And when things didn't go according to plan it was about covering each other's backside.

At Liverpool we understood each other and we socialised together – isn't that what proper teams do? People called us a machine. That's not true. We were a team with great players who cared about one another.

I got some game time in Holland, coming off the bench against Hamburg and starting against Feyenoord, and it was encouraging to be part of new boss Joe Fagan's plans. In his role as Bob Paisley's assistant I had a few dealings with Joe and he'd watched me several times for the reserves so he knew what I was capable of. It was pleasing I didn't have to prove myself all over again to a brand new manager.

After the tournament in Holland there was just enough time to fly back to Liverpool on the Sunday for one night at home before heading to the airport again on the Monday and on to Morocco then Spain. With such a swift turnaround, Eleanor kindly packed my bag for the trips to Casablanca and Andalusia. It was literally a case – no pun intended – of arriving back from Rotterdam, going to bed, waking up then going to the airport. I literally had no time to check what she had packed. Surely I didn't need to…

All of us – the players and backroom staff – were gathered together in the departure lounge at Speke Airport in Liverpool doing our usual; cracking jokes and taking the piss out of each other. It wasn't long before I felt hungry – no shock there – so I rummaged in my bag for a snack knowing fine well that Eleanor would have packed an assortment of unhealthy treats. As I pulled out a bag of crisps something else fell to the floor – a teddy bear with big droopy eyes holding a little banner that read: '*I am Sad Sam. Will you cuddle me and love me?*' What the fuck had she done? Now I may have been a fast mover but this required extreme quickness of hand to somehow get the little fluffy bastard back into the bag, pronto, before anyone caught a glimpse.

Quick, but not quick enough.

As if the lads needed any additional ammunition to annihilate me. I got absolutely crucified for this and rightly so. Eleanor's excuse by the way? She said she was sad that I was going to be away for a week or so and bought me a Sad Sam to ensure I didn't forget her. Well her plan certainly worked!

It was very rare that I had just cause to curse my wife – she's an absolute gem – but that was certainly one of those occasions. And I'm blaming her for what happened in Morocco as well. We were only scheduled to play one match in Casablanca – against local team Wydad in a testimonial for their former Moroccan international Larbi Aherdane – and I was fairly certain I wouldn't be in the line-up. I'd started the match against Feyenoord in Rotterdam three days before and Joe Fagan said he planned to make a few changes. It was only his fourth game in charge since taking over from Bob Paisley and he wanted to see as many players in action as possible. I was just 21 years old and had only started two league games the previous season so, at that time, was a long way from being a first team regular. Therefore I just assumed I wouldn't be in the Liverpool starting eleven for the testimonial.

After lunch in Casablanca we went back to our hotel rooms. Most people satisfy their appetite when they sit down to eat. I'm not most people. In addition to what I'd had at lunch, I munched my way through another six packets of crisps that afternoon. First the teddy bear, now the picnic. The stash Eleanor had packed was meant to last me the full week – including the next trip to Spain – but sheer boredom meant I munched most of the goodies that day.

When we got to the stadium that night you can imagine my surprise, and horror, when Joe named me in his team to face the local select. Not good, but there's no way I could say anything. Prior to kick-off I actually felt fine despite my afternoon binge eating. I was feeling good as we got the game underway so at no time did it cross my mind that the snacking would eventually come back to haunt me.

I scored our first goal before half-time – my first for the club – and felt even better. There was absolutely no sign of what was to come. New signing Michael Robinson, on his debut after signing from Brighton, then made it two-nil just before the hour mark. We were walking back to our half for the restart when I felt this excruciating pain then suddenly my guts collapsed. Fortunately the evidence was minimal, so no-one else noticed. Having to explain that one to Joe would not have been fun.

The whole situation taught me a valuable lesson early in my career. Be prepared for every eventuality, both at Liverpool Football Club and in life. And it was a lesson I learned from going forward.

I know my eating and drinking habits were never the best however after that 'experience' I never once had another issue when food or drink affected my performance. Timing was everything. Eat like a horse? Fine, just not six bags of crisps on a matchday!

The coaching staff expected us to show up on time, give it our all and leave nothing out there. By all means play hard but work harder. That was part of the Liverpool Way.

6

Guiding Hands

'For a bit of fun, we pointed out Graeme's location on the team bus to the furious Dinamo supporters as we parked up outside the stadium in Bucharest. Then in the warm-up, with thousands of home fans beyond angry, we kept giving him the ball. He knew what we were up to but loved it really. He didn't care'

Joe Fagan was in the same mould as Bob Paisley. As seamless a change as there was from Shankly to Paisley, it was no different from Bob to Joe. Even the philosophy was the same. 'Keep it simple and do the job you've been brought to the club to do.'

When Bob was in charge I never truly felt that I belonged in the Liverpool starting line-up. I was still young, not long at the club and was content to bide my time. But that changed once Joe took over because he gave me a chance right from the off – in those pre-season games – and slowly I started to believe that I was as good as some of the players in the team. I also felt comfortable seeking Joe out if I needed a chat, something that started when the new gaffer was Bob's assistant and he was the one the players went to if they ever needed anything. The trusty lieutenant.

After eight games of the new 1983-84 season I'd not had a sniff of first team action. I was an unused substitute on three occasions. Then Phil Neal got injured against Manchester United at Old Trafford and I came on to replace him for the final twelve minutes. 'Mr Reliable' was out for nearly a month – ending an incredible run of consecutive games for Liverpool that stretched back to 1976 – and I took his place at right-back. Finally, this was the opportunity I'd been waiting for.

I made my full European debut in a 5-0 win over Odense at Anfield, also started against Sunderland in the league and played against Brentford in the League Cup. I thought I did pretty well. So did Ronnie Moran and Roy Evans. Then I found myself not only out of the team but also left out of the squad for the trip to West Ham in October 1983 as Phil Neal returned from injury. After training on the Monday, Ronnie and Roy took me aside.

"Have you spoken to the gaffer about getting more game time?" said Roy. This came totally out of the blue.

"Eh, no." At this stage of my career I hadn't yet built up enough confidence to do such a thing.

"Why not?" asked Ronnie, and he just left it at that.

At Liverpool you weren't always told to do things. You were often just given pointers and those pointers were designed to make you think.

It was the same with stuff on the field. It wasn't a case of them telling us where we should be: we were never told to be anywhere specific on a pitch. But afterwards they might ask why we were in a certain position or doing a certain thing. The answer would tell them a lot and allow them to work out what we were thinking.

With preparations already up and running for the midweek European Cup tie at home to Athletic Bilbao I didn't feel that Monday afternoon was the right time to go and see Joe so I left it until later in the week. I'm glad I did. I was one of five unused substitutes against Bilbao at Anfield but at least I was back in the squad. That put me in a better frame of mind when I hesitantly knocked on Joe's door after training on the Thursday.

"Sit down lad, what's up?"

"Er…"

The words dried up. Preparing a speech in advance and practising it on your own is one thing but when the pressure is on – one-on-one in front of the gaffer for the first time – it's another thing entirely. I felt uncomfortable but knew I had to say something.

"I just feel as though I should be playing. I feel as though I'm ready to play. I think I should be playing. I just want you to know that." And breathe. Exhale.

There wasn't much of a response – he just kind of nodded his head and muttered something about being patient. He never did give me a proper explanation why I wasn't playing more regularly. I did, however, get the sense that he kind of knew I was right. He just hadn't yet found a way of getting me in to his team. And I'm 100 per cent certain this is the reason why I began my Liverpool career playing on the left hand side of midfield.

During that game at West Ham – when Phil Neal returned from injury and I wasn't in the squad – Craig Johnston was sent off following a tussle with Billy Bonds. So when Craig was then booked for a heavy challenge on Wayne Fereday in our next away fixture at Queens Park Rangers the coaching staff decided they couldn't afford to risk the possibility of Craig receiving another red card. I was a sub and sat huddled on the rather small visitors' bench at Loftus Road, I heard Ronnie Moran tell Joe: "He might get sent off again."

Joe turned round, looked at the bench and told me I was going on. Not only did I play the last twenty minutes in Craig's wide midfield position but I also scored my first league goal for Liverpool with seven minutes remaining. Graeme Souness played me in with an inch-perfect pass and I hit a sweet left-foot shot past Peter Hucker for the only goal of the game.

Maybe my chat with Joe two days previously had an impact on his decision to bring me on or maybe he remembered I played that same position in both games in southern Spain in pre-season. I wasn't complaining either way. After the easy League Cup win against Brentford the following midweek I started the next 28 matches for Liverpool, all of them in midfield.

The first of those 28 consecutive games was against Luton at Anfield when Ian Rush scored five in a 6-0 win. I provided the assist for his hat-trick with a decent cross into the box which he headed home with his usual accuracy. This was also the game when Craig Johnston served his one-game suspension after his red card at West Ham.

San Mames in Bilbao for the second leg of our European Cup tie against Athletic Bilbao was probably the most ferocious atmosphere I had played in up to that point in my career. Joe named the team the night before and I was picked to start ahead of Craig, who was available again, in left-midfield. After a goalless first leg at Anfield their fans were in confident mood ahead of the return fixture and the place was virtually packed out an hour before kick-off. We came out to warm up and all I remember is a sea of red and white and a hell of a noise from what seemed like hundreds of drums. Rushy continued his form from the previous game against Luton and scored the only goal of the game with a second half header – the perfect way to keep their fans quiet and silence those bloody drums. That was the game when Rushy earned the nickname 'Tosh' – after John Toshack – because the press had been saying he didn't score enough with his head!

My week to remember was topped off with a goal on my Merseyside derby debut three days later. With four minutes to go at Anfield, and Liverpool leading Everton 2-0, Lawro whipped in a cross from the right and I got there before Mark Higgins to head our third in front of The Kop. Right arm aloft and fist clenched in celebration. A feeling unlike any other.

Back at Melwood, you weren't given time to dwell on your successes. The legend of Liverpool in the mid-Eighties according to many outside the club was that we only ever played five-a-sides at training. While that's not strictly true – it was mainly eight vs eight – it's not that far away from the truth either.

During those games we were constantly talking about what we were doing and why we did things, talking about why we didn't close a certain player down or why we took two touches instead of one. So it wasn't just guys turning up at training and having a good time. We were also learning from each other while we were doing it.

The coaches used to pick new teams every day to keep things fresh. We would play two-touch games on different size fields.

To say those games were competitive is an understatement. Each game would usually last twenty minutes and by the end you'd have players going at it big time. Remember, these guys had wonderful touches, so getting the ball back was tough. One side quite often controlled everything and that was when the possibility of injuries increased. There was testosterone all over the place – nobody wanted to lose. If Ronnie and Roy spotted this, and felt things were getting out of hand, they would simply stop the game and take us over to the side of the field where they had set up cones for shuttle runs, just to take the sting out of the situation.

During all this, Joe would simply stand on the sidelines and keep a close eye on everything. Joe would be watching who was training well, who looked as though they might have a problem and if everyone was concentrating fully. If not then why not? Were they hurt? Did they have an issue at home? Was there anything he could do to help? The ultimate father figure.

Niggles were rarely disclosed to the coaching staff while players with slight knocks would do their best to make sure Joe, Ronnie and Roy weren't aware of the issue. We had a fair bit of success in the Eighties so, understandably, no one wanted to lose his place. But pulling the wool over their eyes was never easy. They were too long in the tooth for that and had seen every trick before, probably on numerous occasions.

We were doing 'doggies' one day and I'd done a couple of shuttle runs but was really just going through the motions – I just wasn't feeling it for one reason or another but thought I'd get away with it.

As I turned to go back to the start Roy looked at me and simply said, 'Is that it?'

I asked him what he meant.

'You're either doing them properly or you're not,' he replied.

After training he told me they saw every single thing we did, every single day. They were always watching. And he told me never to forget that. I never went through the motions again. Another lesson learned.

After registering fourteen games unbeaten in all competitions, the wheels came off when we lost 4-0 at Coventry City in the game before Christmas. It was just one of those weird days when nothing went right. We conceded the opening goal in forty seconds, were two-nil down inside twenty minutes and trailed by three at half-time. With nearest challengers West Ham United and Manchester United both winning, our lead at the top was cut to just one point.

That defeat at Coventry was certainly a surprise but so was what happened next: I managed to score in three of the four games that followed! We found form again quickly – the ability to immediately bounce back was a trait of this Liverpool team – and we ended the year with our three-point lead restored at the top of the table.

The visit of Ron Atkinson's Manchester United to Anfield should have been an exciting way to bring in the New Year – first against second in the league – but it wasn't the football that made the headlines in the one-all draw. Just three minutes of the second half had been played when Kevin Moran, wearing a support brace on his wrist, caught Kenny Dalglish with a forearm smash. Intentional? Only Kevin can answer that but it certainly looked that way. Kenny's cheekbone was broken and the injury ruled him out for two months. Needless, nasty and unnecessary.

The FA Cup was next on our agenda – a trophy the club hadn't won since 1974 – and we got off to a decent start by thumping Newcastle 4-0 at Anfield in Kevin Keegan's last ever FA Cup tie as a player. Unfortunately, second division Brighton knocked us out in the fourth round, doing exactly what they'd done in the fifth round twelve months previously.

We were out of one competition but going well in the others and still chasing an unprecedented treble.

The League Cup – or Milk Cup as it was known at the time – had been pretty good to Liverpool at the start of the Eighties. Bob Paisley teams won it in 1981, 1982 and 1983 and under Joe we were drawn against third division Walsall in the semi-final in February 1984. Although they'd already knocked out Arsenal at Highbury in the fourth round it was the draw everybody wanted.

Walsall may have managed a very credible two-all draw at Anfield in the first leg but we ran out comfortable 2-0 winners in the return fixture for a 4-2 aggregate success and a place in the final against Merseyside rivals Everton. I came off the bench at Fellows Park in the second leg but, unbeknown to me at the time, it would be the last time I played in the competition that season.

An ankle injury picked up against Southampton at The Dell in March meant not only a month on the sidelines but I also had to watch the Milk Cup final against Everton at Wembley and the replay at Maine Road from the stands. Luckily it was just a twist, no ligament damage, but unfortunately that still meant the dreaded wax bath the following day in the back corner of the treatment room at Anfield. Half an hour with my foot submerged in boiling hot wax while being supervised by Batman and Robin, aka Ronnie and Roy. What more could anybody wish for?

There was no visible improvement after a day or two so I was sent to see Doctor Calver, an orthopaedic surgeon at Walton Hospital, and he confirmed the initial prognosis of an absence of three to four weeks. So just a European Cup tie away to Benfica, two cup finals against Everton and a couple of vital league games while I recuperated – perfect timing!

I returned to the squad for the European Cup semi-final first leg against Dinamo Bucharest. Although an unused sub, it was nice to feel part of the action again and Sammy Lee's first half goal meant we took a narrow advantage to Romania for the return leg.

Joe was never one to scream from the rooftops so for him to say 'You Beauty' after we won 2-1 in Bucharest was a rare show of emotion. Once Rushy opened the scoring, meaning they needed to score three, we were pretty confident of putting the tie to bed. By the way, our record away from home in the European Cup that season was spectacular, winning all four matches including victories at Bilbao, Benfica and Bucharest.

There's no doubt Dinamo missed Lică Movilă, their best player who was absent after his jaw had an unfortunate alter-cation with Mr Souness's arm in the first leg, but if truth be told, Movilă could just as easily have been suspended for the return leg after punching Graeme three times in the first half at Anfield and getting away with it on each occasion.

I often get asked what's the most intimidating stadium that I played in but to be honest I don't think the Liverpool teams I was part of were ever intimidated playing away from home in

Europe. Noisy, yes, but not intimidating. The stadium in Bucharest for the second leg was certainly loud with 60,000 passionate Romanians in attendance but I think I can speak for the rest of the squad when I say that none of us found it overly intimidating.

The way we viewed it was that we must be pretty good if they were screaming at us all the time. The noise made very little difference and certainly didn't faze us. In fact, guys like Graeme Souness used the hatred of others to motivate him and that rubbed off on the rest of us. We'd experienced hostility from the home fans in Bilbao, at Benfica and in Bucharest but instead of hindering our chances we used the atmosphere to our advantage.

With the Milk Cup already in the bag – thanks to a goal from that man Souness in the replay against Everton at Maine Road – the first part of our attempt at a treble was already secured. And with the European Cup final still more than a month away we were able to fully focus on trying to wrap up another league title. The 2-2 draw with Ipswich at Anfield just three days after returning from Bucharest wasn't as harmful to our chances as it might have been with Manchester United staying two points adrift after a goalless draw at home to West Ham.

The same thing happened the following weekend: we could only draw 0-0 at Birmingham City, but United were held by Everton at Goodison.

So, with three league games remaining, the top of the table looked like this…

1. Liverpool	P39	W21	D12	L6	75pts
2. Manchester Utd	P39	W20	D13	L6	73pts

Unfortunately my game time was limited towards the end of the season as Joe Fagan decided to keep faith with the majority of players who had served him well in previous weeks. I managed a couple of substitute appearances but the time missed due to that ankle injury had given others the opportunity to impress and they took it, just like I had done against QPR earlier in the season. Fair's fair.

The destiny of the First Division title was pretty much decided on the first Monday in May. I watched from the Main Stand at Anfield as we thrashed Coventry City 5-0 – sweet revenge following their 4-0 win earlier in the season – but midway through the second half when the ball wasn't even in play a roar emerged from the Kop. Alan Sunderland had scored for Ipswich at Old Trafford to give the visitors a 2-1 lead over Manchester United. Suddenly the gap at the top was five points with only two games remaining.

We clinched the title in the penultimate league match of the season at Notts County. Normally, a goalless draw for Liverpool at Meadow Lane would be considered a poor result but this 0-0, coupled with Manchester United failing to beat Spurs at White Hart Lane, meant a third consecutive league championship for us with a game to spare. Two trophies down, one to go.

I waited exactly one hundred seconds to get my first touch against Roma after coming on as a substitute in the European Cup final. I picked up a short pass from Souness about ten yards inside their half in a central area, dribbled forward without being challenged then laid it off to Alan Kennedy on the left. Nice and simple and just what I was looking for. I was now officially part of the game and there was no time for nerves.

Joe had put me on to play right-midfield. I'd only played there on a handful of occasions that season but they wanted me to provide defensive cover for Phil Neal while at the same time giving me license to get forward and try to create something. I was as strong as an ox, was predominantly right-footed and had a really good engine, so the role was perfect.

I had one or two defensive duties to attend to but the thing I remember most after coming on happened five minutes from the end of normal time. Kenny played a lovely through ball and picked me out inside the box on the left hand side. Just prior to receiving the pass, I had a quick look in the middle but didn't see a teammate. I would have had a decision to make if I had noticed Rushy making the late run that he did but I thought I was on my own. I tried to shoot across the goalkeeper but it was a good height for him and he saved it without too much trouble. I would have had a better chance of scoring if I had kept it on the ground, but that's easy to say now. I had a split second to make my mind up. Rushy never said a word to me at the time, or afterwards, about not giving him the ball. But Joe did.

As we were sitting waiting in the airport to fly home the day after he came over to me and casually asked: "Did you see Rushy when you took your shot?"

I said 'no'. There were no further questions.

If I had said 'yes', well that's a different story altogether. He probably would have asked me why I didn't pass instead of shooting. What Joe was actually doing was trying to figure out what was going on in my head at that specific time. How clear my mind was in a pressure situation like that.

Joe always wanted to know why his players were thinking what they were thinking on the football pitch. Our answers would help him judge where we were in terms of development and he could then try, where necessary, to help us improve and progress. My answer to his question not only helped him figure out my mindset but also planted a little seed in my head. The next time I found myself in that situation I would try, if possible, to delay my look as late as possible. Most coaches would have berated their players for not seeing a teammate but Joe's Way, part of the Liverpool Way, was different.

The celebrations in Rome lasted long into the night – trebles all round – and continued the next morning as we boarded the flight back to Liverpool. The city's Lord Mayor, Hugh Dalton, was there to greet us on arrival back in England and hosted a small reception at the airport. All the televisions in the room were replaying the goals and the penalty shoot-out from the night before, a nice touch but at that stage I was still embarrassed by my miss and chose not to watch.

I was ready to go home. I hadn't slept and was shattered, both emotionally and physically. The thought of another two hours on an open-top bus didn't exactly appeal at the time. That was only because I had no idea what was going to happen next. Something unforgettable. I was able to enjoy those celebrations on a few more occasions in the years ahead. But that first one, well it's something I'll remember forever.

One of the most incredible things about winning the European Cup – and completing the treble – was how many people turned up for the victory parade. More than 300,000 lined the streets of Liverpool just to wave to us and thank us for doing something we love. They'd been standing there for hours before we even got there, the bus travelled slowly by and then it was over in the blink of an eye. But seeing all those people, and seeing what our achievements that season meant to them, that's when it really hit home to me. Liverpool Football Club means so much to so many.

The parade took nearly two hours as the bus slowly weaved its way through the packed streets of the city but looking back it feels like it was over just like that. Isn't that always the case with special moments in our lives? They pass by too quickly.

While the players were upstairs enjoying ourselves on the top deck Joe was downstairs enjoying a quiet beer with his staff, leaving us to enjoy the occasion from the top deck. Joe was always very much understated. He never looked for attention or a pat on the back. It was never about him. But once the bus reached the city centre the senior players managed to coax him upstairs to receive the adulation he deserved.

The first division title, the League Cup and the European Cup. Not bad for his first season in charge.

7

Tartan Barmy

'There were Scottish punters everywhere. Kilts, bare arses, tartan tammies, flags, the lot. We were in Soho. And we were all looking for the same thing...'

Born and bred a proud Scot, it was always my dream to pull on the dark blue shirt of my country. However, the road to international recognition was often rocky. My Scotland odyssey started like this…

September 1977 – Scotland 3-1 Czechoslovakia:
"What the fuck are you doing?" said the copper as he radioed for back-up. He thought I was taking the piss by *taking* a piss. I was thrown into the back of the police van with two officers for company. Going to watch Scotland for the first time wasn't exactly going according to plan…

I was only fifteen years old and the bus up from Troon was full of beer. Yes, of course I had a drink or three. By the time we got to Glasgow everyone was pissed, myself included.

As we took it in turns to get off the bus I noticed an unopened can on one of the seats so picked it up and hid it down my sock. It was probably a mile to Hampden from where the bus dropped us off and it wasn't long before I was dying for a pee, as usual. I stopped beside a bush by the side of the road. Everyone else walked on.

Next thing I knew I was in the back of a police van with two constables for company. I was shitting myself (well, you know what I mean), but only because I had the beer down my sock. I didn't even contemplate that urinating in public was usually frowned upon.

"Have you been drinking, son?"

"No officer" although it probably sounded more like a Sean Connery-esque "no offisher" given the amount of alcohol I'd consumed.

Grumpy Cop #1 proceeded to call me a 'dirty little bastard.'

So, I'm fifteen years old, I'd just been caught pissing in a bush, I'm in the back of a police van with a can of beer hidden in my sock and two coppers sitting staring and calling me all the names under the sun. 'What the fuck will Dad say?' was the first thing that came into my head.

Then I blurted out "Will I see the game, officer?"

Silence.

Grumpy Cop #2 took my name and address then, all of a sudden, told me to get out. "And don't do it again!" I was now standing right outside Hampden. They'd only gone and given me a lift to the game! How very nice of them.

I already had the ticket for the match against Czechoslovakia in my jacket pocket so I went through the assigned turnstile at the Rangers end of Hampden. All my friends were in the same section of terracing and I was lucky there was still plenty time before kick-off, so I was able to find my pals without too much trouble.

"We weren't sure if we would see you again tonight – what happened?" they asked. So I told them the story, embellished of course to make me sound more of a hero than a dickhead.

After hearing the tale, my big brother Ken reckoned the police might not do anything because it wasn't exactly the crime of the century and they would probably just let it go without taking any further action. So I decided not to tell Dad.

Six months later a letter arrived at the house…

I was lying in bed when Dad came storming in to my room. He put the letter on the duvet and asked what it was. He obviously knew something was up because the writing on the front of the envelope explained it was from the offices of the Magistrate's Court in Ayr. Dad then asked what had happened and I told him I'd been lifted for peeing in the street prior to a Scotland game the previous September.

I fully expected him to go apeshit. He looked at me for a few seconds, although it felt much longer than that.

"Right, open it up and let's see what it says."

It informed me that I had to go to Ayr Police Station at a certain time on a certain date to see the superintendent. "Right," said Dad. That was it. Nothing else. He then walked out of my room and headed to work. No raised voice, no anger, nothing. I'd only heard Dad swear once in his life and was convinced this would be the second time, but that was all he said.

On the day of the appointment he parked the car and we walked the few hundred yards to the police station. As we were walking, Dad told me that he would do all the talking. If the policeman asked me anything I was just to say that I hadn't been allowed out since the incident as punishment (even though I had been in the pub at least twice a week without telling him!)

I was informed why I had been lifted – the official term used was 'urinating in a public area' – and asked if this was true. I said 'yes', admitting my crime. The superintendent also said the arresting officer had noted a smell of alcohol on my breath. I said I had one can on the bus but it had been forced upon me by peer pressure.

The superintendent eventually told me they had decided not to take the case any further, but he did give me the classic line usually reserved for naughty kids: 'I don't want to see you here ever again, do you understand, son?' On the way back to the car Dad told me exactly the same thing. And that was it. Nothing was ever said about it ever again.

May 1981 – England 0-1 Scotland:

My first experience of Wembley came as a fan. My brother, Kim, said he had two tickets for England versus Scotland and asked if I wanted to go with him. We travelled up from Troon to Glasgow on the Friday before getting the train from Central Station to King's Cross.

Several beers later, shortly before midnight, we set off in search of a London bed and breakfast. (Of course, organising a hotel in advance would have been far easier but why make life easy for yourself?)

Prior to making the trip down south, a lot of talk among the Tartan Army had been about Soho. Me and my brother had been told this place was legendary and you could even see porn, which at the time was only available in magazines that were, er, too high up on the newsagent's shelves for us to reach. Kim and I wanted to find out more so it was our first port of call on the Saturday morning.

Walking down a flight of stairs towards one of the gentleman's clubs, we reached the front door of said establishment and were greeted by a burly bouncer, a right miserable bastard. "Are you both members?" he asked with a straight face. Now he might have been taking the piss but we were certainly not about to ask him if he was.

"No, sir, we are not," we replied. He then demanded two pounds from each of us for a 'daily membership'. After paying the money, we walked into what I can only describe as a dark grotto similar to the black hole of Calcutta. We couldn't see a fucking thing. Well, apart from a screen with fornication taking place. Eventually we found somewhere to sit – Kim stayed put and I tried to find my way to the bar in the darkness.

"Two pints of lager please, love."

The first noise I heard was the sound of a can opening. The second noise was the running of a tap.

"That'll be four pounds please."

Eight pounds for two 'day memberships' and two pints?!

I took the pints back to where Kim was sitting and simultaneously we each took a drink. It was the equivalent of drinking piss out of a plastic cup. We asked around and it appeared that every other gullible Scotsman in the building was drinking exactly the same as we were: fifty per cent beer and fifty per cent tap water. As much as Kim and I wanted to complain, it was probably best if we said nothing considering the size of the security men in the club. I was so pissed off I can't even remember if the entertainment was any good or not.

When we walked up Wembley Way later that day, I can honestly say that I have never seen so many Scottish people in one place in my life. A sea of tartan. We certainly live up to our national stereotype, don't we?!

Once through the turnstiles and having climbed what seemed to be thousands of steps I looked out across the stadium. I have never had my heart warmed as much – Wembley was absolutely full of Scotland supporters. The only comparison I can make is standing in front of the pipes at Hampden Park on my Scotland debut against Yugoslavia listening to Scotland the Brave being played (the song that should be our national anthem by the way).

For a Scotland fan, seeing your team beat England at Wembley is like the Holy Grail – John Robertson's penalty meant it was a result that required celebrating. On the way out of the stadium I got separated from my brother and ended up with a couple of lads from Edinburgh that we had met during the game. With no mobile phones in those days there was no way of getting in touch with Kim to tell him where I was. I didn't see him again until the next morning.

Several 'proper' pints were sunk that night – not watered down and costing a lot less than two pounds each – but by 1am most of the pubs were closing and I was ready to call it a night and head back to the bed and breakfast. Except I gave the taxi driver the wrong address for the B&B. After getting out of the cab in the middle of nowhere I started walking – to where I do not know. I saw a man coming towards me so asked him if he knew of a nearby pub that was still open.

"No, but if you really want a drink then you're welcome to come with me and have a couple of beers at my house."

The Nicols: A family portrait taken in Troon, 1969. I am back row, far right. Also on the back row are brothers Kim and Ken. Front row: Sandra, dad Jim, Susan, mum Helen and sister Helen

Early days: (Clockwise from top left) Eleanor's parents Jim and Helen McMath; watching Scotland in the 1982 World Cup with father-in-law Jim; with Eleanor before we were married and wearing my Scotland under-21 shirt as we look after dog Holly's new litter

Step up: (Left) My size 11 feet made headlines when I signed for Liverpool in 1981. Top: At Ayr United. Above: Eleanor's moped – my main mode of transport in the early days at Anfield! Dog Jess is in the basket

We are sailing: With Alan Hansen and his wife Janet on board the MS Mikhail Lermontov. Top: My wedding day in June 1982. Right: Liverpool squad shot, 1983

Local rivals: Evading a sliding challenge from Manchester United's Ray Wilkins and (right) celebrating my first Merseyside derby goal against Everton in November, 1983

Off target:
That penalty miss in Rome...

Big stage:
Coming off
the bench to
face Roma
in the 1984
European
Cup final.
Below: My
shot is saved
late on. Far
right: Personal
snaps of the
post-match
celebrations
in Hotel
Cavalieri

Champions of Europe: Celebrating (back row, third from left) in the Stadio Olimpico after Barney (aka Alan Kennedy) had saved my blushes by scoring the winning penalty in the shoot-out

Beware of Gaz: (Above) Smelling danger as a young Paul Gascoigne goes on the run during Newcastle United's visit to Anfield in 1985

Have boots, will travel: I eventually got a boot deal – no thanks to Kenny and Co!

Black night: With Kenny at Brussels' Heysel Stadium in 1985. It was the second European Cup Final I was involved in – and it ended in tragedy

High five: (Above) Celebrating the moment we won the league at Stamford Bridge in 1986 with Bruce and Craig Johnston

Hitting the right notes: Recording our Wembley song; in action during the final and (below, right) arms aloft at the final whistle

If the cup fits: (Right) Trying on the FA Cup for size during the lap of honour at Wembley. Above: Celebrating with Eleanor after the match

The class of '86: After Big Al had lifted the Cup, we enjoyed our usual team celebration – nobody in the press ever picked up on the song we were singing!

MERSEYSIDE'S

Make mine a Double: Enjoying some celebratory lager and champagne as Kenny, Steve McMahon and Craig Johnston join me at the front of the open-topped bus in 1986

World at our feet: Ready to face Uruguay at Mexico '86. A win would still have seen us progress from the group but we were on our way home after a controversial 0-0 draw

Being young, naive and innocent – and only interested in having another drink – he persuaded me to accompany him to his home around the corner. I sat down in the front room of his flat and he asked me what I would like to drink.

"Do you have any beer?" He sat down beside me. "No" he replied, while trying to touch my arm, "but I do love freckles."

"And you have awfully big hands" he added, as he attempted to clasp my right hand in his left one. "By the way I only have wine."

"Er, that's fine," I replied nervously.

I waited for him to leave the room then I got the fuck out of there as quick as humanly possible.

February 1982 – Italy u21s 0-1 Scotland u21s:

My first taste of international football was with Scotland under 21s and we actually qualified for the European Championships in 1982. I played in three of the four qualifiers against Sweden and Denmark, including the 1-1 draw in Aarhus that clinched qualification at the expense of the Danes and my future Liverpool teammate Jan Molby.

The draw for the last eight wasn't kind – Scotland versus Italy, an Italian squad that contained the likes of Franco Baresi, Giuseppe Bergomi and Mauro Tassotti. The tie would take place over two games with the first leg away from home. With the full Scotland team also in action that midweek – they were away to Spain in a friendly – I was able to travel up to Glasgow on the Sunday night with a certain Mr Dalglish, Souness and Hansen to meet up with our respective squads.

I felt like the cat that got the cream. Just 20 years old and yet to play a competitive game for the Liverpool first team but

I was about to spend the next three hours in a car with three proper football legends. I remember thinking to myself: 'I'm sitting here with THESE guys?'

Then things took a turn for the worse.

The road conditions were hellish, driving sleet and at times heavy snow. About an hour into the journey Graeme pulled over. "There's something wrong with the windscreen wiper," he said.

Someone needed to go out so I volunteered. Well, I say volunteered. The three of them just sat staring at me. They didn't say a word. Didn't need to. Point made. I just had a t-shirt on because they had the heating up full in the car but surely fixing a windscreen wiper would take no time at all. So I didn't bother putting my jumper back on and out I went to get the job done.

They pulled away.

I walked towards the car but every time I got close they moved forward another twenty yards or so.

There was six foot of snow at the side of the road and this went on for a full twenty minutes.

Eventually, once it dawned on them that I could easily suffer hypothermia, they let me back in the car. Probably only because they didn't fancy explaining to Jock Stein and under 21 coach Ricky Ferguson why they started the journey in Liverpool with four in the car and arrived in Glasgow with only three.

Frank McAvennie's first half goal in Catanzaro earned us a fantastic 1-0 win in the first leg and turned out to be the only goal of the tie.

Meanwhile the big team, with Dalglish, Souness and Hansen all starting, lost 3-0 to Spain in Valencia. So I had the last laugh...

September 1984 – Scotland 6-1 Yugoslavia:

Pre-match was just a blur. It was my full debut for Scotland, at Hampden Park as well, but I remember very little between arriving at the ground and just before kick-off. Sitting there in the dressing room encased in a bubble trying to make sense of the fact that I was among my heroes and about to represent my country for the first time. Jock Stein's team-talk? Didn't take in any of it. The captain's speech from Graeme Souness? Nope, not a single word. All I was concerned about was making sure I kept it simple and didn't make any mistakes – just like my debut for Liverpool. I do remember the red jerseys that were laid out for us and thinking it was strange that Scotland were playing at home but wearing our away kit.

Standing in line, just in front of the massed ranks of pipes and drums, they started to play Scotland The Brave. That's when it hit home. Every hair on my body was standing to attention as well. The bubble had finally burst and I was able to fully experience the atmosphere and take it all in. Standing there proud as punch looking up trying to locate Dad and Uncle Billy in the stand. Thinking of all the times I had stood on those very same terraces as a fan. Now I was on the pitch and about to make my debut for Scotland.

Right from kick-off they had a chance – what a welcome to international football! The cross was drilled in and it fizzed across the box. I was facing my own goal so let the ball run across me before picking it up, proceeding to then casually stride up the park with it. I must have looked like the coolest man in Glasgow. Actually I was shitting myself. I then attempted a simple pass to Jim Bett in front of me and it went straight out of play. From Pele to smelly in seconds.

Yugoslavia took the lead after just eleven minutes when Fadil Vokrri opened the scoring with a great header. But Davie Cooper equalised within a couple of minutes and Graeme Souness scored soon after and we never looked back after such a shaky start.

October 1984 – Scotland 3-0 Iceland

Mum wasn't well so unfortunately couldn't be at my debut against Yugoslavia but she was at my second game for Scotland, our first qualifier for the 1986 World Cup. It was the first time her and Dad were able to attend a match together so that was another proud moment for me. It was also the first time I was able to pull on the classic dark blue shirt for my country.

Once again I started at right-back and once again there were nerves, just not as many as on my debut. My game at that point in time was built on doing the simple things but doing them well. I was usually pretty good at decision-making and looking as though I belonged on that stage. Actually, the feeling I got from other Scotland players who hadn't played with me at club level was that they were more than happy I was playing in the same team as them. As a 22-year-old, that felt good.

So, a 6-1 win on my Scotland debut followed by a 3-0 victory in a World Cup qualifier. Not a bad way to start my international career. Things were going well for club and country but the lessons I'd learned at both Ayr United and Liverpool meant it wasn't difficult to keep my feet firmly on the ground. Mum on the other hand got a little bit carried away. Proud as punch she showed up at the front door at Hampden after the Iceland match and just walked right through. She thought because she was my mum that she could just walk in and nobody would care. There was no players' lounge in the stadium in those days – you just met your family in the reception area. Eventually someone stopped her and explained the official protocol. I love how she thought everyone would just know who she was despite me only playing two games for my country!

While my dad was low-key and never wanted to attract undue attention my mum was the opposite. This was her wee boy and she wanted everybody to know. That's fair enough, isn't it? From that day forward Mum would introduce me to people she met by saying 'this is my son, Steve Nicol, who plays for Liverpool and Scotland.' She'd never called me Steve! To her I was always Stephen. But I think the second part – about playing for Liverpool and Scotland – was slightly more important to her than which version of my name she used.

November 1984 – Scotland 3-1 Spain:

It was the first time I can remember this particular corner kick routine resulting in a goal. Just before the setpiece was taken, we would have two players standing right outside the box – one on the left and one on the right. That meant if the ball wasn't knocked away properly then one of those two players could either attempt a shot on goal or help prevent a quick break by the opposition. On this particular occasion, the ball was headed away by a Spaniard to just outside the penalty box, on our right hand side. I volleyed it first time with my left foot, one of the sweetest shots I've ever hit, and it was heading full pelt towards the top corner. Not only was this about to be the best goal I would ever score in my life but it would also fulfil a childhood dream – scoring for Scotland. Then Spanish goalkeeper Luis Arconada proceeded to produce what I still consider one of the greatest saves I have ever seen, leaping to his left and somehow denying me opening the scoring. The silver lining was that Maurice Johnston – as usual – was in the right place at the right time and nodded home the rebound.

I don't think Spain realised just how good a team we were. It was probably the most complete Scotland performance I was involved in, and it needed to be against excellent opposition. If you look at the balance of our side – from Willie and Alex at the back to Souness and Jim Bett in the middle of the park, then Mo and Kenny up front – great partnerships throughout the spine of that team plus, of course, Jim Leighton in goal.

The other thing about that side was that it was very together. We used to meet up on a Sunday night in the Macdonald Hotel on the outskirts of Glasgow – there were characters everywhere you looked.

Some of the press used to suggest there was an issue between the Anglos and the home-based Scottish players in the squad – but that was absolute nonsense. If they had seen us socialising together at the hotel they would have quickly changed their minds. We would eat together then go to the bar and drink together. Going to clubs was banned so the socialising was all done in the hotel with the whole team taking part. For me it was very reminiscent of our Liverpool ethos. Plenty of characters, lots of ability plus hard work equals good times aplenty.

8

On The Brink

*'I found it impossible to walk by that sign without
touching it. It's such a small thing as well – THIS IS
ANFIELD – but it means so much to so many. All the
history, everyone who's touched it – when you look
at it you're mesmerised. It's a religion. It's Liverpool
Football Club in a nutshell'*

Twenty-four hours after Liverpool won the European Cup in
Rome we found out that Eleanor's dad, Jim, had been diagnosed with cancer. Talk about highs and lows. I was due to
fly out to Swaziland with the rest of the squad for two end-of-
season friendlies against Spurs at the start of June but I needed
to get Eleanor back home to be with her parents in Ayr. So I
called the club and arranged with Sheila, Joe Fagan's secretary,
for me to come in and have a chat with the boss.

I may have started 32 matches during the 1983-84 season –
a decent amount, I suppose – but the team ended up playing
67 games so I still didn't feel like a regular. "You don't have to
come if you don't want to," said Joe. "Really, it's no big issue."

But I spoke with Eleanor and we both felt that if I didn't go to Swaziland it might count against me in the long run. A compromise was reached and he agreed to give me a couple of days off back in Scotland before flying out to join up with the rest of the squad. That allowed me to take Eleanor to see her mum and dad and for us to spend some time with them before I headed out to Swaziland. Joe meant what he said – it really would have made no difference if I had stayed at home or not, the club was just fulfilling an obligation to go out there – but I was just a young lad eager to impress and thought otherwise. The good news was that the surgery to remove Jim's cancer, thankfully, was successful.

I finally arrived in Swaziland on the Wednesday morning, three days after Liverpool had beaten Spurs 5-2 in friendly number one, and it was clear the players in both squads had pretty much downed tools and were in holiday mode. We were all staying at the Royal Swazi Spa Hotel for the week and it wasn't uncommon to see lads from both teams mingling and hanging out by the pool, especially Big Al and Alan Brazil. The hot topic of conversation was horse racing with the Derby at Epsom taking place later that day. A few of the boys had money on various horses but, of course, the race wasn't being shown live on African television so finding out the winner wasn't easy.

With Alan Brazil sitting beside him, Big Al phoned Alan's hotel room knowing that his roommate Garth Crooks was there. Big Al knew which horse each of the lads had money on – and he was well aware that Garth had a decent amount on a certain nag – so he told him the name of the horse that had won, which of course was Garth's. "Thank you, thank you. That's fantastic. That's brilliant," said a very excited Mr Crooks.

When Garth was reading a newspaper at breakfast the following morning and found out that 14/1 shot Secreto had in fact triumphed in the Derby, and not his horse, he looked over and saw Big Al with a self-satisfied smirk on his face. It was nice to know it wasn't always me on the end of one of Hansen's pranks.

I know footballers travel thousands of miles these days to play for club and country but I'd be surprised if any of them have played in as many countries as Liverpool players did in the Eighties. Another pre-season and another five places for us to visit in August 1984 with trips to Germany, Belgium, Switzerland and Iceland, plus a game in Dublin against Home Farm as part of the deal that saw Brian Mooney and Ken DeMange join Liverpool the previous summer.

Time at home was always scarce before a season started, but we always finished our preparations at Melwood in the week leading up to the first game. On the Thursday before the league opener at Norwich, Joe arranged a full eleven-a-side match as our final proper workout before season 1984-85 began. No quarter was to be asked or given, and I remember it being pretty competitive to the extent that a penalty was awarded for our team. Immediately I wanted the ball. I needed to get rid of those demons from Rome. It may only have been at Melwood but this was important to me. My spot kick was saved and I decided there and then that my penalty-taking days were over. Only once after that did I take another spot kick for Liverpool – in the shoot-out against Celtic in Dubai in December 1986 – and I scored. But that didn't mean I wanted to be considered as a genuine penalty taker again. We were in good hands with the likes of Warky and Jan Molby so I was happy just to leave it to them. I'd done enough damage!

The man who saved my spot kick at Melwood was a certain Bruce Grobbelaar. As you probably know, he had a colourful life story and wasn't shy of telling us a tale or two. I'm convinced he actually believed everything he said. Like the time he was underwater in South Africa when a crocodile swam up and the two of them made eye contact. Bruce said that by staring long enough he was able to out-psyche the crocodile so it turned round and fled. Then he told us about being in the army on a jungle expedition when they all put their shoes on back to front to confuse anyone trying to follow them.

Another time, I remember Bruce telling us that he had meningitis. This was a first. We'd been privy to him coming in on a Monday morning and telling us he'd picked up a concussion or various other ailments in the game at the weekend. But meningitis?! I remember coming in from a warm-up one Saturday to find Bruce already back in the dressing room and sitting in the toilets in total darkness. Someone had told him that exposure to too much light would bring on bad headaches, not ideal for someone suffering from meningitis.

As it turned out he did miss a fair chunk of playing time – four months in total – during season 1988-89 because of illness and injury so on that occasion he was probably telling some semblance of the truth but that was the problem with Bruce, you just never knew when he was being serious and when he was just acting the goat.

The Hotel Vic in Wirral was a regular drinking haunt for me and Bruce and one particular weekend some of his mates were over from South Africa and were staying there. One of his friends – allegedly a diamond prospector – seemed like a straightforward guy and challenged me to a game of pool. Now

I was pretty good back then, in fact between five and ten pints I was virtually unbeatable. We started off playing for a pound per game: Double or Quits. I kept winning. After about eight or nine games – and many more pints – he owed me around 250 quid. I should have walked away but I felt invincible at the pool table. Then he finally beat me. Quits – with no money owed to anyone.

Taking a break from the games of pool we all went upstairs and Bruce's friend produced a big bag of green stuff, which he placed on the bed in his room. I was offered some but told him 'no chance.' I did smoke but I wasn't trying any of that shit.

"Let's play for two hundred quid," suggested Bruce's pal.

I only had a few pounds in my pocket for beer money but having beaten him nine out of ten times when we'd played pool that night I fancied my chances. So I asked my mate Jack who owned the place to stand me the money, promising to pay him back immediately after I'd won.

Game one: I beat him. He said double or quits.

Game two: I beat him again. He said double or quits.

"Look, let's not be daft. We're both pissed. Are you good for the £800 if I beat you again?" He said yes. I beat him again in game three. He'd finally had enough. "Okay, I'm done."

Initially I figured the chances of me getting the money were slim but he told me to follow him upstairs and he paid up straight away. I then gave Jack his two hundred back, plus a little extra, and made my way home at 3.30am thinking I was the bee's knees. I got to the front door and had no idea where the key was, in fact I can't remember if I even took a key, so I knocked several times. After a few seconds Eleanor opened the upstairs window.

"WHAT?" she shouted.

"I'm sorry, I'm sorry but I've won eight hundred pounds – look," I drunkenly yelled as I looked up while simultaneously waving the wad of cash from side to side above my head.

"It's three-thirty in the morning," came the reply. "Stay there, I'm coming down."

Two or three minutes passed without anything happening so I pressed my face against the small glass pane in the middle of our wooden door and tried, unsuccessfully, to peer through to see if she actually was coming down the stairs. The alcohol-induced lack of balance wasn't helping my cause. Eventually I heard a noise behind the door. "Do you want in?"

"Yeah."

"Okay, take a couple of steps back and I'll open the door."

I climbed down the three or four stairs that led up to the front door and stood there like a little lost puppy. Eleanor opened the door and I immediately noticed a huge pail of water in her hands. "Take that!"

After drying off I made it into bed but less than four hours later the door of the spare room swung open and in she came with the kids, offering a bright and breezy 'MORNING!'

"So here's how it's going to work," she said. "I'm going to spend the £800 on Christmas presents for the family and you get to come shopping with me to look after Michael and Katy."

Just what the doctor ordered…

With Graeme Souness having left Liverpool to join Sampdoria during the summer of 1984 there were a couple of new faces brought to the club – Jan Molby and Paul Walsh, the cockney-est cockney I had ever met and a future roommate. A great lad.

The loss of our captain was a tough one to take and I think we felt Graeme's departure most during the first two or three months of the season. Losing the derby to Everton at Anfield in October – one of three 1-0 defeats to them that season – was not only a big blow, it also left us seventeenth in the table after a fourth league game in a row where we failed to even score. But Joe Fagan was not one to panic and we won five of our next seven league games ahead of the trip to Tokyo in December for the World Club Championship against Copa Libertadores winners Independiente of Argentina.

What happened next is not something that happens in today's game anymore. With the upcoming trip to the Far East looming, Eleanor was induced with our first child Michael the day before the team left, thus ensuring I didn't miss the birth but also my place in the Liverpool team wasn't in jeopardy. The whole focus back then, not just for me but for my wife as well, was about ensuring that I was available for selection and able to do my job. In our eyes this was important, not only for my career at Liverpool but also for us as a family. This was our bread and butter.

I was as sick as a dog on the flight over to Japan but a couple of days later I felt much better and told Joe on the morning of the game that I was feeling fine and was alright to play. He trusted me, he trusted all his players, and that was a big thing at the club when he was in charge. Of course we all wanted to play, but even though we were carrying knocks at times we all knew that we could still get the job done. He trusted us to be honest with him.

The big games kept coming and the following month it was Juventus in the European Super Cup. Normally a two-legged affair between the winners of the European Cup and the Cup Winners' Cup, both clubs agreed on a one-off showdown to help ease fixture congestion. Juventus won the right to host the game in Turin and, with more than a little help from the officials, beat us 2-0.

Their first goal was clearly offside. In fact, after watching it again on YouTube, it's even more offside than I remember at the time. Not when the ball is played through to Boniek but just before that from Platini's pass to Massimo Briaschi, who is definitely in front of Alan Kennedy, our last defender.

After any late arrival home from a midweek European away game, I would always have an extra couple of hours in bed the following morning. On one particular day, after a different trip, my peace and quiet was interrupted when Eleanor came storming in to the bedroom.

"What's this?" she screamed while pointing at the headline on the back page of the Daily Star which read 'NICOL HIGH ON CHAMPAGNE.' "Who do you think you are?" she asked in no uncertain terms.

Liverpool had drawn one-all away to Austria Vienna the previous night in the European Cup and I scored our late equaliser. At the airport on the way home, Matt D'Arcy of the Daily Star asked me if I would be having a glass of champagne to celebrate my goal. We always used to travel to away games in Europe with Aer Lingus and he knew that on the way back the boys would have a couple of beers and, following a good result, the airline would also provide an additional couple of miniature bottles of champagne. I rarely touched the stuff – I've always been a beer drinker – but I told Matt that I'd have some anyway.

Eleanor misinterpreted the headline without knowing the full story and thought I was starting to act like Bertie Big Bollocks. A few years later, we were on holiday in Portugal when we ran into Matt and his family at a communal swimming pool. As soon as I saw him I said, "Matt – you need to tell my wife the whole story."

He honestly had no idea about the shit he'd got me into that day because of the headline in his newspaper. So I explained the story and he laughed before adding a customary 'sorry', said very much with a smile. He was one of the old school journalists you could sit and have a pint with. If you told him something was off the record then that's the way it stayed. I had total trust in him. He actually offered to buy me a bottle of champagne in Portugal but I politely declined!

Ken Gorman of the Daily Mirror was another journalist who had earned the trust of the players and that goes back to an incident in Marbella in 1982, my first pre-season with the Liverpool squad. I remember it was a Sunday, our day off, so the boys went down to the beach. Ken was sitting nearby just minding his own business when we spotted him so we invited him to join us for a game of 'Buzz'.

Let me explain the rules. Each player counts in turn, starting from 1. When the number 7, or any number in which the figure 7 or any multiple of 7 is reached, they have to say 'buzz' instead of whatever the number may be. Failure to do so would mean having to take a drink. Big Al was always the chairman and he would decide which particular number was being used for each game.

Ken had never played the game before so was not fully aware of the rules mainly because we didn't really explain them to him properly, intentionally of course. Every time he said something, even when it was correct, we'd all laugh and Big Al would tell him he was wrong and that he had to take a drink. He must have consumed more alcohol in half an hour than he's probably ever had on any night out.

But Ken wasn't for arguing because he was enjoying himself too much and, as a journalist, was getting this rare opportunity to bond with the Liverpool players. He just had no idea what he was getting himself into. Needless to say it wasn't long before Ken was a little bit disorientated. He soon excused himself from the game and we last saw him that day propped up against one of the showers at the beach with water cascading over him.

This was just our way of welcoming those we trusted into the inner sanctum. We were lucky to have reporters like Ken, Woody, John Keith and Matt D'Arcy covering Liverpool in the Eighties because you could have a conversation with them off the record and you knew nothing would ever be published. Unless it involved champagne…

Having witnessed three League Cup wins (1982, 1983, 1984) since joining the club, yet not having played in any of the finals, I really wanted to win a domestic cup with Liverpool. We were drawn against Manchester United in the semi-final of the FA Cup at Goodison Park. I'd been injured after the win at Sunderland at the beginning of April and missed the next two games against Leicester at Filbert Street and the 4-0 victory over Panathinaikos at Anfield in the European Cup semi-final. But I was feeling better and told my brother Kim, who had already arranged to travel down with friends to watch the semi-final, that I should be fine to play.

A fitness test at Goodison at 9.30am on the Saturday morning – the day of the game – suggested otherwise. Me, Ronnie and Roy took a black cab from the Holiday Inn in Liverpool city centre to the ground and I spent ten minutes running, chasing a ball and trying to change direction. I soon knew I wasn't right. Now I could have lied and said I wanted to give it a go, but what good would that have done if I had to hobble off after five minutes or so? Joe demanded honesty from his players so I explained to Ronnie and Roy that I wasn't able to play. But I was fit enough to start the replay at Maine Road four days later after the first game at Goodison had finished 2-2.

Playing on the right hand side of midfield, I put in the cross for our opening goal and then had a really good chance to make it 2-0 just a few minutes later. Johnny Wark set me up perfectly inside the box; the right foot shot from ten yards or so beat United goalkeeper Gary Bailey but went just wide of the post.

Watching the ITV highlights later that evening, commentator Brian Moore called it 'a marvellous chance' and even George Best in the studio said I should have done better. As George was my hero growing up, that hurt a bit. At the time, I felt as though I struck the shot well but looking back at the chance now they were both right – I should have scored! Second half goals from Robson and Hughes meant I had to wait a bit longer to play in an FA Cup final.

In Europe, it was a different story. Back-to-back European Cup finals for the second time in seven years was quite an achieve-ment for Liverpool Football Club. Unfortunately, as everyone knows, the game at the Heysel Stadium in Brussels was to end in tragedy. I'll be honest, I don't remember too much about it. While the tragedy was unfolding, we were told to remain inside, so details were thin on the ground for the players. As a result, my recollection of the evening is pretty vague.

I remember walking around the pitch before the game and looking at the old-fashioned fences separating the two sets of supporters and I recall Joe and Phil Neal addressing the fans.

About an hour before kick-off, I heard a loud crash, which turned out to be the brick wall collapsing. Initially there was talk that the game would be delayed by an hour, then two hours but no one knew anything official. Would it even go ahead at all? Our wives were sat in a part of the stadium right next to where the wall collapsed. They saw everything that happened. It was much worse for them than it was for us and it wasn't until we eventually got out on to the pitch that we saw the full extent of the chaos.

I remember the kick-off with the pitch being surrounded by hundreds of police and the penalty they were awarded. Then I recall Juventus fans storming the pitch at the end to celebrate the win and me shaking hands with Michel Platini on the pitch as we waited to leave the stadium. It all seemed surreal.

Most of all, I remember seeing Joe upset – and that upset us as well. His post-match interview on BBC was a tough listen. "It's dreadful. It's a night I won't forget, and it's not for the right reasons. My last game in football, not just as a manager, and this will stay with me for the rest of my life. Just so tragic."

We already knew this was going to be his final game in charge of Liverpool but he didn't deserve to go out like that, especially after everything he'd done for the football club.

As the story unfolded, we learned about the 39 victims. Going to a football match to support your team and losing your life? No-one could believe it.

9

Oops! I Did It Again

*'Bruce Grobbelaar brought a new meaning to the term
'windy conditions'. It was the day after the Christmas
party and we were only in at Melwood for a walk,
but Bruce farted and Roy Evans nearly choked because
of the smell. Thankfully him dropping one didn't
cost us on this occasion...'*

'Oops, I did it again' – a regular catchphrase of mine during my first couple of years at Liverpool. As a daft lad who was wet behind the ears and, I have to admit, still rather gullible I usually found myself playing the role of victim when my team-mates – well, one in particular – wanted to have a bit of fun.

He became less involved in the banter after taking over as manager from Joe Fagan in the summer of 1985, but before that Mr Kenneth Mathieson Dalglish, our legendary number seven, was mainly responsible for a whole pile of non-malicious mayhem, mostly at my expense...

Strike one...

When I turned up at training one morning, I think it was around 1982, I noticed all the players had envelopes. Kenny asked me where my envelope was.

"Did you not get one?" asked Kenny, straight-faced and serious without a hint of a smile in his eyes.

"No – what's in it?""

"Sponsorship money."

"Why would I get it?"

"Well you're part of the first team squad aren't you?"

"So what should I do?"

"Go and see the boss."

"I can't do that."

"Why not – you have to stick up for yourself?"

"Yeah, you're probably right."

So after training I got showered and changed and went down the corridor and spoke to Sheila, Bob Paisley's secretary.

"Is the boss in?"

"Yes, just knock on the door and in you go."

"Boss," I said after a bit of hesitation, my heart thumping in my chest. "I just wanted to let you know that I didn't get an envelope."

Bob just turned slowly and gave me one of his looks. After a short pause, he gave me his reply. It wasn't what I was expecting. "Fucking envelope? Here, have mine," he said.

Turns out it wasn't a cash bonus for the players – it was exactly the opposite – a tax bill from a sponsorship deal the year before I'd even signed.

And strike one was followed soon after by strikes two and three...

"By the way Bumper, did you get your money from the team photo?" enquired Kenny another time.

"What do you mean?" I replied.

"Well, everybody in the team photo gets sponsorship money from Umbro. You were in the team photo last week, weren't you?"

"Yeah."

"So you should get the same as everybody else."

I asked him what I should do.

"Well, you need to speak to this lad at Umbro," and he gave me his name.

"Call him up. Nice guy. Here's his number. He'll sort you out."

So, without even thinking about the previous envelope wind-up, I phoned him.

"Hi, it's Steve Nicol from Liverpool. I'm just calling to let you know I didn't get my money for the team photo."

"What do you mean?"

"Well, the lads have all said they've had their money for the photo but I've not received anything yet."

"Let me check if there's been an administrative error," he said. "Give me your number and I'll get back to you as soon as possible."

So I got off the phone thinking 'yeah, I sorted him out, nobody's going to try and take the piss out of me.'

He called me back.

'Stevie, you weren't in that photograph.'

Turns out the lads had only just been paid for the team photo taken a couple of months before I joined the club.

Dalglish had got me again.

If it wasn't tax envelopes or team photo bonuses it was fake boot deals.

For at least a year after moving to Anfield I used to buy my own football boots until Liverpool legend Ian St John, who was working with Nike at the time, asked if I was interested in using their boots. Something for nothing – where do I sign up?

Around six months later Kenny approached me after training one day and asked if I fancied a sponsorship deal with Puma. This was a whole new ball game – getting something for nothing AND being paid? Of course I was interested. Kenny's contact at Puma was Derek Ibbotson, an Olympic athlete and former world record holder in the mile.

"I've spoken to Ibbo and they want to pay you to wear their boots." I told Kenny that I was with Nike but didn't get paid so I was interested to hear what Derek had to say.

"Okay, leave it with me."

I spoke with Derek on the phone and explained the situation with the Nike deal, but told him if Puma was willing to pay me to wear their boots then that changed things. He said he would discuss things with Kenny and take it from there.

While all this was going on, I tried to get in touch with Ian St John – I felt an obligation to him and to Nike – but he was on holiday so I spoke with one of his associates. I explained that Puma had been in touch and asked if they would have any issues if I spoke with them. The associate told me that would be 'no problem whatsoever', which I thought was a bit strange. So I let Kenny know it was fine for him to arrange a meeting with Derek.

A short time later: "Sunday morning at Burtonwood Service Station around 10.30 – he'll see you there."

I went home after training that day and told Eleanor that I had a meeting to discuss my first ever sponsorship deal. This was a big thing for both of us.

We got up nice and early on the Sunday morning, had breakfast then travelled the fifteen miles or so from our house in Croxteth Park in Liverpool to Burtonwood Services, just off junction eight of the M62, and arrived there around quarter past ten. Fifteen minutes later, at the scheduled meeting time, no sign of Derek. Half an hour later, fifteen minutes after the scheduled meeting time, no sign of Derek. Then when the eleven o'clock news came on the radio in the car, thirty minutes after the scheduled meeting time, Eleanor asked if I had actually spoken to Mr Puma about the meeting.

"Eh, no."

"Well who told you to come here?"

"Kenny."

"WHAT?! You idiot! If I'd known it was him that set this whole thing up we wouldn't be here. Come on, we're going home."

Unfortunately my wife is a lot more perceptive than me. She's always been the sensible one

"You didn't go, did you?" asked Kenny at training on the Monday morning.

"Of course not."

"Good, because I forgot to call and tell you it was just a windup!"

"Do you think I'm daft? I knew it was a wind up all along…"

The following week all the boys were in the pub for a 'wet the baby's head' night after one of the lads became a father for the first time. After a few beers I told Kenny that I did in fact go to

Burtonwood Services, not only that but Eleanor went with me. I just couldn't help myself. Kenny then informed everyone else and the whole pub thought this was hilarious.

Come on, I was in my early twenties and just a naive young-ster from Troon in Ayrshire who was amongst his heroes. If Kenny Dalglish offered to help set up a boot deal to make some money – considering I'd been on 25 quid a week at Ayr United not long before that – then I'm sure everyone in my position would have done exactly the same.

The funny thing is I did end up signing a contract with Puma the following year, making sure I put pen to paper first before telling Dalglish and Co.

An added benefit of having a boot deal with Puma was getting free clothing from the company before it was officially launched and available to the public. The downside, however, was the mysterious disappearance of the clothes from the washing line after Eleanor had hung them outside to dry. They always went out but they didn't always come back in.

One day we were out shopping in Liverpool city centre when I saw a young lad, who looked about fifteen, coming towards us. The distinctive Puma gear he was wearing was clearly far too big for him. "That's my tracksuit," I said to Eleanor.

"How do you know?"

"Well it's not even on sale in the shops yet and he looks like a drowned rat!"

As the kid moved closer he soon recognised me. The look on his face quickly changed – it was priceless. He got more and more uncomfortable the closer we got and when he walked past us I quickly turned round and followed him. He started to walk quicker. I started to walk quicker.

"Oi you, come here," I shouted.

He looked back, stopped and I told him he was wearing – in the loosest possible terms – my tracksuit.

"What do you mean?"

"I know it's mine. You know it's mine. So where did you get it?"

He told me he had bought it from a kid on the school bus – utter bollocks – so I told him to give me back the tracksuit top. He took it off and handed it to me.

"And the tracksuit bottoms…"

"But I only have me underpants on underneath," said the scally.

"Well, you obviously know where I live, so bring them round to the house at six o'clock tonight and the issue will be forgotten about."

Six o'clock on the dot the doorbell rang. He was standing there holding on to his bike with one hand and with the tracksuit bottoms in the other, which he duly handed over. Then the cheeky little shit then asked for my autograph in return!

"Are you fucking serious?" I asked, trying to curtail my laughter. Talk about a brass neck. I went back inside and found a picture – an official Puma photograph of course – and signed it. I think the irony was lost on him. By the way, we never did have any other problems with things going missing from the washing line.

Summer 1985 was slightly different from the norm. We had a new boss – Kenny had taken over as player-manager – and the passports stayed in the drawer with every pre-season friendly taking place on English soil. No foreign travel for a change –

English clubs were banned from playing any games in Europe after Heysel – although I still managed to rack up the miles playing three games in three days on the weekend before the league opener at home to Arsenal.

Saturday, August 10 – Bristol City 3-3 Liverpool at Ashton Gate (friendly). Smacked in the mouth by one of the opposition players, I lost half my tooth and the nerve was exposed. No emergency dentists, though, so the journey back to Liverpool was a painful one with the nerve still hanging out.

Sunday, August 11 – Sauchie Juniors versus Ex-Seniors Select at Beechwood Park (George Ramage testimonial). At 7am, an impatient Big Al started tapping on the window because I failed to answer my front door within ten seconds of him knocking. The Big Man was in a hurry. He'd kindly offered me the chance to join him on a trip back to central Scotland to make a guest appearance for the junior team he began his career with – all done with Kenny's permission of course. The plan was to get there in plenty of time and go visit his parents' house in Sauchie, but travelling up the M74 motorway we missed the exit for the M73 and ended up not far from Celtic Park – about thirty miles from where we should have been.

Now Big Al and me were both Rangers fans growing up so perhaps it was a bit of a risk asking for help off a local in this particular area, but we spotted someone and rolled the window down. Fortunately, the guy we spoke to had no clue who either of us were. He also had no clue how to speak understandable English. We're both Scottish; well at least I thought we were until I heard this guy speak.

"Magic, thanks very much pal," I said to him after he gave us directions.

Big Al rolled the window back up – I looked at him, he looked at me and we burst out laughing. Neither of us had understood a single word he'd said. Totally incomprehensible. We retraced our route and eventually managed to get on to the M73 and arrived in Sauchie about an hour later – I'm sure the lad's instructions would have got us there quicker but, without the help of a translator, we had to rely on our questionable sense of direction instead.

The testimonial game was hardly enjoyable considering the pain I was in with my tooth but the traditional Scottish hospitality was first class and the beers after the game helped numb the pain – even though I couldn't smile properly in the photos. Big Al dropped me off around midnight – I reckon I must have travelled around 750 miles in thirty-six hours.

Monday 12 August – Liverpool 2-3 Everton at Anfield (Phil Neal testimonial). "Okay Al, I want you to play the first half and Bumper, I'll try not to play you at all if your tooth is still bothering you," said Kenny.

At half-time he told Al he would have to play the second half as well, contrary to what he'd originally said. I saw the blood drain from Big Al's face as he realised there was still another forty-five minutes to go. I had a little smirk, but little did I know what was to follow. Kenny brought me on with twenty minutes left. I couldn't run because my legs were like rubber, however it was a testimonial so in my mind it really shouldn't have mattered considering everything I'd been through over the previous two days. Being the competitor he is, Kenny came up to me after the game, looked me straight in the face and annihilated me. "If you don't want to play just tell me you don't want to fucking play."

What was he expecting? I was absolutely knackered. I'd spent five hours on a bus on Friday getting to Bristol, played the full ninety minutes at Ashton Gate – where part of my tooth got smashed to bits – then five hours back home to Liverpool on the Saturday night. Another five hours in the car up to Scotland on the Sunday – including a detour through the Wild West, or the east end of Glasgow as it's otherwise known – and played the entire match at Sauchie before drinking eight pints of lager ahead of the car journey back on the Sunday night and not arriving home until midnight. All of this while in pain with this nerve hanging out my tooth!

To then get hammered for playing twenty minutes well below the level he desired? It may have been harsh but there were certain standards new boss Kenny Dalglish expected of anyone pulling on a Liverpool Football Club jersey. I was left in no doubt.

Despite all that, I was pretty happy with the way I started the 1985-86 season, scoring in the first two league games we played at Anfield against Arsenal on the opening day and in a 5-0 win over Ipswich towards the end of August.

My recollection of both goals is pretty vague, and with a television blackout lasting until December 1985 there's no video footage to jog my memory, but I do remember enjoying the freedom of playing on the right hand side of midfield against the Gunners and scoring with a header. We were second in the table after seven games, having lost only once, but Manchester United had a perfect record with seven wins and were already seven points clear.

Game number eight was against Oxford United at the Manor Ground in September 1985. We were having our pre-match meal at the hotel. It was the first time Kenny's first signing Steve McMahon had been part of the travelling squad, joining from Aston Villa. As normal when there's a new player at the table everybody is being nice but, at the same time, trying to suss them out. I quickly found out Macca was an abrasive character.

"Oh well, I guess it's the last supper for somebody," he said, making the point that because he'd arrived, someone would soon be on their way out. He was trying to be funny, but I'm sure a couple of the boys whose place he was hoping to take failed to see the funny side of it.

Macca and me would constantly fall out on the bus while playing the card game Hearts but I think we kept everyone entertained with our childish behaviour. That card game, incidentally, was also the reason why Big Al once fell out with me – the only occasion that ever happened during our time together at Liverpool.

I had two cards remaining and had no chance of winning but Big Al could still win, depending on which card I played. Al somehow knew which two cards I had left but I didn't know which one to play. "Don't you fucking dare play what I think you're going to play…"

I was in panic mode. 'Eeny, meeny, miny, moe' but naturally I innocently chose the wrong card which resulted in him losing.

"I'm never fucking playing with you again," said Grumpy Chops.

After a wonderful Liverpool career consisting of many medals and 650 appearances for the club, the sale of Phil Neal to Bolton in November 1985 really was the end of an era. It's amazing to think he started every league game between December 1974 and September 1983 until he got injured in a match at Old Trafford and I took his place at right-back next time out against Sunderland.

Phil had only missed three games for Liverpool between August and November 1985, but at the age of thirty-four the opportunity to become a player-manager elsewhere was one he couldn't turn down. So a big career change for Nealy, and one that also had an impact on me. When I signed for Liverpool in October 1981 Bob Paisley had earmarked me as Phil's eventual replacement at right-back – I doubt he thought I would have to wait four years for the opportunity.

So Nealy had gone to Bolton, I'd gone to right-back and we were going to Arsenal in mid-December having been able to narrow the gap to Manchester United at the top of the table to just two points. It was another busy weekend with the game in London on the Saturday followed by Sammy Lee's testimonial dinner in Liverpool on the Sunday then a trip north to Aberdeen for John McMaster's testimonial on the Monday.

The dinner at the Holiday Inn in Liverpool was a welcome opportunity in the middle of a busy season for all the players and their partners to enjoy ourselves just before Christmas, but unfortunately a drunken idiot (me!) spoilt the occasion.

Eleanor and me were sat at a table with Kenny and Marina plus Alan and Janet and the beers were flowing. I noticed that Janet was wearing a pair of long white gloves that went all the way up to her elbow. I jokingly asked if I could try them on – surprisingly she said 'yes'. After putting them on I started to pretend I was a stripper. I took my tie off, undid a couple of shirt buttons and before I knew it the rest of the buttons were undone and the shirt was off…

The live band had noticed my behaviour and started to play the stripper song, which was quickly followed by a spotlight following my every move. The rest of the lights in the hall were then switched off and the other 199 people in the room were suddenly in the dark and forced to watch the drunken idiot take centre stage.

I got on the table (there may have been one or two drinks spilled in the process) and I put my hands on the top button of my trousers. Out the corner of my eye I saw Eleanor giving me the stare I'd witnessed on many occasions before. She was not happy.

"Don't you dare…"

Too late. I proceeded to take off my trousers and started to swing them above my head. I looked back at where Eleanor was meant to be sitting but she had left. Then, for some reason, I came to my senses. I climbed back down off the table, gathered all my clothes and the house lights came back on and the band started to play again. It was like everything was back to normal. Now I needed to find Eleanor. I headed out of the room, put my clothes back on, and noticed two females outside the front door of the Holiday Inn. She'd gone for some fresh air along with Elaine Whelan, Ronnie's wife. As I made my way towards them I overheard the following exchange.

"Don't worry, he's only doing it for a laugh," said Elaine. I felt bad for her, because she was only trying to help.

"It's not your husband who's pissed, taking his clothes off and making an arse of himself in front of two hundred people," replied a rather angry Mrs Nicol. Eventually I persuaded her to come back inside with me, but she never said another word for the rest of the night and we left soon after.

Big Al picked me up at seven o'clock the next morning ahead of our flight to Aberdeen. Eleanor still wasn't speaking to me. I spent most of that afternoon in my hotel room on the phone to her trying to explain myself and say sorry but she just wasn't having it. Then, during the game at Pittodrie, Kenny started to give me dog's abuse because I wasn't giving him the ball. I had a hangover, my wife was possibly planning to divorce me and all he was concerned about – IN A TESTIMONIAL – was me not finding him with a pass. Give the boy a break!

With English clubs banned from Europe, the Football League organised a six-team tournament – the Screen Sport SuperCup – featuring those that would have played in the European competitions. It was intended to help compensate them financially for the loss of revenue from competing abroad but it was a waste of time. We qualified from the group stage and faced Norwich City in the semi-final. The first leg took place at Carrow Road in February 1986 – a game I won't forget in a hurry.

It was snowing, the pitch was rock hard and our half-time team talk had just been held in a freezing Portakabin because the dressing rooms were being renovated. I stood shivering out by the touchline waiting for Norwich to kick off the second half and there were a million and one places I would rather have been at that particular moment. They launched the ball high into the air from the restart, aimed for Kevin Drinkell out by the touchline and he came sprinting towards me. He managed to make a clean contact with his head, not with the ball but with the side of my face, unintentionally I must add.

Roy Evans – our so-called physio – came running on with a bucket of water and absolutely whacked me across the side of the head with a soaking wet, freezing cold sponge. THEN he asked if I was OKAY! I remember thinking 'I wouldn't be lying here if I was alright, would I?'

"How you feeling, lad?"

I told him I thought I had broken some teeth but he took a quick look and couldn't see any damage so told me I'd be fine. I played on. I remember heading the ball soon after and feeling a shooting, numbing pain right across my face. At the end of the game Roy asked how I was. I tried to respond.

"Tjewu wrpon fddamf."

Total gibberish. Clearly something wasn't right.

One of the first things Kenny did after taking over as boss was to employ a proper physiotherapist – Paul Chadwick – but as he was only available for training and home games, Paul didn't travel. On the road it was either Ronnie or Roy, neither of them medical experts and neither able to offer any advice as to what the problem was.

With the weather in East Anglia getting progressively worse, a decision was taken not to travel back to Liverpool that evening and to stay an extra night in the hotel before heading back on the Thursday morning. The boys went out for a few beers and I thought alcohol would be the best way to numb the pain.

"Any chance of you actually drinking that beer or do you plan to continue pouring it down the front of your shirt?" enquired one of the lads.

It hadn't crossed my mind that the numbness might be masking more serious damage. Feeling sorry for myself, I got back to the hotel room around two in the morning and called Eleanor. Big mistake. She thought I was hammered because I couldn't talk properly and she destroyed me over the phone.

"You can't even speak – where the hell have you been?"

Of course, I couldn't tell her the truth because of my inability to talk properly so she slammed the phone down.

I got up in the morning and my face was completely swollen, as was the area around my chin. There were sandwiches and snacks on the bus on the way back and the lads ripped the piss out of me by continually offering me food. Roy called ahead and spoke to the club dentist and the plan was to go and see him when we got back to Liverpool. With no mobile phones back then, I asked Kenny to call Eleanor from Anfield and explain to my wife that I was on my way to see a dentist.

Straight from the bus I got into a car with Roy and we headed for Rodney Street. The dentist asked where most of the pain was coming from and I pointed to my bottom row of teeth, only because I had very little feeling below that. He took a quick look before confirming the problem had nothing to do with my teeth and told me to go and see the specialist two doors down to get my jaw checked out. The x-ray revealed it was broken in two places and surgery was required – the specialist told me to go home and pack some pyjamas and an overnight bag.

With Roy already back at Anfield I had to get a cab home, arriving back at the house shortly after seven o'clock. Eleanor opened the door and absolutely annihilated me. Kenny had only forgotten to call her!

She had absolutely no idea about my jaw so I stood at the front door for at least a couple of minutes while she berated me and yelled insults – when she eventually stopped shouting I just looked at her and, sounding somewhat like a gargoyle, told her "Ah've bwoke ma fwuckin' jaw." Her facial expression changed immediately and she couldn't have been more apologetic.

After borrowing some pyjamas from George, my neighbour – because I didn't own a pair – I headed to a private surgery in Southport to have the operation that night and my jaw was wired for the next six weeks. 'You can't eat any proper food,' they said, 'so you'll lose plenty of weight.'

I've always loved a challenge so I simply had everything liquidised. Fish and chips, scrambled egg on toast, the lot. I even managed to separate the wiring just enough at the top of my mouth so I could squeeze some Golden Wonder beef and onion crisps through the gap. A broken jaw certainly wasn't going to stop me from having my daily packet of crisps.

We may have been club rivals but Graeme Sharp was also my international teammate. One day I found myself sat next to the Everton striker on a train coming back from Glasgow after recording our World Cup song 'Big Trip To Mexico'. I've helped make a few records in my time – the obvious one, and the best one, being the Anfield Rap – but this was a waste of a trip north.

Anyway, with the train stopped somewhere between Glasgow and Preston while engineers de-iced the track, Graeme and I discussed the respective title challenges of Everton and Liverpool as we sat freezing our balls off in one of those old carriages with compartments that didn't have any heating.

After winning their first league championship in fifteen years the previous season, Howard Kendall's team had become our biggest rivals for the title. Sharpy and Gary Lineker were scoring loads of goals thanks, in part, to a talented midfield that included the likes of Peter Reid, Paul Bracewell, Kevin Sheedy and Trevor Steven, while the Blues were marshalled superbly at the back by skipper Kevin Ratcliffe and had the one and only Neville Southall earning plaudits in goal.

I said to Graeme that I reckoned Everton were now too far ahead for us to catch them. They'd just beaten us 2-0 at Anfield at the end of February to go eight points clear of us with only twelve league games remaining and were due to play Aston Villa on the Saturday before our game at Spurs the following day. If they beat Villa (which they did) the gap would be eleven points. I told him I struggled to see us making up the difference because they were playing so well. With a smile on his face he accused me of sandbagging. I wasn't, I was just being realistic. However, we went on to pick up sixteen of a possible eighteen points in March and they only took eight from fifteen so we drew level with them before we'd even reached April, even though they still had a game in hand. It was part of an incredible run, winning eleven of the last twelve in the league and drawing the other.

The penultimate fixture – a trip to face Leicester City at Filbert Street on a Wednesday night at the end of April – was really special. When I was part of the Liverpool team that won the league in 1983-84 we pretty much won it at a canter. But this season was very different. We'd spent most of it playing catch-up.

Two early goals from Rushy and Ronnie Whelan inside the first half hour at Filbert Street helped ease our nerves, but Everton still had the destination of the title in their own hands. If they won their last three league fixtures – at relegation-threatened Oxford that same night, at home to Southampton the weekend after and their game in hand against West Ham at Goodison – then THEY would win the title.

With time running out at Leicester we were just concentrating on holding on to the ball and protecting the two-goal lead when all of a sudden there was a huge roar, an absolute eruption of noise from the Liverpool fans throughout the ground. I knew instantly that something had happened at Oxford and it was obviously in our favour. I can't speak for any of the other lads but I definitely lost my concentration. From that moment on there was just a cacophony of noise from those wearing red and white on the terraces. I'm glad there were only a couple of minutes left at Filbert Street because all of a sudden I had goosebumps and couldn't think straight.

Once we were back in the dressing room we found out that Les Phillips had scored the winner for Oxford United against Everton with two minutes to go. John Aldridge and Ray Houghton were also in the Oxford team that night. They might have been wearing a yellow jersey but, without knowing it, they were also greatly helping their future employers and soon-to-be teammates.

Saturday May 3, 1986. Chelsea v Liverpool. And so it all came down to this. Win at Stamford Bridge – a ground where we didn't have the best of records – and the league title was ours in Kenny's first season in charge.

All the talk from those on the outside was about pressure and whether or not we could handle it, but for us this was just another game. And the week leading up to the game was as normal as any other week. Why prepare any differently from the previous eleven league fixtures, ten of which we'd won? The experience you get from being at Liverpool teaches you how to deal with that kind of pressure. When you play for Liverpool you're expected to win. And we expected to win. It had nothing at all to do with what the media wrote or what the opposition said.

We knew what to expect from the media in the days leading up to the game: 'How are you going to celebrate when you win the league?' and 'What's it going to mean to win another title?' but our response was simple – we hadn't won anything yet. We had our own built-in censorship within the Liverpool squad – we never talked ourselves up, we never talked the opposition down, we didn't say anything controversial and we never gave anybody any reason to think that we were getting carried away with anything. As far as we were concerned it was business as usual. We had to do what we had to do to get the job done. Crucially we'd been there before so knew exactly what needed to be done.

The journey on the Saturday from the hotel to the stadium was the same as any other journey we'd made previously to Stamford Bridge. We drove past the usual pubs on the way to the game that we'd driven by many times before – Chelsea fans were standing outside them with beers in hand shouting and swearing and making gestures as our team bus went by. To us this was great because it was normal.

Sitting in the dressing room before the game I looked around and saw players of the quality of Dalglish, Rush, Hansen, Lawrenson and Kevin MacDonald, our unsung hero. I knew they would be doing their bit so I'm thinking I just have to do my bit and we're good.

And guess what happened? They did their bit, I did my bit and Grobbelaar, Gillespie, Beglin, Whelan and Johnston did their bit too and we got the win we needed to clinch the title thanks to Kenny's first half goal.

The 1-0 victory will never be remembered as a classic game of football but it was as professional a performance as you will ever see from any team. We always knew we would make chances and we always knew we would score – in this particular game we only really made one chance but we scored from it. And that was enough. Teams today, it seems, are not always capable of shutting games down. If any coach wants to know how to do it properly then get a recording of that game at Stamford Bridge and watch the last seventy minutes or so after we scored. We were never in danger and we got the job done.

Just a week later, I got the chance to play in my first FA Cup final – and Liverpool's first since 1977. The game at Wembley summed up our season in a nutshell. Our road to the final had seen us beat Norwich at home (5-0); Chelsea away (2-1); York City in a replay at home (3-1); Watford in a replay away (2-1) and Southampton 2-0 in the semi-final thanks to two goals from Rushy. Everton, for their part, had overcome Exeter City (1-0) and Blackburn Rovers (3-1) at Goodison, before beating Spurs 2-1 at White Hart Lane and overcoming Luton in the quarter-final after a replay. They had reached Wembley after a 2-1 extra time victory over Sheffield Wednesday.

In the final we were trailing Everton for a decent length of time before turning things around to win the trophy at their expense, just like in the league. All the talk in the build-up to the first ever Merseyside derby final was whether or not Everton could stop us from becoming only the fifth English team in history to complete the league and cup double. And they had a decent chance of doing so when Gary Lineker put them ahead just before the half hour.

Heading back to the dressing room at half-time I tapped Kevin Ratcliffe on the shoulder in the tunnel – he turned round and I think he thought I was going to punch him. But I just pinched my nose with my fingers and started talking with a nasally voice – "You hit me in the nose ya bastard" – reminding him that he accidentally whacked me in the face with the ball in the first half. He saw the funny side, helped of course by Everton's one goal lead.

I know a lot of people think they were miles ahead of us in the first half and should have gone in leading by more than one goal but I disagree. We were still in touch, very much in the game, and with the quality of players we had in our team we were always confident of turning things around. And that's the way it turned out with a couple of second half goals from Rushy and another one from Craig Johnston clinching the Double. Not bad for a starting line-up at Wembley consisting of four Scotsmen, three Irishmen, a Welshman, a Dane, an Australian and a goalkeeper from Zimbabwe.

After climbing the stairs at Wembley and picking up my first FA Cup winner's medal, it was time for the celebrations to begin properly. The first thing we wanted to do was show the trophy to our to our fans. Then it was time for the traditional on-the-field team photo.

Now I'll let you in to a bit of a secret here – we used to sing a rather rude song every time we won something, but nobody in the media ever picked up on it.

So while the snappers were clicking away and the television cameras were filming our every move and beaming the pictures all around the world, me and my teammates were singing this dirty little ditty…

Hairy growlers, paps and vees, [deep voice] paps and vees
Hairy growlers, paps and vees, [deep voice] paps and vees
There's a hairy growler over there
And it hasn't got no hair, [deep voice] got no hair!

I remember seeing Eleanor shortly after the game and she asked how I was feeling. I told her I was absolutely knackered – it had been a long season – then she reminded me I was on the plane to Mexico the following week with the rest of the Scotland squad for the World Cup! Things then got a bit daft.

Someone, in their wisdom, thought it would be a good idea for both teams to not only fly back to Liverpool together but also go round the city together, no matter the result of the cup final. Whoever suggested that in the first place clearly hadn't taken into account the possibility of one team winning both trophies.

The flight home – with the whole plane mixed – was painful. Gary Lineker and his partner were sitting in the row in front of Eleanor and me, and it was kind of awkward for everyone. We'd just won the Double and wanted to celebrate, but obviously couldn't do so in front of the Everton players who just wanted to get home as quickly as possible.

Fortunately, it was a short flight back up to Liverpool; then it was time for the city centre parade. We won so we were at the front of the procession while the Everton lads and their partners were in the bus behind.

Both sets of fans lined the route – which is incredible when you think about it – and those wearing blue and white were just as vocal as our supporters, but the whole thing was embarrassing for everyone involved. Each time I looked behind at the Everton boys on their bus I felt really sorry for them having been so near but yet so far. I kept thinking how I would have felt if the roles had been reversed.

When we eventually finished the tour of the city I said to Everton defender Derek Mountfield – who lived six doors down from me – that he was welcome to travel back to Heswall with me, Eleanor, Bruce and Debbie. His wife was pregnant and hadn't been able to join him on their bus so we gave him a lift home.

Just like on the flight back from London decorum was shown – there was plenty time to celebrate after we dropped Derek off. And celebrate we did that evening, toasting a league championship, the FA Cup and a fine first season for the new man in charge.

10

Cowboys
In The Sun

*"Good luck ya fat bastard..." Alan Rough just smiled.
With that we went back out for the second half. Those
were the last words most of us heard Big Jock say'*

I wouldn't say I was scared of him. But I was in awe of Big Jock
and would have done anything he asked. Jock Stein to me WAS
Scottish football. What he'd achieved at Celtic and throughout
his life – absolutely incredible. It was an honour for me to have
him as my international manager.

Illness prevented me from playing in Scotland's World Cup
qualifying game against Spain in February 1985. We'd been up
late the night before – as was normally the case on a Sunday
evening when the squad got together – but I was really struggling the next morning. Big Jock came to the door. "Oh you
don't feel well, do you? I've got a fair idea why! Now get out of
your bed because we're leaving in thirty minutes." This time,
though, alcohol had nothing to do with the way I was feeling.

I was beside myself with worry – 'holy shit, I've upset Jock Stein' – but I wasn't the only one feeling poorly. Kenny was also coming down with something. It was suggested that the pair of us travel as planned with the rest of the squad and then see how we felt once we arrived in Spain. We did but there was no change in our condition, so it was watching briefs only for Kenny and me in Seville. Scotland lost 1-0, however previous wins at Hampden over Iceland and Spain meant we were still in a good position in the group.

That situation changed when Wales came to Hampden Park in March. This was the game when Alex Ferguson asked the Liverpool contingent of the squad for some inside information on how to counter the threat of Ian Rush. Fergie had taken over from Jim McLean as Jock's assistant in 1984. 'Well he's great in the air, you can't give him a sniff and he closes people down' was what we told him. Fergie took it that we didn't want to divulge things about our Anfield teammate and later on came out and suggested that he felt it was a closed shop. It was nothing of the sort!

It wouldn't have mattered what any of us had told the coaching staff, Rush and Hughes were simply magnificent and practically unplayable at Hampden that night. Scotland didn't play well, but those two just didn't let us out of our own half. I've never seen such a good display of defensive work by a pair of strikers.

Rushie scored the only goal shortly before half-time to give the Welsh a deserved win, but back at Anfield on the Monday he didn't give the Scottish lads any stick whatsoever. We all had far too much respect for our teammates at Liverpool to ever do that. It was the same in the dressing room after Scotland played England. There was always a cooling off period follow-ing games against each other. Plus, it wouldn't exactly please the coaching staff if we were trying to kick the shit out of each other in training as a form of revenge for what had happened on international duty!

Jock was without Dalglish, Hansen and myself for a 1-0 win over Iceland in May (the game, in Reykjavik, was played the day before our ill-fated European Cup final at the Heysel Stadium). It meant that qualifying for the play-off all came down to the final group game against – you've guessed it – Wales.

It was a night no one would ever forget.

Jock ensured it was just a normal build-up to the game in Cardiff, despite the importance of the fixture. We met up in Glasgow on the Sunday night, as usual, before travelling down to our base in Bristol the following day. Alex took us for training while Jock worked with the goalkeepers, like he always did.

Roughie claims the gaffer didn't look well all week, that he wasn't himself, but at no stage in the two days leading up to the match do I remember thinking there might be something wrong with him. I don't think many of us did.

We were well aware of what was at stake. Avoid defeat and Scotland were guaranteed at least a play-off spot. However, Wales had already beaten us at Hampden, deservedly so, and if we allowed Rush and Hughes to dictate proceedings again then the likelihood of going to Mexico would be slim.

Thirteen minutes in and we found ourselves a goal down. Peter Nicholas took a heavy touch and, with the ball there to be won, I was pretty confident I could win the tackle. There was one problem. Roy Aitken had exactly the same thought. I was ready to make the challenge but when I saw Roy also making a move I hesitated, crucially, for a split second. In the end, neither of us made a proper tackle and Peter was able to take another touch and quickly deliver a low cross for Mark Hughes to give Wales an early lead. That was the only goal of the first half. At half-time, Jock Stein was not a happy man. "Sit down, all of you."

Gordon Strachan had replaced the suspended Graeme Souness in central midfield but Jock was not overly impressed by his performance. He told him he was planning to bring on Davie Cooper in the second half as his replacement. Strach was not happy and tried to give as good as he got. Then Alex Ferguson began shouting at Jim Leighton. Talk about a noisy dressing room. When they were both done yelling, Alex asked Jock if he could have a word in private and they went into the toilet area, out of sight from the players but not out of earshot. There was more yelling.

Ferguson was pissed off at Leighton after our goalkeeper told him he'd lost a contact lens during the first half and couldn't see properly. That explained him dropping a routine cross just before half-time. Jim had also forgotten to bring a spare pair of lenses with him. Meanwhile, Stein was pissed off at Alex for not telling him that his goalkeeper wore contract lenses! The trouble was that Fergie didn't know Leighton wore contacts. Nobody did. Up until that point Jim hadn't told a soul, not even Alex, his manager at Aberdeen. Alex emerged from his 'chat' with Jock and told us that Alan Rough would be taking over from Jim between the sticks.

With so much going on and only ten minutes allocated for half-time in those days there was no time for Jock to deliver a proper team talk. As we lined up in the Ninian Park tunnel ready to go back out for the second half I turned to Roughie and asked him what the fuck was going on. He simply laughed – 'ah ha ha' – just like Tommy Cooper used to do. Trust him to act the fool amidst all the mayhem.

As Jock had promised to do, Davie Cooper was brought on for Gordon Strachan after an hour and he went on to have a pivotal role in proceedings. With nine minutes remaining I found myself in space out by the touchline and, with a little bit of time, was able to look up and see Graeme Sharp running towards the penalty box with his right arm aloft. I picked him out with a floated cross and he managed to head it on to David Speedie. David tried a first time shot that hit the arm of Dave Phillips, who was standing less than two yards away. The arm wasn't overly outstretched and the handball certainly wasn't deliberate, however Dutch referee Jan Keizer pointed straight to the spot.

It might not have been the best penalty that Coop had ever taken but it had just enough pace to prevent Neville Southall from getting a full hand on it.

We celebrated on the pitch – none of us having any idea of what was going on near the dug-out until we made our way back inside.

Jock had collapsed.

From ecstasy to shock and concern in a matter of seconds. With information scarce, most of us passed the time just milling around while one or two of the senior players tried to find out more. Around forty-five minutes later Alex came back into the dressing room and sat down near the door.

"Jock's dead."

Two words. That was it.

I felt numb. We all did.

How? Why?

Suddenly Mexico was the last thing on our minds.

Looking back at it now, I was clearly in a haze immediately after the match – understandably so – and found it difficult to comprehend exactly what was going on with Jock.

A few years ago, I read an interview with Professor Stewart Hillis, the Scotland team doc who was also Jock's personal doctor. He explained that Jock suffered from heart muscle disease and was on diuretic medication to help remove excess fluid from parts of his body. The condition was perfectly manageable as long as the pills were taken daily. However, with such a busy few days in the build-up to the Wales game in Cardiff, the gaffer had apparently been skipping the tablets because he wanted to remain focussed on preparation and not be affected by any possible side effects.

"I still believe that had Jock taken his medication he would not have died. But Jock was his own man," said the doc.

Those words still get to me now.

Dad's health deteriorated before we were due to face Australia for a place at the World Cup. He'd had a heart attack and ended up in a coma. With the play-off first leg taking place at Hampden Park it meant I was able to go and see him in hospital while I was up in Scotland, but the doctors said his outlook was not good, so I wasn't comfortable about getting on a flight to Melbourne for the second leg and being out of the country for several days. I explained the situation to Kenny and he was great about it.

"Look, we're going to get through anyway – how are you going to feel if you're in Australia and something happens to your dad?" He said he would speak to Alex Ferguson and the Scottish Football Association. I was excused the long trip and for that I'm grateful.

We were more than happy to face Australia because they were still part-timers. Playing at home first we knew if we took a lead to Melbourne then we'd be fine, and that's the way it turned out thanks to goals from Davie Cooper and Frank McAvennie. We wanted to score more but were confident a 2-0 lead would be enough. Which it was. A goalless draw at Olympic Park secured our place in Mexico.

The draw for the 1986 World Cup took place in Mexico City a week and a half after we secured qualification. El grupo de la muerte – the Group of Death – was how Uruguay coach Omar Borras described Group E, with his nation in with West Germany, Denmark and Scotland. It certainly might have been kinder – instead of the Danes it could have been Canada, South Korea, Iraq or Algeria, all of whom went on to finish bottom of their respective groups. But with four of the six third-place finishers also going through to the knockout stages I was pretty confident we wouldn't be one of the eight nations going home after the group stage.

I made the cut for the initial squad at the end of March. One big name that wasn't included, however, was Maurice Johnston. I was surprised Mo was left out, but there were stories doing the rounds that he'd enjoyed himself a bit too much down in Melbourne.

With England hosting the annual Rous Cup fixture that year I got the chance to play for Scotland at Wembley for the first time. Just five years after being a member of the Tartan Army – and watching from those terraces in London – I found myself wearing a dark blue jersey and playing on the right hand side of midfield. My memories of Scotland versus England growing up were always of games taking place on a Saturday so to run out the tunnel on a Wednesday night was a bit of a weird feeling. Still a proud moment, nevertheless.

Two or three weeks after the game at Wembley, Alex Ferguson named his World Cup squad. 29 became 22 and seven players from the preliminary squad were cut, including Alan Hansen. I was stunned. Big Al had the cigars out during most of that season. Liverpool had won the Double yet one of our key players couldn't even get in the Scotland squad for Mexico. It made no sense to me then and makes no sense to me now. Even if he wasn't going to get picked ahead of Willie Miller and Alex McLeish then surely he should still have been part of the squad, especially with games taking place at altitude where players who were comfortable on the ball were worth their weight in gold.

Did Fergie have an issue with Liverpool players – is that why Big Al wasn't picked? Well, I was included in the squad so I'm not sure that's true, but it's been argued by some that he favoured those from Aberdeen, where he was also the manager, although he denies that. I know Willie Miller and Big Al didn't always gel as a partnership – I get that – but why wouldn't you want a player in your squad who was arguably the best centre-back of his generation? Truly baffling.

With Kenny having to pull out of the squad after injuring his knee in the FA Cup final against Everton, that left seven English-based players – Strachan, Goram, Albiston, McAvennie, Sharp, Nicholas and me – thirteen who played their football in Scotland plus Graeme Souness at Sampdoria and Steve Archibald of Barcelona. A decent squad and one that we believed would do well at the World Cup.

We spent a couple of days in Glasgow undergoing various tests before flying out to America for a few days in Los Angeles then onto Santa Fe, New Mexico for some altitude training to help us acclimatise.

"Where's the rest of your luggage?" I asked Roughie after noticing he'd turned up at the airport for the flight to the States with only one bag. He expected to be stuck in hotels for the next six weeks because that's what happened to the squad in Spain in 1982 under Big Jock, and with Alex Ferguson having a reputation of being a bit of a task-master he thought this World Cup would be no different. "Be prepared for a lockdown," he replied. He couldn't have been more wrong.

Temperatures in Los Angeles were way above average for that time of year and I remember leaving the airport and walking outside into stifling heat, the like of which I had never experienced before. There was a lot more of that where we were going so playing a game against local team Los Angeles Heat at the end of May was ideal preparation to help get used to the conditions. It was classed as a friendly but for me it was much more important. This game would determine whether or not I was fit enough to take part in the World Cup.

I had started to feel some abdominal discomfort three or four weeks before the FA Cup final. I didn't think much of it at the time but I remember just after the FA Cup victory over Everton thinking wow, I'm tired. I told the Scotland medical staff about my condition when we first met up prior to flying to the States – I passed all their initial examinations and was the top performer out of everyone in the squad when it came to the fitness tests. I had an incredibly high pain threshold so I was prepared to put up with a little discomfort as long as it wasn't affecting my performance – this was a once-in-a-lifetime opportunity to play at a World Cup and I was not about to let an issue with my stomach deny me that chance.

After talking it through with the medics it was decided that if I got through the game against Los Angeles Heat without a reaction, then I would go to the World Cup. I scored in a 3-0 win, was named man-of-the-match and although I felt a little discomfort afterwards it was no more than I'd felt in the previous couple of weeks. My ticket to Mexico was stamped.

It's funny the way football works sometimes. The guy between the sticks for Los Angeles Heat that day was David Vanole, who ended up being my goalkeeper coach at New England Revolution twenty years later. Justin Fashanu also played for them while a certain Rod Stewart was among the smallish crowd in attendance. He came into the dressing room after the game and invited all the Scotland players back to his house. A kind gesture, but I'd already arranged to have dinner with a childhood friend, Gordon McBean, and the rest of his family. He may be a music superstar but there was no way I was letting down a pal of mine who I hadn't seen for fifteen years.

Upon arrival at the Sheraton Hotel in Santa Fe we were told to collect our bags from the bus – or bag in the case of Roughie – put them in our rooms and then head upstairs to one of the conference rooms for a meeting.

Given everything that Roughie had told us at Glasgow Airport, this was when we were expecting to be told the plans for the month or so would include training, meals in the hotel, more training and more meals in the hotel. Oh, and three World Cup group games as well.

Instead, Fergie told us that a fair bit of the time spent in Santa Fe would be focussed on team bonding. We wouldn't be spending every evening in the hotel bored out of our skulls. A visit to the local racetrack had been organised while every other night we'd split up into groups with different coaches and eat in various restaurants in the city. Then we'd all meet up after dinner and have a beer or two together before heading back to the hotel for a good sleep, ready for training the following morning. A pleasant surprise indeed.

Roughie couldn't believe his ears. With one bag, not even a suitcase, to last him six weeks he panicked and went on the scrounge. I gave him a pair of shoes because I was the only other player with size eleven feet. He then proceeded to 'borrow' other gear – trousers, shirts and all kinds of clothing – from the rest of the boys. I think he managed to get at least one item from every single member of the squad. Roughie travelled back from Mexico with two full suitcases. That's certainly not what he left with. He phoned me a couple of years later asking for tickets for a Liverpool game that he was coming to watch. I told him I'd only do that if he returned my shoes!

There's no question the group was together and in good spirits. The pre-tournament training camp was more enjoyable than usual – although not for a certain Hugh Allan. Hughie was the kit man and when the staff were out for dinner on the first night we got the keys to his ground floor hotel room and, from the inside, stacked all the metal kit boxes against the door. There was now no chance of him getting back in to his room. We also took the bulbs from all the lights in his room and put them in the sink in the bathroom before climbing out of the window. When he returned to the hotel later that night, good old Hughie didn't take too kindly to our prank – it wasn't long before he gave up trying to get in to his room and decided just to sleep on the masseurs' table in the room next door. At breakfast the following morning he said none of us were leaving until whoever stacked the kit boxes in his room removed them. It wasn't like Hughie not to see the funny side of things. A lovely guy but a miserable so and so...

On one of our days off, we decided to try a line-dancing establishment out of town. I think we broke the world record for the number of people in a limousine at one time – my guess is seventeen. A particular member of the squad, whose alter ego was called 'Philippe', somehow – despite the lack of space – managed to get himself to the front of the limo and sat down beside the driver.

A well-lubricated 'Philippe' decided he was a better driver than the one we had so he proceeded to try and push him out of the way and take over at the wheel. But the driver was having none of it.

Meanwhile, the vehicle was swerving violently all over the road because of the struggle, putting the lives of the majority of the Scotland World Cup squad in a fair amount of danger. When 'Philippe' tried this for a second time the driver stopped the car abruptly, told him some home truths and said to us, in no uncertain terms, that he was done.

Thankfully the exchange of a few dollars, and more importantly the promise that 'Philippe' would rejoin the rest of us in the back of the limo, resulted in him agreeing to back down and us eventually reaching our destination.

Every single one of us bought a cowboy hat at the line-dancing and one of the regulars at the club made the mistake of telling Graeme that he looked like Tom Sellick with his on. That made Charlie's night and we didn't hear the end of it.

The following morning, however, a shadow was cast on all the posers in the Scotland squad – of which there were a few – when Robert Redford walked into the reception just before we headed out for training. He was directing a movie called The Milagro Beanfield War and was staying at the hotel. I think this was the only time in Graeme Souness's life that he felt upstaged. If only he'd still been wearing the cowboy hat from the night before.

Training was tough in New Mexico, with the altitude and stifling heat, but it was the perfect place to prepare for what we would face in Nezahualcóyotl and Queretaro. We played one game against Northern Ireland in Albuquerque – an afternoon kick-off with three periods of twenty minutes – and that gave us a taste of what the conditions would be like in Mexico.

The night before we flew to Mexico City the players were informed of their squad numbers for the World Cup.

"You'll be wearing number 13," I was told.

I'm superstitious and wanted a different one but I was told it was too late – FIFA had already been informed of the squad numbers and that was the end of it.

That was typical of how the Scottish Football Association operated back then. It was like the players were an afterthought. And don't get me started on the blazers getting the best seats at the front of the plane and the best rooms in the hotel.

I sometimes felt that they thought we were doing THEM a favour by turning up.

"Did you ever think that somebody might just have a problem wearing a jersey with number 13 on the back?" I asked.

"Tough shit, it's too late."

The SFA didn't give a fuck about something as menial as this. They also gave us the cold shoulder when we asked for two shirts per game. I wanted to keep the jersey I had worn and swap the other with an opponent, but in true SFA style we were simply told that it wasn't happening – end of story. 'You can either keep it or swap it.'

In previous internationals, Hughie the kit man used to go round making sure we didn't take our shorts or socks as mementoes. I'm sure Hughie wasn't the one who decided this – the order must have come from above – but it was so damn petty. The matter actually came to a head after the opening game against Denmark. Once again we asked if we could have two strips for each of the remaining matches against West Germany and Uruguay. Initially the request was denied but, fortunately, common sense eventually prevailed.

'The best prepared Scotland squad there has ever been…' Graeme Souness was taking part in his third World Cup so he was in a good position to judge. Everything had gone smoothly in Los Angeles and Santa Fe – training in the stifling heat of California and at altitude in New Mexico meant it wasn't difficult to acclimatise once we arrived at our base in Mexico City. The training facilities were fine but the hotel was no more than adequate. The only good thing was we had the entire place to ourselves with no other guests roaming around.

The biggest problem facing players in any team at a major tournament is downtime. When you're away from home all you do is train, eat and sleep – it's pretty dull – but at least having a roommate helps relieves some of the boredom. I'd roomed with Manchester United defender Arthur Albiston in America, and he was good company, but when we arrived at the hotel in Mexico City we were told we'd all be in single rooms. While that was great for getting rest as and when required, it also increased the boredom. Alone in a small hotel room with only six Spanish-speaking television channels for company – at times it felt like being in solitary.

Thankfully, parcels from home arrived every two or three days – Eleanor used to send newspapers and snacks, including a regular supply of my favourite cheese and onion crisps. A healthy diet never hurt anyone.

Wed 04 June – Scotland 0-1 Denmark (Nezahualcóyotl)
Kick-off: 4pm local time
(I played: 90 minutes)

When an opponent later acknowledges that he should have received two years in prison for a tackle instead of a yellow card then it's fair to say the referee may have let him off lightly. The player in question was Klaus Berggreen and the assault was carried out on Charlie Nicholas with only six minutes remaining of our opening group game. Chasing an equaliser, Charlie looked to have a clear run in on goal but Kung-Fu Klaus thought otherwise. The brutal foul saw Charlie – who'd been our best player – stretchered from the field and we ended the game with ten men having already used both subs. It was a day when very little went right for us. Roy Aitken had a goal disallowed for offside shortly after Preben Elkjær had given them the lead; the far side linesman inexplicably raised his flag despite Roy being at least three yards onside. It was one of many ludicrous decisions made by officials at this tournament.

This was my first experience of playing a competitive game at altitude – the prep work in New Mexico certainly helped us but both teams struggled.

The only reason I was able to complete the ninety minutes was because the pace of the game was so slow. Bursts of energy were minimal – it was mainly about being in a good position and not getting ahead of the ball. The stomach didn't cause me too much trouble. It was only when I went flat out that I could feel it, but that maybe happened once because there were very few opportunities to go at full pace.

When we got back to the hotel there were armed guards with machine guns both inside and outside the premises. I know they were there for our safety but it felt like we were in lockdown. Not being allowed outside of the hotel compound – by order of the management – we improvised and decided to have a toga party instead.

We took sheets from our beds and wrapped them around us then used parts of various plants as headdresses before heading to the bar for a few drinks. Every member of the squad took part, we had a few beers and a carry on and it helped us to forget about the disappointment of the Denmark defeat.

The following morning I could hardly move because of pain in my lower stomach. It eased off over the next couple of days but had this World Cup taken place in Europe then I would never have been able to play.

The pace would have been so much quicker and there's no way I could have coped.

Sun 08 June – West Germany 2-1 Scotland (Queretaro)
Kick-off: Noon local time
(I played: 61 minutes – replaced by Frank McAvennie)

Imagine eleven pigs trying to eat food at the same time from a trough that's only large enough to accommodate four or five of them at once. A mass scramble to get there first and secure a prime position then not wanting to give it up. Well that's what it was like in the Scotland dressing room at half-time when we finally worked out that the bizarre-looking things hanging on the wall actually supplied oxygen. Except there were only four or five of them to go around. That first half was tough and we needed all the help we could get.

We came in at the break 1-1 after Rudi Völler equalised Gordon Strachan's opener. Wee Gordon trying to jump over the Camel advertising board is one of the indelible memories of Mexico '86 but it wasn't until I saw the goal on television later that I realised how I reacted. I was over on the left hand side of the pitch near the halfway line when he scored and as much as I would have loved to have gone over and given him a big hug, I was much closer to our dugout so I went over to the bench to get some water instead.

Just a few minutes after they equalised, I went back over to the same side to take a throw and what did I see? Roughie, lying on the ground covered in Ambre Solaire with his shorts tucked up as high as he could get them. He had a big smile on his face and gave me a wink. The big man was topping up his tan while we were running around daft and struggling to breathe.

I think we kept a good shape against the West Germans, but they were a good team with a lot of really good players and the goal by Klaus Allofs five minutes into the second half was enough to earn them a 2-1 win. We tried to keep the pace of the game as slow as we could in order to get in good positions to defend, but sometimes when you play against great players there's only so much you can do. Even after the match – despite having lost two in a row – we still knew there was a chance of going through because the Uruguayans had also lost, so we didn't dwell too much on the defeat.

We stayed in the same hotel as Denmark after that second game against West Germany in Queretaro and the staff had set up a temporary bar in the foyer to recognise their 6-1 win victory over Uruguay earlier that day. But we hijacked proceedings. A couple of hours into their so-called party only Jan Molby, Jesper Olsen, Soren Lerby and Michael Laudrup remained from their squad while we were all still there drinking. The night after a game was the only time when we were allowed beers so we always made the most of it – even if this time the alcohol wasn't meant for our consumption.

And so to our final group game against Uruguay: a point was enough for them to finish third while we had to win. That scenario could easily have been different if Roy Aitken's 'goal' against Denmark in the opener had stood – when he was clearly onside. What was a hard enough task on its own became even harder when Graeme Souness wasn't included in the starting line-up. He'd lost a lot of weight so I understood why he didn't start; what I didn't understand was Alex Ferguson's strange decision to leave him out of the eighteen. Graeme may have struggled with the heat in Mexico but I'm sorry, he should at least have been included among the substitutes. Even Souness at less than one hundred per cent was still an option worth having on the bench. That decision was on a par with the omission of Alan Hansen from the World Cup squad. With Alex McLeish missing out against Uruguay because of 'flu it would have been a perfect opportunity for Big Al. Instead David Narey took Alex's place and partnered Willie Miller in central defence.

Fri 13 June – Scotland 0-0 Uruguay (Nezahualcóyotl)
Kick-off: Noon local time
(I played: 70 minutes – replaced by Davie Cooper)

What a shower of dirty bastards. This might sound daft but the worst thing that could have happened to us was them having a man sent off so early. Defender Jose Batista was given his marching orders after just 48 seconds for a vicious lunge on Gordon Strachan – from then on French referee Joel Quiniou let them away with murder, as though he dare not show another red card. Spitting, pulling hair, they tried every trick in the book – but Quiniou allowed them to get away with it.

The Uruguayans took it in turns to play the role of hatchet man to avoid being singled out and they did it very well. I remember at least another three tackles that were worse than Batista on Gordon, but the punishment never did fit the crime. To make matters worse, I picked up a yellow card in this game for a run-of-the-mill tackle – the only time I was ever booked when playing for Scotland – yet I received the same punishment for my challenge as some of their players did for brutal assaults. They were cynical, nasty and disgraceful and did things that most professionals wouldn't even have contemplated.

We had two or three decent chances in the game; it just so happens that mine was the most obvious and is the one people remember. Once again it was a slow build-up due to the conditions. Gordon Strachan played a ball in behind to Roy Aitken and he delivered a great low cross into the six-yard box. I made a good run inside their full-back but ultimately mistimed the shot. Instead of using the pace on the ball and just redirecting it I tried to generate my own power. However, I hit it into the ground and that took pace off the ball, giving goalkeeper Fernando Alves time to get across and make the save. Scotland's number 13 missing the chance on Friday the 13th. How's your luck?

The first time I saw a replay of my chance was probably more than twenty years after it happened. I thought I didn't need to see it again. Everybody kept telling me I missed a sitter and should have scored and I believed them, so why would I want to watch it back? I knew if I'd connected with it properly then it would have gone in the net. Simple as that. But I didn't make a clean contact. It wasn't until I eventually watched it back that I realised I was further out than I thought. When people used to bring it up, and I thought I'd missed from point blank range, I tried to deflect the blame and tell them it was a great save. But actually it *was* a decent stop. It irritates me now when people say I missed an open goal because I didn't. Was it a great chance? Yes. Should I have scored? Yes. But at least my mind is now at rest having watched it again and I don't feel as bad as I did.

There were so many frustrating aspects that afternoon, and that was just one of them. It's one thing when you don't play well, but another thing entirely when you're just not allowed to play. They weren't even that good a team. Enzo Francescoli up front was a superstar but most of the others were just a bunch of spoilers. They just sat tight and hoped Francescoli on the break could make something happen and sneak a goal. At the end of our game they tried to console us as if what they had done was just normal practice. They had no problem with their behaviour and were surprised we didn't want to shake their hands.

If we'd beaten Uruguay we would have qualified as one of the best third-place finishers and faced hosts Mexico in the Azteca Stadium. Ifs, buts and maybes – we've always been pretty good at that in Scotland. Instead, we arrived home before the post-cards.

I suppose our whole Mexican adventure can be summed up in four words – what might have been. We had decent players but certain things transpired against us. Roy Aitken's goal against Denmark that should have been allowed. The vicious tackle by Klaus Berggreen that meant we lost Charlie Nicholas for the West Germany game. Then one of the most ridiculous refereeing performances ever seen at a World Cup cost us victory against Uruguay – a Frenchman allowed a team of butchers to get away with murder.

This was a good Scottish team that just never got a break when it really mattered.

11

Doctor And
The Medics

*'Some of the stories of the old treatment room
at Liverpool are legendary. Injured players not
responding to ultrasounds then discovering the
machines hadn't been working for months. And
those wax baths used for treating ankle injuries –
players were celebrating when they got rid of them.
Thankfully Kenny introduced a slightly more
professional approach'*

You always had to be on your toes when Kenny was around and
have the ability to second-guess what was coming next. Even
when he took over as manager you could see he still wanted
to be involved in the banter, without overstepping the mark of
course. And this is a perfect example...

Wednesday, January 14, 1987 was the date. We were in the
hotel prior to the FA Cup replay at home to Luton and one or
two of the boys had heard rumours about our opponents not

showing up because of problems with their flight due to snow. After the usual sleep in the afternoon, followed by tea and toast in the room, Ronnie Moran came round to let us know that Luton had indeed not been able to travel. However, we still had to go through the whole rigmarole of going to the stadium to satisfy the official rules and regulations of the competition. I'd just been ruled out for the season but Kenny asked me to travel with the team on the bus to Anfield.

Fellow Scot Alan Irvine had recently joined Liverpool and was actually staying at the same hotel until he found more permanent accommodation. But Alan didn't know about Luton's problems because his room was on a different floor in a separate part of the Holiday Inn, so Ronnie hadn't told him. On the bus on the way to Anfield, we figured out pretty quickly that Alan was still completely unaware there would be no game, so Big Al went down to the front of the bus and told Kenny.

Spotting an opportunity for a wind-up, the boss asked Alan to come and join him at the front of the bus and explained that he needed him to play centre-back. Now Alan was a striker and told Kenny he didn't think he could do it because he'd never played there before.

"Well, if I move one of the midfielders back into defence could you play in the middle of the park?"

That scenario was more to Alan's liking, but Kenny told him not to tell anyone when he went back to his seat because the team hadn't been announced yet. When we got to Anfield – nice and early as usual – the whole area around the stadium was like a ghost town, but the doormen were standing waiting to greet us as normal.

Everybody went into the first team dressing room and all the kit had been laid out. Kenny sat us all down and, before confirming the team, said he wanted everyone to go to reception and sort out their allocation of complimentary tickets for the game. Everybody trooped out of the dressing room with one exception – Alan Irvine. Kenny knew that Fraggle (that was his nickname) didn't have anyone coming to the game so the big lad just sat there while we went home.

Ten minutes later, Kenny went back into the dressing room and Alan was still sitting there. His boots were on. His shorts were on. But not his top.

"Fraggle – there's nae game. The game's aff."

"I knew it was off, gaffer," replied Alan, pretending to go along with the wind-up but failing miserably. Kenny gave him a look that only Kenny could give and walked away, shaking his head. Good old Fraggle!

Alan got that nickname because someone said he looked like a puppet from the TV programme Fraggle Rock. It was typical of the daft names we gave each other at Liverpool in those days. I was given a few myself…

Bumper – I said 'bumper' instead of 'bouncer' at training one day and it stuck. When I phone my old teammates most of them call me Bumper. Big Al still calls me 'Bump'.

Chico – after one of the Marx brothers.

Chops/Chopsy – I liked eating chips but Terry Mac claimed I pronounced them 'chops'.

Hannu – apparently I looked like the Finnish rally driver Hannu Mikkola.

Henderson – Kenny called me this when I played right midfield – after the former Rangers midfielder Willie Henderson.

Nico – not very original.

Soash – because Mo Johnston said I was the social convener on Scotland duty.

As for the others, here's what I can remember…

John Aldridge – Stonks or Aldo – he turned round one day and told one of us to 'kiss his stonks.'

John Barnes – Digger – after Digger Barnes in Dallas, with particular emphasis on the letter D in case any onlookers who didn't know better thought we might be racially abusing a teammate!

Jim Beglin – Dex – once came in wearing a pair of denim dungarees and looked like one of the members of Dexy's Midnight Runners.

Bob Bolder – The Rock – the original Rock. It's a little known fact that the WWE wrestler and actor was named after Bob Bolder…

Jimmy Carter – Jimmy the Jumper – he used to wear the most ridiculous looking jumpers. These days he'd be in his element at Christmas with all these ugly sweaters.

Nigel Clough – Young Man – because his dad said that all the time. A lovely lad.

Kenny Dalglish – Dogs – Souness called him the dog's bollocks.

John Durnin – Goyly – one day at training someone said he looked like a gargoyle.

David Fairclough – The Whip – because of the way he struck the ball when he took a shot at goal.

Gary Gillespie – Smithy – he once said Ian Baker Smith instead of Ian Baker Finch when talking about the golfer.

Bruce Grobbelaar – Parlez-Bleu – I wish I knew!

Alan Hansen – Big Al or Jocky.

Ray Houghton – Roy – Big Al's missus, Janet, called him Roy one day by mistake and it stuck.

Alan Kennedy – Barney, after Barney Rubble in the Flintstones.

Kevin MacDonald – Machine Gun Louis or Albert – he looked like a gangster and once wore a pin-stripe suit on the team bus to an away game. The last thing on our minds when getting changed was the match because we were still laughing at the state of his clobber. And Albert because he was always miserable, just like the Coronation Street character Albert Tatlock.

Mark Lawrenson – Lawro.

Steve McMahon – Macca or Billy – we were taking part in a pro-celebrity golf day and each group was announced on the opening tee, with the footballer always named first. Except when Macca prepared to hit his opening tee shot. His group was introduced as Billy Ingham and friends.

Jan Molby – Sergeant Slaughter – because of his sharp tongue.

Ronnie Moran – Bugsy – after Bugs Moran, Al Capone's rival and the Prohibition-era gangster.

Phil Neal – Nealy.

Ronny Rosenthal – Rocket – Rocket Ronny because he would explode at the slightest opportunity on the field.

Ian Rush – Tosh – we played Athletic Bilbao in the European Cup in 1983 and he finally scored with his head. The press used to say he never scored headers so when he did we called him Tosh after John Toshack.

Graeme Souness – Charlie – he built up a substantial champagne bill at the Holiday Inn after signing from Middlesbrough, so Champagne Charlie.

Michael Thomas – Lester – after Lester Piggott because none of us could understand a word he said. A top man, though.

Phil Thompson – Tonka – no idea why!

Paul Walsh – Juice – "pass the fucking juice mate" were the first words he uttered at a pre-match meal shortly after signing.

John Wark – The Jink – playing cards on the bus one day he he flipped over three jacks but said he had 'three jinks'.

Ronnie Whelan – Dustovic – when he said the word 'just' it sounded like he was saying 'dust'. And we added 'ovic' because he always played well in Europe.

Mark Wright – Ralph – the spitting image of Ralph Malph from Happy Days.

David Johnson – The Doc – because his toilet bag always contained creams, aspirins, anti-inflammatory tablets and various other medical supplies. By the way, the only Liverpool player I know who had to leave the pitch to do a number two!

And finally… *Graham The Bus Driver* – Helmut. One day he turned up having just had a haircut. It was atrocious. It looked like he was wearing a German war helmet.

As soon as I got back from the World Cup in Mexico I called Kenny. I'd been experiencing pain in my stomach while playing for Scotland and it still didn't feel right, so he arranged for me to get checked out.

The Liverpool club doctor examined me: 'How's this?' as he poked and 'how's that?' as he prodded but that was about the extent of it. With two weeks before the start of pre-season training, the doc told me to rest for the full fortnight and it would calm down.

Twenty minutes into day one of pre-season training and even though we were only jogging I didn't feel right, so I told Kenny. This time he bypassed the club doctor and arranged for me to see a specialist, Dr Richard Calver. To this day I still don't know why the doc didn't refer me in the first place – surely that would have made more sense.

The examination at a Liverpool hospital didn't take long. They initially thought it was a hernia, and sent me for surgery, however when they opened me up they realised I had torn a stomach muscle in my lower abdomen as well.

There's no way of knowing if I made the injury worse by playing for Scotland in Mexico but it certainly wouldn't have helped. I had a high pain threshold so playing with a hernia is probably why I tore my stomach muscle. Anyway, I was ruled out for six weeks.

Kenny had no real replacement for me at right-back. He could have played Gary Gillespie there but Gary's best position was in the centre of defence. So I was called in to the manager's office at the end of July and told that Barry Venison was about to join from Sunderland.

Now Kenny Dalglish might come across to some people as dour, hard-nosed and self-opinionated but he's actually very clever and you always knew where you stood with him. As much as he would join in when he could with the fun and games, we all knew where the line was, the one not to be crossed. Kenny didn't have to tell me that he was signing Barry, but he made a point of bringing me in to explain what he was doing. That is proper man-management.

By that stage of my Liverpool career I knew I was an important member of the squad. I had already played more than one hundred games for the club and felt there were four positions in the team where I could play if required: right-back, left-back, right-midfield and left-midfield. So the signing of Barry did not faze me. I was confident that once I regained full fitness I would get back in the side, and that's the way it panned out.

Feeling pain-free and ready to return, my first game back from injury was a Merseyside derby. Okay, it was only the first leg of the Screen Sport Super Cup final but I was just glad to be back out on the pitch. And I was lucky enough to be involved in one of the best Liverpool goals I saw during my time at the club. Leading by two goals to one, Kenny started things off with a quick pass out wide to me. I fired it first time in to Rushy at the edge of the box. He took it straight away and fired past Bobby Mimms. The whole move took less than five seconds. Two killer passes and one fantastic goal. When we knocked the ball around like that, no-one could live with us. It's worth checking the goal out on YouTube.

Missing the first six weeks of the season was a blow but it was great to come back and feel one hundred per cent again. And it wasn't long before I was back among the goals, netting our tenth in a 10-0 win against Fulham in a League Cup tie at Anfield. I had to laugh when I picked up a copy of the Fulham pro-gramme for the second leg – there was a paragraph on the back page reading *'Should the tie be level on aggregate after 90 minutes there will be extra time and penalties'* and the front featured a photo of Diego Maradona praying! Even the Argentina legend couldn't have saved them from losing 13-2 on aggregate.

After a year of highs and lows for the family in 1986 – our daughter Katy was born but Dad died in February – I was looking forward to the festive period hopefully signalling some stability and normality. Except I got within two days of Christmas when disaster struck. While training at Melwood ahead of the home game against Manchester United on Boxing Day I felt a sharp pain in the base of my stomach – exactly the same pain as before. As soon as I felt it, I knew. I'd started twenty-one straight games since returning to the team against Everton in September but the previous match against Charlton on the Saturday before Christmas was to be my last action of the campaign. More surgery required.

Dr Calver explained that although the first operation had been a success to remove the hernia, the stitching hadn't taken as well as he would have hoped. So this time he was going to 'double-mesh' it. He told me the procedure, plus recovery time, would normally be around six weeks but because of what had happened in the summer – and having to perform another surgery so quickly – he recommended it would be best if I didn't play again that season. I wasn't about to argue with him.

The loss of my dad really hurt. When he initially came out of the coma following his heart attack he just wasn't the same person. I don't think he recognised us or had any idea who we were, even though my mum was there every day. He never used to swear but after the coma that all changed – he was swearing a lot and behaving inappropriately around the nurses. I drove up to see him as often as possible, depending on fixtures, and it was heartbreaking each time he didn't recognise me.

Dad eventually passed away six months after coming out of the coma. He had to get an operation on his teeth to ease his discomfort but had another heart attack while he was in theatre and died on the operating table. He was only 69.

I was the last member of the family to find out that he had died. After breaking my jaw and being out of action, Eleanor and me went away for a week at the start of the year to an isolated cottage in the Lake District. It felt like it was in the middle of nowhere and I don't think we saw another human being for the first few days until there was a knock on the door.

A friend of Eleanor's family, Jim Porter, was a superintendent in the police force in Ayr and they had managed to track us down. They passed on the message to the local constabulary in Cumbria and a policeman delivered the news. It was met with a rueful smile because Dad hadn't been himself since the coma and I was just relieved his pain was over.

Dad was classic old school. He'd come home with his pay cheque, give it to mum and get his pocket money in return. That was his job done. She was the one who then ran the household and sorted everything else out. If Mum asked Dad to pick up a pint of milk he'd come home and demand the ten pence back. It was his money. That's just the way he was.

On a Saturday he'd go down to the bookies and put a line on the horses, but only on a Saturday – talk about a creature of habit. I remember one afternoon when I was a kid hearing him in the other room screaming and shouting. We all ran through thinking he'd won a fortune because he had the biggest smile on his face. He told us he'd won 50 pence on an each-way bet.

One of my favourite stories about Dad took place right at the start of my career. I signed for Ayr United as a semi-profes-sional – I was only part-time but in my eyes I was a pro despite being unemployed at the time.

My first ever game for Ayr was meant to be for the reserves in pre-season against a local junior team. I was supposed to get picked up half a mile from the house by teammate Ian Cashmore but there was still no sign of him thirty minutes after we'd arranged to meet. So I ran home and begged Dad for a lift to the game. He did the maths and worked out it was a forty-five minute round trip and he had fifty pence on the next horse race thirty minutes later. He was not happy.

After eventually persuading him to take me – "I can't be late for my first ever game for Ayr United" – he drove at 29.5mph the whole way. All the roads had 30mph limits. At this rate I was going to be late for kick-off.

"Do you think I am going to break the law so you can get there quicker?" he asked. When I got to the ground the teams were warming up.

"Well, this is a good start", said Willie McLean, the manager. I was named among the substitutes and didn't get on. "If you don't turn up on time then you can't expect to play," said the boss.

When I got home later that night Dad was in his usual chair in the living room, just about to head up to bed.

"By the way," he said. "You owe me petrol money."

As a footballer, all you want to do is play, so being stuck on the sidelines for a decent length of time is an absolute nightmare. Kenny asked me to travel with the team on the bus for the game (that never was) against Luton but that wasn't a regular occurrence when I was out injured.

I used to get bored and was always on the lookout for something to do – I hated going to games I wasn't playing in. There were even a few occasions when we decided to take the kids up to Scotland to see our families.

One particular Sunday afternoon I told Eleanor I was going down to the pub at Ayr harbour for an hour or so to meet Stephen and Doug, two of my brother-in-laws. She was well aware that the '*or so*' part of '*an hour or so*' usually added another five or six hours on when drink was involved…

Doug arrived at the pub directly from work and brought with him a big fish that he'd been given by a mate of his – perfect for dinner that night. When Stephen left to go home around six o'clock, the sensible thing would have been to do likewise. But I rarely did the sensible thing when drink was involved. So Doug and I went on to another pub in a hotel, and we took our fishy friend with us.

We spent the next couple of hours with a beer in one hand and a pool cue in the other. Mr Fish spent the next couple of hours just lying there quietly on the ledge keeping himself to himself. Smartly dressed posh couples and not-so-happy families spent the next couple of hours wondering what on earth the pungent smell was while trying to eat their dinner.

After exploring various other options to find the source of the pong the bar manager eventually came over to us and enquired what was in the bag on the ledge. He then issued an ultimatum: either the fish goes or we do. So we left and went to another bar. And the fish came too. I eventually got home at ten o'clock that night. Surprise, surprise Eleanor wasn't happy.

"Oh it's only the nine hours this time since you left the house."

"But I brought you a fish…"

Nope, that didn't exactly help matters.

Like a naughty schoolboy she sent me straight to bed. I stumbled upstairs, got to the top then realised I wanted a drink of water. I then fell down the stairs – head first – but somehow

I had the wherewithal to use my hands to minimize the damage to the rest of my body. I went downstairs in the morning and Eleanor's mum was being weird and wasn't talking to me. So I asked Eleanor what was up with her.

"Well, considering you tried to climb in to bed with her and my dad last night when you were stark bollock naked, how do you think she was going to react when she saw you?"

Apparently I went in to the wrong room when I came back upstairs with the glass of water but I have absolutely no recollection of this. Oops…

Season 1986-87 was probably the first time we weren't quite right since I arrived at Liverpool. And I don't know why. We were knocked out of the FA Cup in the third round by Luton Town after a second replay, lost to Arsenal in the League Cup final – the first time we'd been beaten in a game when Rushy scored for us – and finished a distant second in the league behind Everton. Finishing second at Liverpool was no consolation whatsoever for a team used to winning titles.

Kenny obviously thought it was a transitional season as well because he started to make changes to his squad. He signed John Aldridge from Oxford United in January 1987, bought Nigel Spackman from Chelsea the following month and came close to getting full-back Derek Statham from West Brom, until that move fell through on medical grounds.

With Rushy heading back to Juventus in the summer – having already signed for them in July 1986 and then loaned back to us for a season – Kenny was on the lookout for a striker to replace him. The likes of Charlie Nicholas, David Speedie and Danish international Preben Elkjaer – who I played against at

173

the World Cup – had all been linked with Liverpool, but Kenny decided to sign a 28-year-old from Oxford United. And what a signing John Aldridge turned out to be...well, eventually.

It was just as well Aldo was patient because he only started twice for the club during the rest of that season after signing in January (scoring on both occasions by the way). Clearly seen as Rushy's replacement rather than his strike partner, he was used mainly as a substitute and it frustrated him that he wasn't getting much of a chance. But this was all part of Kenny's grand plan. Always ahead of the game. Why wait until the summer to try and sign a replacement for Rushy when the number one target may no longer be available? Aldo might have found his first few months at Liverpool frustrating due to a lack of game time but Kenny knew what he was doing.

When you think of it, an incredible number of top-class strikers moved on from Liverpool over the years and were quickly replaced by other top-class strikers. Hunt, St John, Keegan, Toshack, Rush, Aldridge, Fowler, Owen, Torres and then Suarez. And don't forget Dalglish replaced Keegan. What other club in English football has been able to do that – to recycle their main goalscorers – as many times as Liverpool have? I don't think there is one.

So with Rushy away to Italy and Aldo primed and ready for his chance, with Kenny pretty much hanging up his boots and concentrating on management and with the arrivals of John Barnes and Peter Beardsley, the squad had new impetus and a much-needed freshness. The new season couldn't come quick enough. Now all I had to do was get myself fit over the summer so I could be part of the plans.

12

Red Machine
In Full Effect

*'Liverpool FC is hard as hell...United, Tottenham,
Arsenal...watch my lips and I will spell... 'cause they
don't just play, but they can rap as well'*

"Oh shut the fuck up Nico – there's fuck all wrong with you."

Subtlety was never Paul Walsh's strongpoint. I remember the night vividly, sitting on my bed in a Danish hotel room with tears coming down both cheeks wondering aloud if my career might be over.

But Walshy did have a point, even if it was delivered using language as filthy as a sewer rat.

Sunday, July 27, 1987 – I'd already made my comeback from injury against Bayern Munich in a testimonial in Germany three days previously and, although the game was played at a sedate pace, I was back on a football pitch for the first time in seven months.

So why was I worrying?

Dr Calver had already explained and gone through what would happen after being out for so long – there was a lot of scar tissue so I would initially feel some discomfort because of two lots of surgery in the same area of my stomach but the pain wouldn't last long and, more importantly, shouldn't affect my game.

The doubts about my fitness eased with each pre-season fixture I played in. Then came the big test – Arsenal away in the first game of the new season. In the hotel the night before the game at Highbury my mind was racing – 'would I still have problems with my stomach?' and 'what if there's a recurrence of the injury?' Remember, I hadn't played a competitive game since December of the previous year so I thought those were legitimate concerns after being out for so long. Ninety minutes later and all doubts had been erased. We won 2-1 and I scored the winner late on. More importantly I was pain-free.

Beardsley to Barnes to Aldridge for the opening goal inside ten minutes – our new-look Liverpool side was off and running. Then, after they'd equalised and with time running out, we were awarded a free-kick deep inside their half, about ten yards from the touchline, after Barnesy was obstructed by Perry Groves.

I went over to take it but Digger told me to leave it for him so I took up a spot nearby at the edge of the box. He whipped the ball into a dangerous area just in front of goalkeeper John Lukic and it was only partially cleared by Tony Adams. Straight into my path.

As the ball was coming towards me first of all I wondered if I could head it back into that dangerous area, then I realised I had a chance to go for goal. All I wanted to do was make good contact and force Lukic to make a save.

Instead, I made perfect contact with my head and the ball flew into the top corner of the net from all of twenty yards out. All those fears about my future? Gone in an instant.

The result got our season off to a flyer and the performance convinced us all that we had a team that was once again ready to challenge for honours.

Plus, any doubts I had about my stomach had totally disappeared and I felt I was back to the level I had been playing at prior to the World Cup twelve months earlier. It was the day when all the pieces of the jigsaw came together. This was a proper team.

A collapsed sewer underneath the Kop meant our opening three league games all had to be played away from Anfield. So next up was a trip to face the FA Cup holders, Coventry City. Each of the players were meant to take it in turns to write a weekly match report for the Liverpool Fan Club Magazine. Here's how I described my contribution to a 4-0 win at Highfield Road:

'... I was in the goals again. Don't worry, it won't last for long! My first midway through the first half followed a short corner which Digger took back to Stevie Mac. I just hung around avoiding their half-hearted offside trap. Stevie played a great ball back into the box where I held off Dave Bennett and then had all the time in the world to pick my spot. I was going to slip it to Oggy's left, but as he went down anticipating a shot, I just walloped it straight in the middle of the goal. I got the next one too, early in the second half. Aldo was involved in the build-up, Digger played it into Peter Beardsley and went on for a return. But I ran on past him and Pete's pass fell perfectly for me to score again...'

Just how much of that I actually said or where it came from is up for debate because I've never written a column in my life!

Exactly one month after my tears and fears in Denmark, and that Paul Walsh pep talk, I'd suddenly scored three goals in two games and felt as right as rain. Isn't it funny how things can change so quickly? Some of the football we were playing was breathtaking – Coventry boss John Sillett even said our performance against them was probably the finest he had ever seen from a team in the top flight in England.

Why? What had changed?

Well, the biggest difference was the way we played – we got it forward a lot quicker and were more dynamic. But that was only possible because the players Kenny brought in – John Barnes, Peter Beardsley, John Aldridge and Ray Houghton – settled in so quickly and were able to gel with the quality already in the team. As a player, Kenny always wanted it played early to him. He was constantly getting on at us in defence to get it forward as soon as possible, whether it was a thirty yard pass to him or Rushy or a ball out wide, but he always wanted it to be a positive pass. And when he became manager that's the way he wanted his team to play.

Previously, from when I joined Liverpool up until Kenny taking over, the style of play was possession-based with a more precise build-up. When you had Graeme Souness in the middle of the park then it made sense to go through him whenever possible. The teams I played in during the early to mid-Eighties looked to get the ball forward when it was on – keeping possession followed by a measured pass – ball retention was a key component of our success and teams just couldn't get the ball from us.

Remember, Kenny was initially dealing with a lot of the same players Joe Fagan had so his idea of a quicker, more dynamic way of playing had to be gradually phased in over a period of time. Once he had the players he wanted, playing in the style he wanted, we became a real force to be reckoned with. On many occasions, opponents just couldn't handle us. Everyone was at the peak of their powers – physically and mentally – and our ability was second to none.

I've always wondered whether not being involved in European competitions helped us do that because we used to play a hell of a lot of games in a season. Of course, Kenny's way of playing and the players he had at his disposal was the main reason for our success but I just wonder if not having those extra fixtures in Europe helped give us some additional energy.

It was Aldo's fault...

He was standing in an offside position as I curled the ball beyond Newcastle United goalkeeper Gary Kelly. The laws were a bit different back then and the goal was disallowed. That would have been my second of the afternoon at St James' Park, in front of the live BBC television cameras as well. Thankfully we ended up winning 4-1 and, playing on the right hand side of midfield, I scored my first ever hat-trick.

The first goal was a simple finish with my left foot from twelve yards after good work from Barnes and Beardsley, who was returning to the North East for the first time after leaving Newcastle. Goal number two was a tap-in from two yards (which I miss-hit, but don't tell anybody...) and the third was a cheeky chip with the right foot after a nice reverse pass from Aldo put me in the clear. Off I went with my arm raised aloft in triumph.

I was so surprised to score a hat-trick I left the pitch at the end of the game and forgot to ask referee Keith Hackett for the match ball. It wasn't until I was sitting in the dressing room afterwards when one of the lads asked me where it was that I realised. Kenny tried to tell me that the ref had decided to keep the ball but this was a wind-up too far and one I wasn't falling for this time.

I eventually got my hands on the ball and all the boys signed it for me. It may only have been mid-September but this game was one of the highlights of a great season, and what's more a nationwide audience watching live on Match of the Day got to see what Liverpool fans already knew – this was a special team with some very special players.

Incidentally, my hat-trick helped make up for missing my twin sister's wedding on the Isle of Arran, which took place on the same day. When the fixtures originally came out, the game against Newcastle was supposed to take place twenty-four hours earlier, on the Saturday, which was perfect for me because I was meant to be giving Susan away the following day (Dad had died the year before). Then it was moved and put back for live BBC coverage, so our dad's brother, Uncle Billy, gave her away. At least the wedding ceremony took place early enough to allow guests at the reception to watch most of the game on TV before the speeches took place.

Another goal at Blackburn in a League Cup tie made it seven in seven for me – equalling my goal tally for the whole season in 1983-84 and 1984-85. But that strike at Ewood Park was to be the last time I would score that season as Kenny moved me back into defence. Thankfully, Aldo, Digger and Peter kept finding the back of the net.

We ended the year ten points clear of Nottingham Forest and had yet to taste defeat in the league.

After going twenty-nine league games unbeaten from the start of the season – and equalling the record set by Leeds United in 1973-74 – we finally lost, to Everton, on Sunday, March 20, 1988. It had to be them. They'd also beaten us in the League Cup at Anfield the previous October but this one hurt more.

The consolation was a fourteen-point lead over Manchester United at the top of table as well as having two games in hand. Nottingham Forest were the only other team to get the better of us in the league that season, at the start of April, but we certainly got revenge eleven days later.

It was one of those strange quirks of fate. We hadn't played Forest at all that season then faced them three times in eleven days. The first game at the City Ground, when they beat us 2-1, was billed as the dress rehearsal for our FA Cup semi-final at Hillsborough the following weekend. Thankfully we won the right one and beat them 2-1 in Sheffield to secure a place in the FA Cup final against Wimbledon. But it was the final part of the trilogy that some people still talk about to this day, mainly thanks to Tom Finney's now famous quote afterwards.

Fans of a certain age will know what happened but I'm sure even they won't mind a quick reminder of the events of Wednesday, April 13, 1988…

• Liverpool 5-0 Nottingham Forest.

• Our team: Grobbelaar, Gillespie, Ablett, Nicol, Spackman, Hansen (c), Beardsley, Aldridge, Houghton, Barnes, McMahon.

• Goal one – Ray Houghton's one-two with Barnesy.

• Goal two – Beardsley's wonderful through ball then Aldo's delightful chip.

- "Barnes…Houghton…Aldridge… GILLESPIEEEEEE!" screamed BBC commentator John Motson for goal three as 'Smithy' smashed home our third from close range.
- Ask Steve Chettle about goal number four — the Forest defender's legs weren't even that wide apart but Digger still managed a nutmeg in the corner in front of the Kop before setting up Peter to score from twelve yards.
- Goal five — Aldo's second, after Nigel Spackman cut it back perfectly for him.
- Should have been more — Steve Sutton, the Forest goalkeeper made four or five incredible saves and had a strong claim to be named man-of-the-match despite conceding five!
- What Finney said: 'It was the finest exhibition of football I've seen the whole time I've played and watched the game. You couldn't see it bettered anywhere, not even in Brazil. The moves they put together were fantastic.'

Because of that quote this game is still remembered, but I reckon we played just as well on several occasions that season. The significance was the quality of the opposition because Forest were one of the best sides around at the time. When we were all fit and everybody was flying we had a really good team and when everything came together at the same time — like it did against Nottingham Forest — it really was magic.

We clinched the title with four games to spare thanks to a 1-0 victory over Spurs at Anfield — fittingly Peter Beardsley scored the goal to cap a wonderful first season for him at the club. It was Liverpool's ninth title in thirteen seasons and was probably the most stylish of the lot. It also backed up Kenny's decision to slightly change the transfer policy of the club. Up until the mid-Eighties Liverpool managers were still bringing in young players and teaching them the Liverpool Way, getting them ready for an eventual step-up to the first team. In the late Sixties, we signed Ray Clemence from Scunthorpe United and Emlyn Hughes from Blackpool. Then Kevin Keegan also arrived from Scunthorpe while Phil Neal came from Northampton Town in 1974. You also had the young ones, guys like Steve Heighway who was plucked from junior side Skelmersdale United, plus the likes of Brian Hall, Chris Lawler, Tommy Smith, Sammy Lee and Phil Thompson. They all came through the ranks at Liverpool.

But things changed in 1987 when Kenny signed Aldo, Beardsley, Barnes, Spackman and Houghton in the space of a twelve-month period and they all pretty much went straight into the team. These players were bought to play immediately, signalling the end of the buy-them-young, put-them-in-the-reserves and turn-them-into-something era. And these players played a huge part in not only our success that season but also the manner in which we won, scoring 87 goals in 40 league games and only conceding 24.

'Is this the greatest Liverpool team of all time?' was the opening paragraph of the match report in the Daily Mirror after we beat Spurs to clinch the title. That's not for me to say – it's very hard to compare teams from different eras – but it was certainly the most entertaining side I was lucky enough to be involved in. Wimbledon in the FA Cup final now stood between us and a second Double in three years.

Before we could think about the game, there was the Cup Final song to do – get a squad of footballers drunk, put them in a recording studio for a couple of hours and see what happens.

What could possibly go wrong? Well, apart from me nearly breaking Bruce Grobbelaar's neck...

Think of pop stars and you probably think of glamour and wealth. Well none of that was evident at The Pink Museum recording studio in Hesketh Street when a bunch of tracksuit-wearing scallies got together to record Liverpool Football Club's FA Cup final song for the princely sum of one hundred pounds each in expenses.

[Me] We're Highland lads
[Gary] Och aye the noo
[Kevin] And there's four of us
[Big Al] And only two of you
[Me] So if you want nae trouble
[Gary] And you don't want a slap
[All] You'd better teach us
[All] The Anfield Rap

The Anfield Rap, or Anfield Rap (Red Machine In Full Effect) to give it its full title, got as high as number three in the Official UK charts, behind only Wet Wet Wet and Fairground Attraction and ahead of musical luminaries such as Kylie Minogue, New Order, Prince, Belinda Carlisle, Michael Jackson and, of course, Harry Enfield. At least he had Loadsamoney...

Written by Craig Johnston, the lyrics centred on the two Scousers in our squad – John Aldridge and Steve McMahon – and the quest to get the rest of us to talk like them.

We split into groups based on where we were born and I was with fellow Scots Kevin MacDonald, Gary Gillespie and Big Al. Kenny wasn't singing because he was the boss and trying to act all cool, although he did make a cameo appearance in the video.

As for our gear? Absolutely honking. I was wearing a wee bespoke number by Puma – a black tracksuit with white diamonds on the shoulder – along with a black baseball cap sitting sideways on my head and some white high-top trainers. And to complete the 'look' we all wore long gold chains. I was also wearing a pair of aviator sunglasses but if you watch the video closely you'll notice one of the lenses gets knocked out amidst the shenanigans.

Just before we filmed the video, Bruce was acting the goat and trying to do a headstand on a football. So I thought it would be a good idea to not only push him but also kick the ball out from under his head. I'd love to blame alcohol for being that daft but even a drunk person would know that was a stupid and dangerous thing to do. Thankfully, Bruce was not harmed in the making of the video, although maybe a bang on the head might have knocked some sense into him!

Not many people know this but Juventus striker Ian Rush was also present at the recording. It was done at the end of April so maybe he already knew he was on his way back to Liverpool that summer but Rushy certainly didn't say a single word about that. Even if he didn't know I'm sure spending that day with us cavorting in the studio made him wish he was back at the club.

Although we were all well outside our comfort zone, the whole day was a blast. None of us were any good at singing – although I'm sure one or two will suggest otherwise. They gathered us together at the start and told us just to 'relax and enjoy it.'

It felt awkward at first but the more alcohol we consumed the more relaxed we became. The pressure was off, the league title was already in the bag and it was the perfect way to help prepare for rounding off a perfect campaign.

Sadly, two games at the end of what would be known as the Samba Season stick out in my memory for the wrong reasons.

Liverpool v Wimbledon. Saturday, May 14, 1988…

Apparently we were intimidated by their antics in the tunnel pre-match. Apparently, according to Vinnie Jones, we were also running scared after his ninth minute 'tackle' on Steve McMahon. Utter bollocks. We were so intimidated that there are pictures of us laughing and joking in the tunnel. We were so scared that we spent the remaining 81 minutes attacking their goal. Total shite. This was just one of those days when nothing went right for us and they took their chance when it came. These things happen in football – all credit to them for taking advantage.

We had a feeling that it wasn't going to be our day when Peter Beardsley had the ball in the back of the net ten minutes before half-time but referee Brian Hill said no goal. Inexplicably he'd blown his whistle for a supposed foul on Peter by Andy Thorn as he was running through on goal. It was that bad a foul that Peter didn't even go to ground and we ended up with a free-kick instead of a one-goal lead. A ridiculous decision.

Then, two minutes later, another ridiculous decision, this time by the linesman. I was chasing down Terry Phelan and the two of us were tussling near the corner flag. There was absolutely nothing in it, it wouldn't get a second look these days, and Terry didn't even appeal for a foul as the ball rolled out of play. But the free-kick was awarded which led to the only goal of the game. Talk about things conspiring against you.

We set up defensively exactly the same as we would for a corner. We had three players picking up and everyone else in a zone, including me. The delivery from Dennis Wise went over the head of Alan Cork leaving Sanchez sandwiched between myself in front of him and Gary Ablett in behind. Fair play to Wisey, the ball in was perfect – just too high for me to get my head to it and not enough pace on it to reach Gary as Lawrie flicked it past Bruce and into the back of the net.

There was no panic in the dressing room at half-time, no raised voices. We knew we were better than them and would get chances in the second half. The most glaring chance of all came after an hour from the spot. Now, I'm honest enough to admit that the decision to award us a penalty was an absolute joke – as bad a decision as the ones in the first half that saw Peter's goal chalked off and Terry Phelan get a free-kick for absolutely nothing.

Wimbledon defender Clive Goodyear produced a perfectly timed tackle on Aldo, yet Mr Hill pointed to the spot. Was this a case of him trying to even things up, an acknowledgement from the referee that he had messed up earlier? Only he can answer that, but it's fair to say the officials did not have their finest day at the office. Anyway, we weren't complaining about the award of a spot kick, especially with John Aldridge having scored all eleven penalties he'd taken that season.

There was to be no successful twelfth spot kick and some would say justice was done when Dave Beasant became the first goalkeeper in history to save a penalty in an FA Cup final, leaping to his left and palming the ball behind to prevent Aldo from equalising. I'm totally convinced that if that had gone in then we would have gone on to win the game, but it didn't and you've got to give them credit. They did what they had to do. It doesn't matter if they deserved to win the game or not – the name of Wimbledon Football Club is on the trophy and it was a disappointing end to an otherwise fantastic season.

I remember sitting at the hotel after the game with Ray Houghton and I told him I had no fizz in my legs, and I couldn't run properly but I didn't know why. He said he felt the same way.

We'd wrapped up the league title three weeks before that and had maybe just lost some of our edge and our focus, unintentionally of course. That's why footballers can't just turn it on and off when you want. All the ability in the world is no use if you don't have the physical strength to go with it that you normally have.

All they had to do after going a goal up was to sit tight. The onus was on us to break them down but when you don't have that extra bit in your legs then it becomes more of a level playing field. I'm not looking for excuses; I just think we were the victims of our own success by wrapping up the league as quickly as we did. Would we have won the FA Cup if the title race had gone down to the final weekend of the league season? I think we would have.

Things didn't improve a week later when England beat Scotland 1-0. I was put up to speak at the pre-match press conference and was asked about coming up against my Liverpool teammates, John Barnes and Peter Beardsley. I told the journalists that I hoped the game went as well for them as the previous weekend at Wembley.

Unfortunately, the press took it the wrong way – as they have a habit of doing – and suggested that I was criticising their performances. What I meant was they'd had had a rotten weekend seven days previously – as we all did – and I just hoped it would be the same.

No surprise, Peter and Digger knew exactly what I meant so it wasn't a problem, but that was all I needed after a tough few days which also included helping Eleanor cope with the imminent death of her father.

It wasn't a great month all told but dealing with everything that happened is one of the reasons why I'm as grounded as I am. Highs always seemed to be followed by lows in my career – from winning the European Cup then finding out your father-in-law is diagnosed with cancer the next day to winning the league at a canter as part of a team that played some sensational football then losing two big games at Wembley in the space of a week. You never know what's around the corner.

12+1*

* I've always been a bit superstitious.
That's why I'm not having a chapter 13 in my book!

Horseplay

'Christmas parties at Liverpool were legendary. One time, a player turned up in fancy dress wearing a Ku Klux Klan costume. 'You can't come in dressed like that,' said Steve McMahon, 'because John Barnes is in there!' 'No,' said the man as he removed the hood, 'he's in here!''

Prior to the start of season 1988-89 I took part in one of those question and answer sessions for Shoot! magazine. It was one of those interviews with some offbeat questions – and some even more offbeat answers!

Any remaining copies of the issue I appeared in are probably at the bottom of a pile in attics up and down the country and will never see the light of day again.

So, with belated apologies to Chris Waddle, Nigel Spackman and Jimmy Cricket (but not Bonnie Langford), here's how the Q&A from August 1988 went…

What would you do if you could be invisible for a day?
I'd stand in the opposing penalty box on a Saturday afternoon.

Who would you most like to meet and why? Freddie Starr,
because we share the same sense of humour.

What, if anything frightens you? Heights.

What do you want for your birthday? Another League
Championship medal.

*What's the worst Christmas present you have ever
received?* A pair of socks four sizes too small.

Outside football, what is the biggest risk you have taken?
Being a passenger in Nigel Spackman's car.

Have you ever been mistaken for anyone else? 'Oor
Wullie' from the Sunday Post.

Do you have any superstitions? Too many to mention.

Who is your most difficult opponent? Bruce Grobbelaar in
training.

What is the biggest disappointment of your career?
Losing this year's FA Cup final against Wimbledon.

What's the highlight of your career? Winning the FA Cup
against Everton in 1986.

Who's got the worst haircut you've ever seen?
Chris Waddle of Spurs.

Which pop star would you most like to be and why?
Chubby Checker because he sings with the Fat Boys!

Where are you going tonight?
The Hotel Victoria (my favourite haunt).

If you ever cook a meal, what do you usually make?
Nothing. I'm just hopeless in the kitchen.

Who is your favourite TV personality? Fred Flintstone.

What frightens you most about going to the dentist?
The injection.

*Who would you most like to be stuck on a desert island
with and why?* Bonnie Langford. I can't stand her so I could
annoy her for a change.

Who is the worst comedian you have ever seen?
Jimmy Cricket.

What was your most embarrassing moment?
Being sick in front of someone very important.

*If you could come back in another life as an animal, what
would you most like to be and why?* A bear, so I could sleep
half the year.

What subject did you most like at school? None!

What is your favourite away ground and why?
Old Trafford. I just love playing there.

*If you had to go to a fancy dress party, what would you
go as and why?* A fairy, so I could wave my magic wand.

Which household chore do you hate most and why?
All of them – only under extreme pressure do I do any.

It was all going so well until that penultimate question about the
fancy dress party…

We went to Spain before the campaign started. The Teresa
Herrera Trophy – named after a local Spanish woman who
was famed for her work with the region's poor – is an annual
pre-season tournament in La Coruña. And it played a big part
in shaping my season.

Thirteen minutes into Liverpool's opening game of the competition, against Atletico Madrid, Big Al suffered a serious knee
injury. Not only did it keep him out of action for nine months
but it also meant a positional switch for me – I replaced him
in central defence. I also started every league and cup fixture
that season and ended up winning the Football Writers' Player
of the Year award. Maybe a fairy did indeed wave a magic
wand…

I don't know why but I would often have a problem with my
groin when we reported back for pre-season training. It was
just one of those physical quirks I had and it would sometimes

bother me when I stepped up my fitness regime ahead of a new season. Liverpool took part in seven Charity Shields during my time at the club yet I only played in two – I missed three of them because of that exact same injury.

It wasn't anything serious in 1988 but there was enough discomfort so I didn't risk playing and watched from the stand as we beat Wimbledon at Wembley. In their match reports the day after some of the newspapers claimed we got revenge after losing in the FA Cup final, but to be honest beating them meant nothing to us. That loss in May hurt then and still hurts now.

A bigger story that week was the return to Anfield of Ian Rush after a season in Italy with Juventus. Maybe him being present at the recording of the Anfield Rap three months before helped make his mind up to return to Liverpool…

It had taken until March of the previous season before we lost our first league game. Unfortunately, we didn't have the same consistency in the first few months of this season and the home defeat at the hands of Newcastle at the beginning of October signalled the start of a poor run of form – no wins in four – that left us playing catch-up early doors. I can't put my finger on why we weren't able to recapture the form of the season before. Ian Rush had arrived to strengthen the squad and we hadn't sold any players, but the loss of Big Al certainly didn't help. Suddenly we were dropping points in games that twelve months previously we were winning quite comfortably.

Losing to Manchester United at Old Trafford on New Year's Day, 1989 – our fifth league defeat of the season – left us trailing leaders Arsenal by nine points at the halfway stage and we'd played a game more than them.

What followed, however, was a 24-game unbeaten run and

that tells you everything you need to know about the spirit and belief we had in that particular squad. We also didn't carry any passengers. Everybody played his part. And when that happened, coupled with the real quality we had in the team, we were a totally different proposition.

You're at Liverpool because you have that extra ability, part of a squad of players that can make things happen, and we all knew that if things weren't quite working out for us individually on any given Saturday there were plenty others in the team who were able to step up to the plate. It's all about attitude, ability and consistency. If the majority of our players produced on a matchday then a decent result usually followed. But if all eleven players showed those three qualities at once then we were a hard team to beat, practically impossible. That's why, most of the time, we didn't lose.

Just as important, however, was the coaching staff never allowing us to get ahead of ourselves. If, for example, any of the lads failed to help put the kit hampers back on the bus then Ronnie Moran would go apeshit. Don't forget where you came from. That was the message regularly drummed into us.

Kenny's role in all this was quite simple: he made sure we did what we were supposed to do. He was all about standards. If he thought standards were dropping then he'd be on you like a ton of bricks. It certainly wasn't done intentionally but if our standards did drop for whatever reason – no matter who you were – he'd be all over you like a rash, big time. Even though he was the boss he held himself to those standards as well. And he expected us to do likewise.

I'm not going to pretend that everything was always perfect at Liverpool. It wasn't. Arguments took place in the dressing room, as I'm sure they do at clubs the world over, and there was the odd occasion when things threatened to get out of hand. As they did at a hotel in Dundee in February 1989.

I'd been in Cyprus during the week for a World Cup qualifier with Scotland but had to be replaced after only nine minutes in Nicosia because of pains in my chest. When I got home to the Wirral on the Thursday, I called Kenny and told him I didn't feel right. He suggested I go and see the club doctor at his house before we travelled north to Scotland. The doc – in his pyjamas – answered the door, offered us a drink, got out his stethoscope, tapped a couple of times on my chest and said I was fine. An in-depth medical examination it was not. But the hospitality was excellent.

No further forward in the quest to find out what was wrong with me it was agreed it was best if I sat things out at Dens Park. I might not have been included in the playing squad for goal-keeper Bobby Geddes's testimonial but I travelled to Dundee nevertheless. A couple of days away with the boys and a few beers on the Saturday night – there's no way I was passing up that opportunity.

The initial plan after the game was for the lads to hit the town, but a huge rainstorm put paid to that idea. It was impossible to go outside without getting utterly drenched, so the squad set up base for the night at the hotel bar. Usual stuff; taking the piss out of each other when all of a sudden – after about ten pints – all hell broke loose.

I was sitting with Steve McMahon and Barry Venison and a few others when an argument about shopping, of all things, got out of hand and things got pretty heated pretty quickly. Bruce stepped in and tried to split Steve and Barry up but Macca told him to mind his own fucking business. So Bruce stuck the head on Macca – properly nutted him – and there was blood everywhere. Our goalkeeper then disappeared and our midfielder was left running around looking for ice.

With Bruce concerned that Macca would come looking for revenge, he decided to try and swap rooms to secure a better hiding place.

Initially he was in with Craig Johnston before I stupidly agreed to accommodate him because I had a room to myself. Bruce took himself off to bed and, I thought, took the sting out the situation by doing so. How wrong I was.

About an hour or so later, I went upstairs. I opened the door in the room and there was nobody there, at least that's what I thought at first. Then I put the light on and found Bruce sleeping on the floor between the two beds. He'd put pillows in his bed to make it look like he was in there, but instead was using my pillows to ensure his comfort on the floor.

His explanation was just as bizarre as his antics and it went something like this: "If Macca finds out I'm in this room and gets a key then he'll think I'm in my bed because of the pillows and then he'll jump on me and attack me but really I'm not in my bed so he won't be able to attack me because I'm actually on the floor!"

Around half past three, there was a loud bang outside our room followed by someone trying to break the door down. It was Macca. He had knocked over a lamp in the corridor and was now trying to persuade Bruce to come out of the room. This is the point where our stories differ.

Bruce claimed that he hid in the bathroom while I opened the door then watched Macca enter the room. He says he then tapped Macca on the shoulder before smacking him across the nose for the second time that night.

Now, Bruce has been known to tell a tall tale or two over the years and most of them I would take with a pinch of salt, including his version of events in this one. For a start, this particular incident happened in February 1989, not October 1987 as he claims, because Macca wasn't even in the squad for that trip to Dundee. Secondly, there was no way on God's green earth that I was going to open the hotel room door to a revenge-seeking madman in the middle of the night!

Heavy snow the following day meant the journey back to Liverpool took a lot longer than it should have done, but at least with Macca and Bruce at opposite ends of the bus there was no chance of a repeat of the shenanigans from the night before.

The snow got progressively worse and shortly after Penrith the bus came to a stop, along with every other vehicle on the M6. We were going nowhere. Worst of all we'd run out of beer.

Remembering that a Tennent's Lager lorry had passed us, slowly, a few minutes earlier, I figured it would also be stuck and therefore couldn't be too far along the road. So I volunteered to get out, put on my club jacket and wander off down the motorway in search of beer.

I must have walked for about ten minutes but the lorry was nowhere to be seen. I soon realised the predicament I was in. It was snowing and I was freezing so I did an about-turn and headed back. Staying alive was slightly more important than returning with a few cans of lager.

Fifteen minutes later I still couldn't find the bus and was beginning to panic. I was in the middle of a snowstorm and my body temperature was getting progressively colder. Eventually I spotted Helmut, our driver, and was never as happy to see him as I was then…

Arsenal continued to lead the way as we approached the busy Easter period but Norwich City were also making a title charge and were the Gunners' nearest challengers. Then we beat the Canaries 1-0 at Carrow Road at the start of April and moved up into second, just two points behind George Graham's men.

After four games in eleven days – and with no midweek league card – we could have done with a rest. Instead we had to fly to the Middle East to take part in a match against Celtic for the Dubai Champions Cup. Billed as the unofficial 'British Championship' it was basically a glorified friendly between the title winners in Scotland and England. We lost on penalties but it was actually nice to get away from it all for a few days. And my hero, George Best, presented me with the man-of-the-match award so it was worth the 7000-mile round trip just for that.

Back to the league campaign and in all my years playing for Liverpool, I never once lost a match at Anfield on the day of the Grand National. There's a good reason for that. There was always that little bit more intensity to our play because of the possibility that Bugsy and Roy might one day say it was a distraction and ban us from attending. If we were playing at home and there was racing at Aintree on the same day then our games used to kick-off at 11.30am. I think the early start used to affect the opposition more than it affected us because we were always trying our bollocks off and used to come flying out the traps.

The 5-1 win over Sheffield Wednesday at Anfield on Grand National Day not only kept us hot on the heels of leaders Arsenal – three points behind but now with a game in hand –

it also gave us the green light to go to the races. And that was the day when John Barnes decided to take to the Aintree turf himself.

When the racing was finished, we walked back to where the bus was parked. The quickest way to get there was across the racetrack so, having consumed a fair amount of alcohol, Barnesy and Big Al decided to have a race on the course. Unlike the Grand National there were no fences involved, but the upshot was that Barnesy tweaked his hammy.

There were rules in place that if a player had a knock after a game then you had to go in for treatment with Ronnie Moran at 9am on the Sunday morning. Considering the amount we'd had to drink at Aintree it was no surprise when Barnesy failed to show. Now, if you were hurt when you went in on the Monday morning having not turned up on the Sunday then Ronnie would have you for breakfast.

Barnesy knew this so didn't let on that his hamstring was a bit tight until after the warm-up at training on the Monday. Of course, we all knew the real reason but we kept our mouths shut.

It was just as well he didn't go in for treatment. I've got this wonderful vision in my head of Ronnie asking him when he first felt his hamstring tighten and Barnesy responding that it was "when he was crossing the Melling Road." Somehow I don't think that would have gone down too well with Bugsy!

Thankfully it was only a minor tweak and John played in midweek, scoring the equaliser at The Den in a 2-1 win over Millwall. It was the first time we were top of the table all season.

With six games to go, and Liverpool leading Arsenal on goal difference, we were in pole position to win our fifth league championship in eight years. Things were going well. And we knew that victory in the upcoming FA Cup semi-final against Nottingham Forest at Hillsborough would only help build momentum when the title race resumed.

14

Tell Me
It's Not True

'I can't speak for any other club but I think if you play for Liverpool you understand it's not just a football team. It's not just a job. It's a way of life'

I should have left Liverpool Football Club long before I did.

That sounds like a terrible thing to say, but it's true. I loved the club – still do, always will – but I simply could not rid my mind of Hillsborough. Consciously and subconsciously it was eating away at me.

Eventually, I just couldn't take it any more.

God alone knows how the survivors and families have coped. In terms of my story, it's only now, looking back, that I realise just how much of an effect it had on me as a player. Three years, I reckon.

Three years of being unable to focus properly. Three years of playing in a bubble. Three years on autopilot. It was hard to realise that was the case at the time. Impossible, in fact. Trying, and failing, to deal with the aftermath was obviously having an effect but no-one knew how to properly cope with it.

At the time, the club asked us if we wanted counselling. It was our choice. They left it up to us.

How were WE to know what we needed? We were just foot-ballers. We were not equipped to do all those things we had to do. Counselling should have been mandatory. Every time I think about it now I keep telling myself to shut up because we never lost anybody. Others did. It's the first thing that goes through my head. It always goes through my head when I talk about it.

Saturday, April 15, 1989.

The day itself was a blur. Still is. I remember sitting in the dressing room listening to what was going on outside. Wonder-ing. Once or twice a policeman would come in and try to give us updates, but proper information was scarce in the immediate aftermath.

The day after the tragedy, we got a call from the club asking us to come to Anfield on the Monday morning. Apart from that telephone call, I cannot remember any other detail of what I did or what happened that Sunday. I was numb.

I recall now that it was the PFA Player of the Year Awards evening in London that night. I was in the running and ended up finishing second to Mark Hughes. I was meant to attend the ceremony. No chance. Didn't even consider it. Never crossed my mind.

Everything snowballed in the days after Hillsborough. Over the weekend, fans started leaving flowers and scarves at the Shankly Gates, then the club allowed supporters access inside

Anfield to put flowers down in front of The Kop. By Monday there were so many floral tributes that they started to use the pitch as well.

After arriving at Anfield at 9am on the Monday morning, as the club had requested, we got on the bus and travelled back to Sheffield to visit those who'd been hospitalised.

Meanwhile, the wives stayed in Liverpool to do what they could to help. On the way back from Sheffield later that day we were told to report to Kenny's office the following morning at 10am.

On the Tuesday morning, in Kenny's office, were all the players and our partners. We were told that there were people in the Candy Lounge who had lost loved ones or been traumatised by what had happened and didn't know where else to go. Kenny suggested if we could help them, in any way, then we should go and talk to them.

That's how it all started. People were sitting at tables in the lounge. The players and wives dispersed and started to mingle. We introduced ourselves. Asked them to introduce themselves. Eventually you get to the point where you have to ask them who they have lost. Ask them how they feel.

Eleanor and I were sitting talking with Ginger – one of the fans who'd been at the game. Like everyone else, he couldn't understand what had happened or why it had happened. We were talking but we weren't really getting anywhere.

I suggested we went for a walk out on to the pitch. We saw the flowers and I said 'let's go and stand on the Kop.' We went to the spot where he stands every week and just stood there in silence.

We grew up quickly in a short space of time. I think those

of us with children were able to relate more to what had happened. Some of the younger players who didn't have kids probably struggled at first because they were unable to grasp the enormity of it all.

I think we actually did a lot of good. Those affected came to the stadium, some with no idea why they were even there, but they saw us – players and wives – talking to them and consoling them and having an affinity with them. They didn't all get it. Not everyone was like that. Some were still angry. But I think a lot of them really appreciated how much we cared.

I remember getting in the car one afternoon after being at Anfield and I just started howling. I had spent the day at the club with families, talking to them and trying to be supportive. Once I got back to the car the magnitude of what had happened suddenly hit me. Tears streaming down my face. Wailing. Then a sudden change of emotion. The tears stopped. I now felt guilty. Why am I howling? I didn't lose anybody. I wasn't in the middle of it. A real strange bunch of emotions going round my head. It still happens from time to time, no matter how many years later.

There was no training that midweek – football was the last thing on our minds – so the players spent time at the club instead trying to help in any way possible. I suggested to Bruce on the Wednesday that we go for a pint before we went home. Just to take our minds off things and maybe try and relax a little bit. We went to the usual haunt, Hotel Vic on The Wirral.

We were halfway through the pint when Angie, the barmaid, told us that one of the regulars, an old boy who we used to talk to from time to time, had passed away the day before. He had died of old age – nothing at all to do with Hillsborough – but that was enough for us. We'd only just come in but we looked at each other, our eyes welling up. We didn't even speak. We put down our glasses and left, both in tears. I then howled all the way home in the car. I had only come in for a bit of solace and relaxation but I had ended up an emotional mess. Again.

It came to the time when we had to decide which players went to which funerals. We told the club we would prefer to be with those families that we had spent time talking to – those who had lost someone or were traumatised by what had happened. We wanted to be at some of those funerals where we had made a connection with loved ones – apart from that, we'd go anywhere we were asked.

When you walk into a church and there's a coffin at the front and everyone there has a Liverpool strip on and the organist starts playing 'You'll Never Walk Alone' – my God that's powerful. Sitting there, tears streaming down your face. You're always trying to be the strong one, but at times you just can't help yourself.

Jon-Paul Gilhooley was only ten. We hadn't met the family before so I said to Eleanor that I didn't want to just turn up at his funeral. I didn't want it to come across like I was some kind of candyfloss decoration representing the club because I'd been told to attend. I wanted to see his family beforehand. I wanted them to know that I wanted to be there. That was important to me.

So we went to the house the day before. Jon-Paul was in the front room in an open casket. I asked his parents if I could go and see him. I cared. And I needed to show them that I cared. Jon-Paul's was one of probably five funerals I attended. Fans were thanking us for attending at some funerals we went to. I'm sure they just wanted to reach out to us, to show their appreciation, but it felt a little strange. We weren't there to be anything other than supportive and to show that Liverpool cared, both as a team and as a city. We were not there as celebrities or footballers. We were simply there as human beings affected by a tragedy so close to home. We were there because we wanted to be there.

It wasn't just the guys who played for us who attended those funerals. Former Liverpool players were also involved. I can't speak for any other club but I think if you play for Liverpool you understand it's not just a football team. It's not just a job. It's a way of life. Sometimes things do go wrong, and it's important to show you can cope when bad things happen as well.

I think what we, the Liverpool players, wives and staff, did after Hillsborough showed exactly what our fans meant to us, how close a bond there was between us. I know we weren't able to cover all the cracks simply by talking but we just wanted to be there for them in their time of need. It wasn't contrived. It wasn't a PR stunt. These people came to watch us every weekend and gave us their support. Now it was time for us to give them our full support and help in any way we could. It was heartfelt. But it was difficult. Bloody difficult.

Each player will have stories of trying to help different families. Eleanor and me are still in touch with some of them, still trying to help if we can. I think we helped. I hope we did. But I still can't comprehend that I've done something really good because it wasn't me who lost a family member or a friend.

It's important to mention the players' wives who were just as involved as we were. Eleanor still speaks to some of the families on the phone and we remain friends to this day with several of those who we tried to help.

We are godparents to Ryan Moran, whose dad was left completely traumatised by what happened. In absolute bits. It was Eleanor who met his dad, Roger, initially. Roger just couldn't figure it out. Couldn't understand why it had happened. Different people were affected in different ways.

How many more were indirectly affected? Can you imagine? Hillsborough changed the way Liverpool thought, both the city and the football club. Before that, everything revolved around the first team. That changed in an instant.

To this day, none of the players, when in each other's company, talk about Hillsborough. We never brought it up back then, we don't bring it up now and, I imagine, it will never be brought up in the future. We just don't know how to talk about it among ourselves. It's too close to home.

After Hillsborough, and up until I finally left Liverpool in January 1995, I never had the same focus that I'd had before the tragedy. Everything I had done before April 1989 was simply geared towards playing my best on the Saturday. But from the end of that season, and until I left, I was not the same player or anywhere near as focussed as I was before Hillsborough.

I went from drinking at the right time to doing so whenever I got the chance which – surprise, surprise – shows on the field, right? I had friends who had drinking establishments and I went there too often. Far too often. But that was because I could. Previously I would go at the right time, not all the time. Then I started doing it at the wrong time. A couple of pints here. A couple of pints there. Then more and more. In the eyes of some I may have got away with it, but there's only one person who knew I wasn't at my best. And that was me.

Five months after Hillsborough – in September 1989 – we beat Derby County 3-0 at the Baseball Ground. The night before the game, I went to see Kenny in his hotel room. I knew I wasn't right but I didn't know why and had no idea what to do. I was lost. I trusted him and wanted to share my thoughts and feelings. He asked what was wrong. I told him I was drinking too much. I told him I didn't feel myself. I told him I wasn't focussed. I told him I wasn't where I'd been. I told him I wasn't where I should be. I just wanted him to know all that.

I was half-expecting a response along the lines of 'Right, get a grip of yourself and don't be so stupid. If you know you're drinking too much then you just need to look after yourself better.' The real Kenny would have told me off. Told me to stop drinking. Told me to get my arse in gear. But this version of Kenny didn't say that. Instead I got something like this: 'Look, you're doing fine. You might not be at your best but you know what you need to do to sort yourself out.'

At the time I was shocked at his response. But now it makes sense. He was in the same boat as me. He just couldn't let it go either.

Me and Eleanor love Blood Brothers, the musical by Willy Russell. I used to drive home from training – through the Mersey tunnel – with the tape in the cassette player and the soundtrack blaring.

After what happened in Sheffield on April 15, 1989, however, the opening lyrics of one of the songs suddenly took on a completely different meaning...

'Tell me it's not true
Say it's just a story
Something on the news
Tell me it's not true
Though it's here before me
Say it's just a dream'

The first six lines of Tell Me It's Not True. For a few days after Hillsborough it was the only song I listened to driving home from Anfield. When the song ended, I would simply rewind the tape and play it again. On repeat until I got home. That was also my routine on a number of other occasions in the weeks and months after Hillsborough if I was in the mood for con-templation.

Singing along every single time while tears were streaming down my face. Trying to understand why. Not being able to understand why. It killed me to listen to it but I just couldn't turn it off. I could easily have taken that cassette tape out of the car. But I didn't.

'Tell me it's not true, say it's just a story, say it's just a dream…' those words etched on my brain forever.

It used to be my favourite song. Used to be. Not anymore. Every time I hear it these days I think about going through the Mersey tunnel on my way home from Anfield. It's weird. Just really weird.

15

Lap Of
The Gods

*'I was so proud to wear my primary school strip.
The fact it was an old Arsenal top from their
Double-winning team of 1971 made no difference. But
after what happened on the final day of the season in
1989, the last thing I want to do now is look back at
those old school photos'*

I don't think we could have picked better opponents for our
first game after Hillsborough. The reception we got from the
Celtic fans inside Parkhead was unbelievable – they sang You'll
Never Walk Alone just before kick-off and there wasn't a dry
eye inside the ground. Both sets of supporters were absolutely
magnificent that day.

Once the game kicked off, it probably took us twenty minutes
or so to get going properly but when Kenny opened the scoring
we were soon back into the swing of things. A realisation it was
time to get back to work. Every game after that we were playing

for somebody who had either lost someone or was affected by the tragedy. We had a job to do.

Training was put on hold following events at Hillsborough. The fixture against Arsenal at Anfield – scheduled for Saturday, April 22 – was postponed and most of the boys then went away on international duty. I think Aldo and me were the only two who didn't go. For some of them, it was a case of getting away from it all for a short time – a chance to clear their heads in a different environment. Everyone was different. I didn't want to get away from it all. I didn't feel right doing that. I wanted to stay. I was more interested in what was going on at home and how I could help.

Our first training session after Hillsborough took place two days before the game against Celtic in Glasgow – nearly two weeks after the tragedy. Trying to focus was hard. I looked at Aldo and, of all those involved, he was the one who was still not with it. No surprise, of course. He was Liverpool through and through.

The first league game after Hillsborough was against Everton at Goodison, but this wasn't your normal derby. We received an amazing reception from the Everton fans – they were different class. Everyone is intertwined in our city and so many households on Merseyside are split, red and blue. It's totally unique. Barcelona and Real Madrid. Celtic and Rangers. River Plate and Boca Juniors. Do you think fans of any of those clubs have feelings for the opposition? The game at Goodison ended in a draw. I don't think either team minded a share of the spoils that day.

Nothing changed football-wise after Hillsborough. The training was the same, the preparation was the same but it was all on us both collectively and individually to make sure we did what we had to do.

When we turned up at Old Trafford on Sunday, May 7, 1989, to replay the FA Cup semi-final, there was simply no way we were going to lose. I actually felt bad for the Forest players because they, too, were on the pitch at Hillsborough the previous month witnessing the tragedy unfold. As far as I know, nobody has ever spoken at great lengths about how the Forest players or fans felt about that day. It must have been traumatic for their supporters being there as well. They could easily have been traumatised after everything they witnessed but it seems to me like they've never really had a voice.

It's difficult to explain but I had a different feeling on the day of the game – both consciously and subconsciously – and I don't think I was alone among my teammates. I just knew we would win. Aldo scored after just three minutes and we were off and running. Even when Neil Webb equalised twelve minutes before half-time our mindset never changed: 'Okay, don't panic, we'll just score again and win the game.' Aldo got our second just before the hour mark and we never looked back, eventually winning 3-1 and securing our place in the FA Cup final. And after everything that had happened our opponents just had to be Everton.

Three games in six days would decide our season. The FA Cup final; our penultimate game at home to West Ham and the league decider versus Arsenal on the Friday night. And things got off to a good start at Wembley.

After Hillsborough, every time I stepped on to a pitch, I was riding a wave of emotion.

The Cup Final. Against Everton. No way were we losing that. Not for one minute. It just meant too much to too many people. And the game couldn't have started any better. I intercepted a long ball a few yards outside our penalty area and exchanged passes with Peter Beardsley. Everton were trying to play a high line. As usual, Steve McMahon made a run in behind. I found him with a through ball. He played it across the middle, first time, and Aldo stuck it in the back of the net. Ahead after just four minutes. The perfect start.

We were never really in much trouble and they rarely threatened us, until the last minute of the game. The ball was played across the six-yard box and Bruce couldn't hold onto it. Stuart McCall got there just a fraction of a second before me and poked it home from close range. As he got up to celebrate I found myself doing probably the stupidest thing I've ever done on a football pitch. For some inexplicable reason, I took a swing at him. Luckily for me, his leg lifted up as part of his stride and I just missed him. Had I made contact, and referee Worrall had seen it, there's no doubt in my mind I would have got a red card. And deservedly so. What a fucking brain dead thing to do. With the importance of the game and, especially, with everything that had happened over the previous few weeks I would never have been able to forgive myself. Fortunately I escaped punishment. A lucky boy indeed.

At the start of extra-time Kenny made a second change. Barry Venison came on for Stan Staunton and I moved to left-back – Ian Rush had already replaced Aldo with twenty minutes to go in normal time. We were soon ahead again. I found myself in space on the left hand side with a bit of time, looked up and saw Rushy. I knew where he wanted it. He made the run, I played the pass, and he controlled it, turned 180 degrees and fired a shot into the roof of the net.

When Stuart McCall equalised for a second time we still didn't panic. We knew we were better than them and within sixty seconds or so we were in front for a third time. And this time there was to be no comeback. Barnesy whipped in a ball from the left – from a similar spot where I'd provided the assist for the second goal – and once again Rushy found space and stooped low to head home the winner. There was relief that we'd won but we knew we were going to win because we had to win, if that makes sense!

This triumph was made so much more special because of the Hillsborough tragedy. If somebody said to me that I was only able to win one trophy during my time at Liverpool – and I would have to give the rest of my medals back – then the FA Cup final in 1989 would be that trophy. It's the one I cherish the most.

Everything happened so quickly. The FA Cup final on the Saturday, West Ham on the Tuesday, Arsenal on the Friday. We didn't start thinking about West Ham until after we played Everton. And we didn't start thinking about Arsenal until after we played West Ham. Already brainwashed – 'one game at a game' – even if we wanted to get ahead of ourselves and think about the possibility of winning another Double there simply wasn't enough time to do so.

We had a nice meal and a few beers at our hotel in Leicester Square after winning the FA Cup but nothing too daft because of the upcoming fixture against West Ham. It certainly wasn't our normal piss-up after winning a trophy.

On Sunday we travelled back on the bus, Monday we went in for a run and a stretch then Tuesday we had the game. There simply wasn't time to think about anything else or do anything else.

I don't ever recall during my time at Liverpool plans changing depending on circumstances. A midweek fixture at home meant doing the same things we always did to prepare for a midweek fixture at home – nothing changed just because we were in contention to win the title: Morning – a jog and a stretch at Melwood then back to Anfield for a bath. Lunchtime – straight to the Holiday Inn hotel in Liverpool after training for our pre-match meal. Afternoon – to bed for a couple of hours then tea and toast at 5pm. Leave the hotel at 6pm.

We were flying and beat West Ham 5-1 at Anfield. Even when Leroy Rosenior equalised Aldo's opener we just continued playing as normal and ran out comfortable winners. So, with one game left, we knew we could even afford to lose to Arsenal – as long as it wasn't by more than one goal – and still win the title. Even with a league championship at stake our preparation did not change one bit: Wednesday – in for a bath at 1pm. Anyone with knocks and niggles would get treatment. Thursday – a jog and a stretch. Friday – exactly the same routine as West Ham on the Tuesday

The only difference was when we got to Anfield. The biggest problem in the build-up had been sorting tickets out. Unsurprisingly the demand far exceeded the supply. I had millions of requests as, I'm sure, the rest of the boys did. Normally we got four comps plus two lounge tickets. I asked for a total of ten tickets for the game – I'd paid for six in addition to my four comps – so it took a bit longer than usual to sort them out before leaving them at reception to be collected. The time it took to do that was the only difference from our normal matchday routine. The game itself went by in a blur…

1-0 Arsenal – Alan Smith, 52nd minute: I misjudged the flight of the ball. He's my man. I got underneath it. He got in behind me and scored. We surrounded the referee because we were desperate. I was hoping it might have been offside but the rest of the lads were claiming that Smith hadn't touched the ball and, because it came from an indirect free-kick, the goal shouldn't have stood. I was close enough to him to know that he glanced it in with his head. Just not close enough.

2-0 Arsenal – Michael Thomas, 90th minute: Lukic throws it. Dixon thumps it forward to Alan Smith. Gary Ablett goes to challenge Smith. Big Al moves across to cover Ablett. I go across to cover Big Al. Smith plays the ball over the top to Michael Thomas. He miscontrols it. It hits me. Then it hits him again and falls right into his path. By this stage none of us can get to him in time. He shoots. He scores. Game over. Title lost on goals scored.

No question about the first goal, I made a mistake and hold my hands up. For the second goal it's just one of those things, although it was a composed finish. A miscontrol and two rico-chets – how's your luck? Sometimes in life you just don't have any say over what happens. Only someone above decides that. The ricochet off him could have gone anywhere. The ricochet off me could have gone anywhere. I was where I should have been. Big Al was where he should have been. Gary was where he should have been. The football gods decided that was the way it was going to end.

When referee David Hutchinson blew his whistle 38 seconds after the restart to signal the end of the game we were numb. Totally numb. I can't remember what I did in the immediate aftermath but I do remember the Liverpool fans staying behind and, after showing their appreciation for us, applauding Arsenal when they were presented with the championship trophy. This was the team that had just beaten their team to the title. Of course they were hurting too, really hurting, but I don't think another set of supporters in the world would have shown the class that the Kop and the rest of Anfield showed that night.

After getting changed I headed upstairs to the Candy Lounge and bumped into Arsenal manager George Graham, who was heading in the opposite direction. I'm thinking 'He's the last guy I want to see.' However, one of the many things drummed into us as Liverpool players was the ability to lose with class. I shook his hand and congratulated him. He said thanks; he must have known how I was feeling so I appreciated him avoiding any additional small talk.

Being a Liverpool player was always about responsibility. As bad as the situation was that we found ourselves in, we still had a duty to meet sponsors and various others in the lounges. Many players at other clubs, given the same scenario, would have brushed aside that responsibility and just made an excuse for not doing it – but not us. That's what being a player at Anfield was all about – the Liverpool Way.

There were two or three of us on duty after the match. If none of us had gone up to the lounges I think people would have understood, I get that. But we were better than that. We met stuff head on. It's always easy to meet stuff head on when things are going well, but it takes a special kind of person to meet stuff head on when things aren't going well. You don't realise until you get older that all those things we did actually made a difference. That's how the club was run. It wasn't just the players. It was the whole organisation. From chairman John Smith at the top all the way down – we were Liverpool Football Club and that was the way we did things. And everybody knew that. If you shirked out then you stood out.

A few days later I went to Anfield to pick up some stuff and I saw Roy Evans. I just looked at him. "Fucking hell."

That was all I said.

He looked at me and told me, 'we wouldn't even have been in that position without you.' It was only a five-second chat. A 'chin up' message in a bid to lift me from the doldrums. I appreciated the sentiment. And I also appreciated being named the Football Writers' Player of the Year that season. But neither made up for the heartache of seeing the title slip away with just 38 seconds to go of the final league game of the season.

I've told you before in this book – my career was a series of peaks and troughs. This time it was winning the FA Cup then losing the league in the space of only six days. Those football gods certainly have a strange sense of humour.

16

Not This Time, Big Al

'How we won the league in 1989-90 is beyond me. We weren't even half the team we'd been the year before when Arsenal pipped us on the final day but we still finished nine points clear. That's some achievement'

Eleanor and me had the worst summer break in 1989. We went to Malta on holiday but were miserable throughout. A really nice couple were staying in our hotel and they offered to babysit the kids if we wanted to go out one night, which we did. But I was miserable company and we had a horrible time. So much had happened over the last six weeks of the previous season that I'd been left in a daze. It was a daze that, ultimately, would last another couple of years.

My whole life was focussed on football. I always did everything I could to ensure I was one hundred per cent ready for action. But that changed. I lost focus on what I was supposed to be doing. My family life changed too. I started slacking. I was drinking more. Much more. I wasn't the footballer I used to be. More importantly, I wasn't the husband and father that I used to be. I don't think I was the only one at Liverpool who experienced a change of emotions, a chance of circumstance. As I've said, there is no question that we, as players – and I include Kenny in this as well – should have been forced into receiving some sort of counselling post-Hillsborough. It should have been mandatory. But it wasn't. We had to deal with all these issues on our own. And it wasn't pleasant. Trust me.

Unlike most professional footballers, I didn't mind it when we had to report back for pre-season training. And part of that was due to the fantastic team spirit we had at Liverpool. Usually there were smiles on faces because everyone was back together again, exchanging stories from the summer and raring to go for the new season – it was always an exuberant time. But reporting back for pre-season in 1989 was different. There was no exuberance. No smiles on faces from them or me and no exchange of stories from the summer. This time it was a lot tougher to be in a positive frame of mind.

The end of the previous season was manic. Those three games in six days that decided the FA Cup final and the league championship – there was hardly any time to think. Then I had a miserable time in Malta during the summer. I wasn't the only one who went away and didn't enjoy their holiday.

So why did this happen? Why were we all feeling like this?

Well, it was the first time any of us had a prolonged period of time for reflection, to be alone with our thoughts. There was intensity about our play immediately after Hillsborough – we felt a duty to play for those who were affected – and maybe that led to an emotional letdown once the season was over.

Or maybe it was the way the game against Arsenal ended, suddenly no more football for a couple of months, therefore no way to seek solace on the pitch. I don't know what the biggest obstacle was. Maybe it was a combination of both. To this day I still can't figure it out.

I felt a sense of deja vu when referee Allan Gunn blew the final whistle at Wembley. It was the same feeling I'd had twelve months previously – although that time I was in the stands and not on the pitch. We'd just won the Charity Shield again by beating the team that had beaten us in the final game of the previous season, yet it didn't mean anything. This time it was Arsenal, twelve months before that it was Wimbledon. But I couldn't have cared less. Journalists asked us post-match if it was pleasing to gain some revenge. Absolute nonsense. All we'd done was win two glorified friendlies. The last time I checked I didn't have a 1988 FA Cup winners' medal or a league championship medal from season 1988-89. Revenge my arse.

I mentioned previously about the time I went to see Kenny in his hotel room the night before we played Derby County in September 1989. I was drinking to excess and needed to tell someone. I didn't get the immediate response I expected.

Well, in the dressing room the following day at The Baseball Ground, just before I was going out on to the pitch, I walked past him and he just gave me a little nod and a look that told me that I was okay. Not to worry about it.

That nod meant he knew what I was going through but I also took it to mean that everything would be fine going forward. That little look and nod meant everything to me. I knew that the night before hadn't just gone over his head. When you've got a manager that you know is thinking about you then you'll run through brick walls for him. I always did for Kenny. He probably understood exactly what I was going through so I wanted to repay him. I wanted to go out and play for him. Unfortunately, however, off the field was a different story and things didn't change.

I scored twice against Crystal Palace the week after we played at Derby – forty-six goals in 468 appearances for Liverpool isn't too bad a record for someone who played the majority of those 468 games in defence – but those goals weren't the main memory from that day.

John Aldridge was on the verge of completing a move to Real Sociedad, so the game against Palace at Anfield was going to be the last time he'd play for Liverpool before moving to Spain. Named among the substitutes, it was always Kenny's intention to bring him on for one final wave to the Kop, where he'd stood as a youngster supporting the club.

I opened the scoring early on and further goals from McMahon, Rush, Gillespie and Beardsley gave us a 5-0 lead. With 24 minutes remaining, referee Keren Barratt pointed to the spot after Gary O'Reilly brought down Ronnie Whelan. John Barnes would usually take our penalties when Aldo wasn't on the pitch and I remember watching him go over to get the ball just as a huge roar emerged from the terraces. Aldo had taken off his tracksuit top and was getting ready to come on. Kenny knew this was the perfect opportunity, so he signalled to Peter Beardsley to come off.

Aldo ran out to a huge ovation, Barnesy threw him the ball and, with his first touch, he scored goal number six, in front of the Kop of course. That produced the biggest cheer of the night – his 63rd and final goal for Liverpool in just 104 appearances. Just slightly better than my goal ratio!

My second goal of the night rounded off the scoring and made it 9-0, but my highlight of the evening was immediately after the game when Aldo tossed his shirt and boots into the Kop and was given a rapturous farewell as he left the field for the final time.

What a player, and what a top lad. He was a super teammate and was great in the dressing room. He kept the banter going and, most importantly, he scored goals. And plenty of them. But he was also smart. He knew his place was the penalty box – I could randomly put a ball into the area and I knew there was a good chance that Aldo would get on the end of it. He was just as good a goalscorer as Rushy – Ian just had that little bit more to his game outside the box. But that's the only thing that separated them. We were incredibly lucky to have them both at the same time.

On Saturday, November 29, 1989, just over seven months after that fateful day, we returned to Hillsborough for the first time since the tragedy. It was a fixture none of us were looking forward to. Two or three of us were injured – including Big Al and me – but the whole squad travelled to Sheffield. We all wanted to pay our respects to those who had died.

The Leppings Lane terracing behind the goal was empty except for a handful of Liverpool scarves, flags and some flowers, which had either been placed there by supporters before the game or thrown down by Liverpool fans occupying the seats in the tier above. Big Al and Sheffield Wednesday goalkeeper Chris Turner laid wreaths in front of the terracing before we all stood on the edge of the eighteen-yard box, facing the empty pens, for a minute of silence. At the other end – on the Spion Kop – two giant banners were displayed by Wednesday fans: 'For all you Reds a new tomorrow' and 'Hillsborough will always share your sorrow.' A classy touch.

Kenny had told the press before the game that we would go out and do our best to put the horror of what had happened to the back of our minds. But that was never going to be possible.

As always, a decent number of Liverpool fans were in attendance – more than 4,500 had travelled – but understandably, given what had happened previously, several had chosen not to attend. Those who did were told that a decision had been taken to delay kick-off by a quarter of an hour due to heavy traffic in the surrounding area. If only the same decision had been taken before the FA Cup semi-final against Nottingham Forest seven months previously...

Going into the game they were at the bottom of the table and we were top. David Hirst opened the scoring ten minutes into the second half and a decent solo effort from Dalian Atkinson in the closing seconds wrapped up the points for them. We lost 2-0. Apparently it was Liverpool's first defeat at Hillsborough for 25 years. I didn't care. None of us did. The result was of secondary importance. The only positive of the day was that both goals were scored at the Spion Kop End and not in front of the empty Leppings Lane terracing.

After the game there was no hanging about. We all wanted out of there as quickly as possible. I shared a car journey back to Liverpool with Kenny, his wife Marina, Big Al and Eleanor but very little was said. The relief of just getting out of Sheffield and back onto the motorway was huge.

Having beaten Crystal Palace 9-0 at Anfield in September, and 2-0 at Selhurst Park in January, we were pretty confident of beating them again in the FA Cup semi-final at Villa Park in April. I was injured and didn't travel with the official party, but there was another bus leaving from Anfield to take the wives, reserves and club staff to the game so I travelled down on that one and enjoyed one or two beverages along the way.

For the first fifteen minutes or so, the bus was pretty quiet so I went down to the front with a pile of music tapes to try and persuade the driver to put them on. About an hour later I asked the driver to change the tape.

On the way back to my seat Glenn Hysén's wife, Helena, stopped me. "Did you enjoy those videos you borrowed from my husband?" she asked.

I could feel myself turning a bright shade of red. I had borrowed some blue movies from Glenn a couple of weeks before and I had absolutely no idea he had told her.

"Um, yes, thanks," I mumbled, before scarpering to the back of the bus as quickly as I could. Needless to say, I didn't bother asking for the music tape to be changed during the remainder of the journey. I kept my head down and arrived in Birmingham well-oiled as I took my seat in the stand at Villa Park.

Liverpool battered Palace in the first half and should have been further ahead than the one goal lead we had at half-time. The second half turned into an absolute nightmare – Mark Bright equalised within a minute of the restart and we ended up losing 4-3 after extra-time.

Prior to the game – and no doubt thinking we would win – Kenny had organised a post-match meal at the Mandarin Chinese Restaurant on Victoria Street in Liverpool for the players and their wives. After the incident on the bus I was more than happy to see that Helena and Glenn Hysén were absent from proceedings. I was in no mood to answer any awkward or inappropriate questions in the presence of my wife.

I ended up sitting beside Gary Ablett's wife at the time and after the meal (washed down by several bottles of beer) I was lighting up a cigarette at the table while, at the same time, staring at Debbie Ablett and her huge lion's mane of hair.

Like a child, I was fascinated by it. Then, for some inexplicable reason, I decided to see what would happen when I put my lighter next to her rather large mop…

WOOOOOOFFFFF!!!

It went up like a ball of flames. I started bashing her on the head with my hands to try and put the fire out. "What the hell are you doing?" enquired Gary, understandably, with more than a hint of anger in his voice.

Thankfully, I was able to stop the flames before they caused too much damage. At least that broke the ice after the disappointing result earlier in the day.

Despite what was happening off the field, everything went according to plan in the league. We wrapped up the title pretty comfortably, winning it by nine points from our nearest challengers Aston Villa.

We had enough quality in the team to win 23 of our 38 games but the football certainly wasn't as much fun that year. We played with an emotional hangover and I'm sure that was evident in our style of play. It wasn't as exciting. It wasn't as dynamic. It wasn't as enjoyable. But the ability we had in the team got us through the season. And we still won the league.

Job done.

The next season, 1990-91, may have started well – eight league wins out of eight right off the bat then an eight point lead over Arsenal after thirteen games – but things started to unravel in December. We lost for the first time in the league, going down 3-0 at Highbury to our nearest challengers.

Then, a draw at QPR – described by The Guardian newspaper as 'one of our least convincing displays of the season' – was followed by defeat at Crystal Palace, which, according to The Times, 'completed a miserably unproductive month in the capital for Liverpool.'

I can't put my finger on exactly what went wrong. There's no doubt we'd set the bar high with our start to the season, a consistency which in all honesty would have been impossible to maintain, but to then go on a run of only one win in six over the festive period was simply not good enough. We'd set standards and were unable to maintain those standards – whether there was one specific reason why that happened or a whole host of them, I don't know.

Having been chased for the first half of the season, we were eventually overtaken at the top of the table by Arsenal in the middle of January.

Now we were doing the chasing.

A 3-1 win over Everton at Anfield helped us reclaim top spot. It was only temporary and a poor run of form meant we wouldn't be back there anytime soon. But there were bigger changes on the way that would impact us in the longer term.

Picture the scene.

It's the FA Cup fifth round replay of Wednesday, February 20, 1991 and things aren't exactly going according to plan.

> I'm leaving it…
> He's leaving it…
> I'm getting it…
> He's getting it…

The ball bounces at an awkward height. I get there first and knee it back towards Bruce. Unfortunately, by this point, Bruce is standing right beside me at the edge of the box. Oops. A total fuck-up. Graeme Sharp – who is lurking in the box, hoping for such a mistake – takes a touch and takes full advantage. I try to chase him down, try to rectify my mistake but it is already far too late and despite my desperate lunge, Sharpy bundles the ball home.

Everton 2, Liverpool 2.

When Rushy scores with thirteen minutes remaining, I think to myself 'it's the winning goal.' Tony Cottee equalises with a minute left to make it 3-3 and force extra-time.

Kenny gathers us together on the pitch. His last ever team talk as manager of Liverpool. Little did we know. "Keep doing what you're doing, stay focussed." There is no shouting, despite the concession of a last-minute goal, and he stays calm, just telling us to try and "tighten things up at the back."

Barnesy makes it 4-3 two minutes before the end of the first period of extra-time then, unbelievably, Cottee's second of the game levels it up at 4-4. Goodison goes wild. A second replay is necessary to decide whether Liverpool or Everton are going through to round six.

It's a game remembered by many as one of the classics of our generation. For us, however, it was anything but memorable. Playing in it was a nightmare at times. It's painful to watch because, despite scoring four great goals, we let in four of the most horrendous goals you're ever likely to see. Looking back, those four we conceded are consistent with mistakes made due to a lack of concentration. That's because the team wasn't properly focussed on what was going on. A lot of us just weren't there mentally. And that was borne out when we got in the dressing room after the game.

Normally there would be an inquest – 'what went on?'…'how did we let those goals in?'…'why did we do what we did?' But there was this strange vibe afterwards as we sat there waiting on a backlash. Nothing ever came. Instead, a kind of acceptance – 'it's fine, we're still in the FA Cup.'

That attitude wasn't normal in our dressing room, particularly from Kenny – a guy who usually held people to standards. Previously during his tenure if something similar had happened he would let every single player know their standards had dropped, irrespective of whether they were new to the squad or a trusted veteran, and he would tell the whole team it was unacceptable. This time, Kenny said very little.

Did I think something was up? Not at all. I don't think any of us did. Yes, he might have been acting differently from the norm but what else do you expect from a manager who has just watched his team take the lead four times in a game yet still not come out on top?

As we left the away dressing room at Goodison Park that night headed for the bus, we did so completely unaware that we would never again be in a dressing room on a matchday with Kenny Dalglish talking to us as manager of Liverpool Football Club.

I came in to Anfield as normal on the Friday morning. We

were all getting changed to go to training at Melwood when Kenny walked in.

"I'm off," he said. "That's me finished with the club."

That was all he said. You could see it was hard for him and he was choking up. Then he walked out again.

Ronnie Moran piped up, "Okay then, let's get on the bus and let's get to training." And that was that.

We lost 3-1 at Luton on the Saturday. The defeat was excusable. There were one or two other things occupying our minds that day.

In his book, *Dalglish: My Autobiography,* Kenny explains that Hillsborough was a huge factor in his decision to leave Liverpool, and that he actually wanted to do so in 1990, the year before his resignation. I totally get that and completely understand where he's coming from. He speaks about becoming unpleasant company at home. He speaks about shouting at the kids. He speaks about drinking more than he used to. I was guilty of all three things as well, in addition to a few others.

Kenny also talks about the 4-4 draw at Goodison and how he knew beforehand that it would be his last game in charge, regardless of the result. It's easy to look back, with hindsight, and see now the signs that we clearly missed at the time – his lack of anger in the dressing room at the end of the game being the obvious one. But you've got to realise that we were all in the same spot. Hillsborough affected everyone. A lot of the focus after the tragedy was centred on helping others. And when you're in the midst of doing that then it's hard enough to sort yourself out, never mind look around and see how it's affecting everybody else. I missed the signs from Kenny. I think we all did.

Things didn't go well immediately after Kenny left. After losing at Luton the following day, we were then knocked out of the FA Cup by Everton in midweek. It was one of those games when we did everything but score. Dave Watson got the only goal of the game early on, although Neville Southall was named man-of-the-match – he was simply unbeatable. I was denied twice in the second half when he produced saves that were out of this world and Big Nev did the same to Rushy on more than one occasion. Ronnie Moran was in temporary charge and he told us afterwards there was very little else we could have done at Goodison that night.

It hadn't been the best of weeks so the mood around the place was pretty sombre when we reported to Anfield for training on the Friday morning.

At the time there was all kinds of speculation about who would replace Kenny. Big Al was mentioned, as were many others, but as usual the players were the last to find out what was actually going on.

I was sitting in the dressing room, in my normal spot, getting ready for training when Big Al came up to me and said, quietly, that he wanted a word and told me to follow him to his office. *His* office? Had I missed something?

Thinking I'd misheard him, I got up and followed him down the corridor. But what if I'd not misheard him? There was plenty of speculation linking him with the job. Now I'm thinking it might be possible he actually does have the job. But on the other hand, he always told me he never wanted anything to do with management.

By the time we got to the manager's office, my head was spinning.

Sheila was sitting at her desk outside the office. "Morning Sheila," said Big Al, as he walked nonchalantly into the office. "Morning Mr Hansen," replied the manager's secretary. Wait a minute. *Mr* Hansen? I followed him into the office and was told to shut the door.

"I just wanted to tell you that I've got the job."

"You've got the job?"

"Yeah. We've got a few problems here and I need you to back me up."

"What do you mean?"

"Well, I'm in charge now and I want to make you captain."

"Is this another one of your wind-ups?"

"No. Not this time. We've got to change a few things and you're my captain. I want you to speak up, say something to the players."

"Like what?"

"Well, say something like we're all in this together."

There it was! As soon as he said 'we're all in this together' I knew it was a wind-up. I could smell it. He was at it. Full of shit. Him and I used to take the piss all the time when coaches would say 'we're all in this together.' It had become our code phrase and we always used to laugh when other people said it. That's what immediately suggested to me this was a wind-up. However, in the back of my mind I still wasn't one hundred per cent sure. What if he was telling the truth for once? By this stage my brain was mush.

"Look, we're going to have a team meeting in five minutes and that's when I want you to speak to the players."

I said 'okay', despite being highly dubious this was actually happening. Hansen was replacing Dalglish? This was nuts.

So I went back up the corridor to the first team changing room and I just sat there not knowing if it was New Year or New York.

Two minutes later, Roy Evans and Ronnie Moran came in, along with all the pros at the club. They shut the door. By this stage there must have been nearly thirty people in a space designed to hold half that number.

Then Big Al entered. We had this old, creaky treatment table in the middle of the dressing room. He stood behind it and, right on cue, it creaked as he put the palms of both hands on it. "I've got some news. I'm taking over from Kenny."

Gasps all round. Most of me thought he was at it, but there was also a part of me that thought he might not be bullshitting.

"There's too many things going wrong at this club so there's going to be a lot of changes. First of all, you guys from Southport, drinking in your local, and those of you over the water – this has to stop. We have to be far more professional. We have to move on from the past. Barnesy – I know you're partial to a Kentucky Fried Chicken. Those days are over. Bumper – no more going to the pub," (he somehow said this to me with a straight face).

"Also, we're going to video the games then you'll all come in the next day and, over a light lunch, we'll go over the tape together. Oh, and Glenn [Hysén], I'm going to make Nico captain. Bumper – have you got anything to say to the boys?"

By now I'd decided it was a wind-up so I said nothing. He gave me a stare.

"Anyone else with anything to say? Nope. Okay, then. I'll see you down at Melwood."

Then he walked out.

"Who does he think he is, telling me where I can drink and when I can drink?" said Rushy, less than five seconds after the door had closed. The dressing room then got really noisy as the players discussed what Big Al had just said. Two minutes later he came back in. It all went silent again.

"Only kidding. I'm just retiring," and he walked back out.

Big Al had actually done the same thing the day before with Ronnie Moran, Roy Evans and Tom Saunders. He'd gone in to the room next to the manager's office – a tiny little place where the coaching staff used to get changed – and told them he had the job and was replacing Kenny, and that he was going to be making some changes before describing what they'd be. Then he walked out, shut the door and listened in through the flimsy wall. A few minutes later he came clean and told them that he was going to do the same thing to the players the following day. That's how Roy and Ronnie were able to round up all the pros and get them into the first team dressing room the next morning.

A nice try, and some pretty good planning from the big lad, but for once he didn't fool me. This guy had been winding me up forever. However, for the first time in my life, with the biggest wind-up of all, he never got me.

Not this time, Big Al.

17

Kindergarten Cop

'I was married with two children. I was not a kid in a school playground. Tuck your shirt in. Pull your socks up to your knees. Take your hands out your pockets. Do this. Do that. It was far too regimental for my liking. It wasn't fun anymore'

I'd never really noticed Andy Roxburgh before he replaced Alex Ferguson as Scotland boss in July 1986. He'd been part of the backroom staff but was mainly involved, I think, with the youth teams. He certainly wasn't a prominent figure.

After missing a large chunk of season 1986-87 due to injury – including seven Scotland games – I didn't play for him until September 1987 when we beat Hungary 2-0 at Hampden.

Fifteen months had passed since the World Cup in Mexico so it was a relief to finally be back in a Scotland squad. We met up on the Sunday night at the Macdonald Hotel on the outskirts of Glasgow. It may only have been a friendly but I was just glad to be playing international football again.

"I suppose you've only come up to see us because none of

your Liverpool pals play for Scotland anymore?" asked Alex McLeish with a smile on his face after opening the door of his hotel room. It was the Sunday night, we weren't flying out to Riyadh until the Monday morning and I was bored. So I went up to see Alex and Willie Miller. I'll let the big man take up the rest of the story...

"Stevie came bounding into the room carrying a pretty full plastic carrier bag. I asked him what was inside and he proceeded to empty the contents all over the bed. Fourteen packets of crisps – I counted them all – and somehow each of them was a different flavour, no two were the same! Worcester sauce, salt and vinegar, cheese and onion, smoky bacon, beef and onion, barbeque, tomato ketchup, ready salted, pickled onion, prawn cocktail, roast chicken, scampi, ham and mustard plus those Salt 'n' Shake things. He offered us a packet. We declined. Over the next two hours he sat and drank six pints of lager top and ate every single bag of crisps. I've still never seen anything quite like that. Willie and me were starting to get tired and wanted to go to our beds but Stevie didn't quite take the hint. Instead he phoned reception and asked for three boiled eggs to be sent up to the room. How on earth could he still be hungry?! I'm not sure I've ever seen someone have such a horrendous diet yet still be one of the fittest guys at training. He's some boy. Truly one of a kind."

Whose idea was it to arrange an international friendly in Saudi Arabia in the middle of the season anyway? The game was played on a Wednesday night in the middle of February 1988. It was a weird trip. Andy Roxburgh thought it would be a good

ow you're Gunner believe us: Jumping for joy after my late long-range header had given us a 1 win in the first game of the season. We played some wonderful football in 1987-88

aying hard: On a pre-season tour in Scandinavia, 1988. The bosses at Liverpool trusted us. e were allowed to have a good time, as long as we made up for it in training

Three and easy: (Above) celebrating at St James' Park in September 1987. I scored a hat-trick in a 4-1 win

Tragic day: (Above) Leaving the pitch at Hillsborough on April 15, 1989. Left: Paying our respects — we did everything we could to support the families and those affected by Hillsborough

Personal honour: I was named Football Writers' Association Footballer of the Year in 1989 – but everything was overshadowed by what happened

Team of stars: I found myself in illustrious company (below) when I was asked to join a celebration for the 50th Footballer of the Year award in 1997. Included in the line-up were Sir Bobby Charlton and Sir Stanley Matthews

50TH FOOTBALLER OF THE YEAR AWARD

50TH FOOTBALLER OF THE YEAR AWARD

One hundred years old: For Liverpool centenary in 1992 we posed for a team picture wearing the club kit from 1892. I decided not to keep the centre part!

So this is Christmas: The squad in fancy dress for our 1992 party. I'm the one in camouflage, hiding under the hat

Scotland cap: Posing for a photocall with Mo Johnston, donning the obligatory Tartan tammy. I was so proud to pull on the famous dark blue shirt of my country but circumstances forced me to call time on my international career

Souness years: With Jamie Redknapp after he is sent off in a 5-1 defeat at Coventry in December 1992. Right: At home with Eleanor, Michael, Katy and my dogs in Wirral the same year

That winning feeling: (Above) Enjoying a sing-song with the team in 1992 after we had beaten Sunderland to lift the FA Cup and (right) posing for a picture with the family. I look happy and it was another proud moment but I didn't get the same trophy buzz

The Liverpool family: Saluting the fans at my testimonial (right). Michael and Katy pull on my number four shirt (above) and (bottom) a team shot featuring Sammy Lee, Torben Piechnik, Mo Johnston, Julian Dicks, David Johnson, Big Al, Joey Jones and Kenny

Mac attack: At Notts County, sliding in on my old Anfield teammate, Swindon's Steve McMahon

Mr Versatile: I played in every position during my professional career – including goalkeeper at Sheffield Wednesday! Above: Keeping an eye on Paul Ince on a return to Anfield in 1997. Left: I loved my spell at Doncaster Rovers

Nicol for your thoughts: In contemplative mood, standing on the Kop in 1993, shortly before I left Liverpool. My successes at Anfield mean even more to me now than they did then

New life: It was a big step moving to the USA but I have had some wonderful experiences. Above: At New England Revolution in 2003 and (right) with Paul Mariner

idea to have a cards competition on the flight on the way over, which was fine, but he made taking part mandatory for all the players. Richard Gough point blank refused but everyone else just went along with it to keep the peace.

Andy also decided to invite all the club managers of the players who were taking part to join the squad on the trip to Riyadh. I remember chatting with Celtic boss Billy McNeill on the flight back and somehow the topic of conversation turned to Brazil. By that stage of the flight I'd had a few beers and managed to turn the Brazil chat into a Monty Python-style Life of Brian conversation – I asked him what Brazil had ever done for world football. Before Billy could say a word I answered my own question and said 'Pele'. Then, before Billy could say anything, I said 'Okay, the Maracana'. Billy was desperately trying to jump in. I opened my gob again – 'Okay, Rivelino'. This continued. The Brazil strip, the samba drums and the banana free-kick – I gave them all a mention. Then a group of Scotland players, including Roy Aitken and Mo Johnston, joined the debate and the chances of Billy getting a word in went from slim to none. His mood wasn't helped shortly afterwards when him and Mo became embroiled in a rather heated row...

A short time later, I was sitting having a smoke with Frank McAvennie in the flight attendants' quarters in the middle of the plane. "How the fuck did he find me?" he said, "I just changed my number yet he still managed to get in touch." Frank had been lying in his bed at home with a female stranger for company when the phone rang. Not knowing who was calling he wasn't sure if he should answer. He wished he hadn't.

"Hello, is that Frank?"

After a pause, Frank confirmed it was indeed him and asked who was calling. To his horror, Andy Roxburgh was on the end of the line. He asked Frank if he wanted to join the Scotland squad for the friendly in Saudi Arabia. With Macca failing to come up with a reasonable excuse in time as to why he shouldn't go, he reluctantly agreed. It wasn't a case of him not wanting to play for Scotland; Frank was simply pissed off at Andy coming cap in hand after he'd been overlooked for the original squad.

Almost a year later, we travelled to Cyprus for an important World Cup qualifier. We were getting changed in the dressing room before the game in Limassol when the door opened and in walked Roxburgh, followed by Fabio Capello. Andy loved doing things like that. I'm not sure a lot of the boys even recognised our guest because it wasn't until 1991 that he took over as AC Milan coach, but I remembered watching him score for Italy at the 1974 World Cup in West Germany and he hadn't changed a bit.

I was expecting Andy to go round and introduce Fabio to us individually to try and keep it low key ahead of an important World Cup qualifier. Instead, Andy told us all to settle down and take a seat before accompanying his guest into the middle of the room – "boys, this is Fabio Capello."

Everyone just sat there in silence. What else were we supposed to do – clap and cheer? Now I don't know how Capello felt, but I was embarrassed for him. That kind of told me where Andy's head was – an hour before a vital qualifier and the Scotland boss was acting like a cross between a starstruck punter and a big kid. At times he treated us like children, too. When you're 27 years old and the father of two children yet somebody is telling you to take your hands out of your pockets and pull your socks up – and I mean that literally – that sure is irritating.

During the warm-up before the game I felt a sharp pain in my chest. It wasn't something I'd felt before. I could jog, but as I tried to run quicker the pain got progressively worse. I told the manager, who was free to listen now that his pal had left. He asked if I'd ever felt that kind of pain before, I said 'no' but told him I'd probably be fine once the game started. After just nine minutes, I felt it again and I was worried – the chest pains were in the same area as my heart. I came off immediately, replaced by Ian Ferguson, and watched the rest of the game from the bench. I may be wrong, but I don't remember being examined until I got back to Liverpool and I returned to the club a couple of days later.

Nearly six minutes of stoppage time had been played in the second half when Richard Gough got on the end of a Roy Aitken free-kick and bulleted a header into the back of the net. We'd won 3-2 right at the death. Mayhem on the pitch. Mayhem in the dugout. The dressing room was buzzing afterwards – we knew how important it was not to drop points against the minnows in the group.

Amidst all the backslapping and congratulating each other, a voice could be heard near the door. It was that of Craig Brown, Andy Roxburgh's assistant. He told us all to take a seat because he wanted to say something. We were expecting him to congratulate us on a vital win and for showing great resolve and character. Instead, he explained that the reason we had been able to score a goal so late was because Andy had spent the previous night at the team hotel with the UEFA delegate and had informed him that the Cypriots would waste time at every possible opportunity – free-kicks, throw-ins, corners, goal-kicks – so we should thank Andy when he came back into the dressing room. Again, silence – everyone just stared at him. You know I could have sworn that Richard Gough scored the winning goal, not Andy Roxburgh.

In September, we flew to Zagreb to face Yugoslavia. The flight on the Monday was delayed, so we arrived several hours later than expected. SFA secretary Ernie Walker showed up at the hotel reception first and ensured his cronies were looked after when it came to accommodation, before then sorting out plans for the evening for all the SFA blazers. Meanwhile, all the Scotland players were still sat in the foyer – we weren't able to check in until the suits were taken care of.

Most of the bigwigs seemed to have no interest in the players. They were only interested in themselves. I wasn't used to that. At Liverpool, the players were always checked-in first at hotels. The directors and other guests of the club were then accommodated. The Board realised that we were the most important part of any trip. Being away on Scotland duty was totally different. The players, more often than not, were usually an afterthought. And that's embarrassing.

Two months after the game in Yugoslavia, we travelled to France for another World Cup qualifier. It was around this time – seven months after Hillsborough – that I was having major problems at home and things were seriously in danger of unravelling. My body may have been on the pitch in both Zagreb and Paris but I was a basket case and my mind was elsewhere – I was trying to focus on how to save my marriage to the person that meant everything to me. The only reason I had the career I had was because of Eleanor.

She told me that if I continued doing what I was doing – drinking heavily – then she wanted no part of it. She said that although she wouldn't leave me she would lead her own life with the kids and it wouldn't directly involve me. A stark ultimatum. From then on, I pulled back a bit, but I was still miles away from returning to my normal self. It would be a lot longer before that happened.

During a match for Liverpool against Queens Park Rangers at Loftus Road in November 1989, I put my hands out in front of me to help cushion a fall and minimise the damage. At the time, I didn't feel much discomfort and played the full ninety minutes. It wasn't until a couple of days later, when I was on international duty with Scotland, that I knew there was a problem. I tried to put my top on before training but couldn't raise my arm above my shoulder – something wasn't right, so I alerted the medical staff.

Professor Hillis from the SFA examined the shoulder then accompanied me to hospital where I found out I had damaged tendons. I withdrew from the Scotland squad to face Norway in the World Cup qualifier at Hampden and went back to Liverpool, where I saw a specialist who told me I needed surgery but it could wait. In my absence, the boys got the draw we needed against the Norwegians to secure a place at the World Cup in Italy – finishing second in group five, a point ahead of France. As it turned out the damage to my shoulder was actually the best thing that could have happened to me. The four-week lay-off not only allowed the injury an opportunity to heal properly, but it also meant I was able to spend additional time with Eleanor and try to repair some of the damage I had caused.

The recovery time after shoulder surgery – depending on the severity of the injury – is normally around three months, but with Liverpool challenging for the title it was decided that I would hold off getting it done until the end of the season. Doing that minimised the number of games I would miss for my club and would also mean I'd be ready for the start of the new campaign. But it also meant I wasn't able to play for Scotland at the World Cup.

Now, as much as I would have loved to represent my country in Italy, I didn't want to jeopardise my Liverpool career for a second time, especially after what happened in 1986 with the torn stomach muscle and hernia. Miss a couple of months of the season when we were challenging for the title – then possibly struggle to get back into the Liverpool team – or miss the World Cup? Sorry Scotland, there was only ever one choice I was going to make.

My next involvement with the national team came in May 1991, when we travelled to San Marino.

We were getting ready for training the day before the game – ensuring our socks were pulled up to our knees, of course, like he always wanted – when Andy informed us that Scotland fans would be allowed access to watch the session that morning.

It was one of those ideas that might have sounded good when it was thought up but it didn't turn out that way. It became impossible to get things done without being interrupted. Every time a player with a connection to Rangers touched the ball, the Celtic fans booed him. Every time a player with a connection to Celtic touched the ball, the Rangers fans booed him. Then, just before the end of training, we practised our finishing and anyone who missed the target was laughed at, irrespective of which club side they played for. The whole morning was a total shambles.

At the end of the session, the Scotland supporters were allowed access for autographs as we got on the bus, but it turned into a complete melee and somehow THEY got on the bus as well! One lad even found his way into the toilet, as I found out when I went for a piss. There were fans everywhere – I even saw one of them crawl through the sunroof on top of the bus and ask Gordon Strachan for his autograph.

As a supporter it must have been fantastic to get that kind of access to the Scotland squad, but as a player it was totally unprofessional. It's not the sort of situation your manager should be putting you in. This was another supposedly bright idea from Andy. The day before an important European Championship qualifier away from home, albeit against San Marino, we should have had a closed-door training session concentrating on what needed to be done. I'm no killjoy – I'm all for fan engagement – but this was ridiculous. Such a thing would never have happened under Jock Stein.

The Stadio Olimpico in Serravalle is not exactly Wembley Stadium. It was like a glorified construction site with fans sitting on benches either side of the tunnel. On the way out before the match the atmosphere was decent with Scotland fans smiling, cheering and singing. It wasn't quite like that as we made our way back to the ramshackle dressing room at half-time after failing to score in the opening 45 minutes.

Our supporters at the training session the day before couldn't have been nicer. Now they'd turned into an angry mob after watching our piss-poor first half performance.

There was no smiling. There was no cheering. There was no singing. One guy even shouted to me that he had "paid a fortune to watch this shit." I couldn't get inside quick enough.

The second half wasn't much different – they still had all eleven men behind the ball but fortunately Gordon Strachan's penalty and a goal from Gordon Durie saw us scramble a 2-0 win. Thankfully, the reception from the Scotland fans at full-time was a little more cordial than it had been at half-time.

I wasn't happy with my performance. I was a Liverpool player up against a bunch of part-timers and should have been someone who made a difference. Instead, I was substituted after 73 minutes and couldn't argue with Andy's decision to replace me with David Robertson.

After the game against San Marino I received some criticism in the Scottish press, which was probably fair. What I didn't expect was Andy to agree with that criticism in public after being asked by a journalist for his thoughts on my individual performance. Whether you played well at Liverpool or not you were never criticised in public. Privately? Absolutely. Just not in public. For Andy to tell the press that I wasn't at my best was not something I was used to. I thought it was unacceptable. If he had a problem with my performance he should have told me directly after the game, or he should have somehow side-stepped the question from the journalist. But he didn't and, in my opinion, he hung me out to dry.

I think he chose this course of action because he wasn't experienced enough. I don't think he understood the psyche of what it took to be a top manager. Jock Stein would never have done that. Bob Paisley would never have done that. Alex Ferguson would never have done that. Kenny Dalglish would never have done that. I had bad games in my career but none of my managers criticised me in public, even though in private they had gone right through me. I would have accepted that from Andy as I knew it was true.

A few days after the game against San Marino I spoke with the manager on the telephone.

"Well, I said some things about you, and you said some things about me..."

Now I'm the most mild-mannered, most accommodating person you could meet but when someone says something about me that's not true I become a totally different animal. I was pissed off. I wasn't having that.

"Don't you dare suggest I said anything about you," I replied. "You said some things about me but at no time did I ever say anything about you. In fact, just don't bother picking me for Scotland again."

He then asked if I was going to announce my retirement from international football.

"No, but don't pick me again."

To say I was surprised when I received a phone call a few months later from Andy would be an understatement.

"We've had some call-offs and we need you for the trip to Switzerland," he said.

"So I'm playing?" I replied.

"Yes, absolutely, you're playing."

But I made it clear to him it was a one-off and would not be repeated in the future. I was still having problems at home – still drinking too much – and saving my marriage was far more important than my international career.

After everything that happened after the San Marino game I was convinced I had played for Scotland for the last time. Call me a hypocrite if you like – I know I told him not to pick me again – but I wasn't doing this for Andy Roxburgh. I was doing it because I was asked to help out my country.

Hearing the national anthem again on the night of Wednesday, September 11, 1991 took me back to my first cap against Yugoslavia at Hampden in September 1984 when I stood in front of the pipes and drums and listened to Scotland the Brave. I knew it would probably be the last time I would ever pull on a Scotland jersey so I was determined to enjoy every minute of it.

At half-time in Berne I wouldn't say there was much enjoyment in the dressing room. We were 2-0 down and our hopes of qualifying for the European Championships in Sweden were hanging by a thread. But second half goals from Gordon Durie and Ally McCoist earned us a 2-2 draw – and two months later that comeback proved vital when we finished top of Group 2 by a single point from Switzerland and Romania.

As kids growing up we dream about the future and what it might have in store for us. My dream was to play for my country and to do that 27 times was very special. It's something that can never be taken from me. But things changed. Circumstances changed. I used to enjoy going away with Scotland. When it stopped being enjoyable – and with all the other things on my plate at home – I knew it was time to give it up.

18

The New Breed

*'We were 2-0 down at half-time against Bolton in the
FA Cup and the gaffer was absolutely raging. Using
the back of his hand he sent twenty plastic cups – all
filled with hot tea – flying across the dressing room.
The players got soaked. The clothes hanging on the
pegs got soaked. Ronnie Moran got soaked. Tea was
dripping off the end of his nose but he stood perfectly
still throughout. If we had dared laugh...'*

Graeme Souness didn't give a fuck. He thrived on confrontation. Planting a huge Galatasaray flag in the middle of the pitch at the Şükrü Saracoğlu Stadium, home of rivals Fenerbahçe, after his team had just won the Turkish Cup. Signing a high-profile Catholic while manager of Rangers after Celtic had already announced THEY had signed the player. Charlie was not afraid of anything.

On the last weekend of freedom before the start of pre-season training in the summer of 1989, Eleanor and me went down to

London for the weekend to meet up with my old Ayr United teammate Billy Hendry and his girlfriend.

"What the hell are you doing here?" Mo Johnston was the last person I expected to bump into. We'd managed to get ourselves into the VIP area of Browns nightspot in Shoreditch and that's where I saw my Scotland teammate acting rather sheepishly.

"Well, what brings you to London?" I asked once more.

"I can't tell you," he replied.

If he'd just responded by saying he was on a night out with his pals I would have ceased with the inquisition, but this made me even more curious. I knew it had nothing to do with football – well at least I thought it had nothing to do with football – because he'd been pictured in the newspapers six weeks previously wearing a Celtic shirt, having supposedly sealed his return to Parkhead. So what was the reason?

I tried again. "Look, Mo, how long have you and me been pals? You know I'm not going to say anything."

I'd known the wee man for years – from the early days with Scotland under 21s when this youngster from Partick Thistle was as quiet as a mouse, to the days of 'Hurricane Mo' and his time with Celtic and Nantes. After every couple of beers I kept asking him why he was in London, but he continually refused to let the cat out of the bag.

Two days later, at a press conference at Ibrox, it all became clear. Maurice Johnston had performed THE biggest U-turn in the history of British football by signing for Rangers. As it turned out, the deal was apparently being finalised in London over the weekend and that's why Mo was in town. The signing was typical Graeme Souness, who even admitted several years later 'there was a bit of mischief in it.'

He knew there would be repercussions but he always did what he thought was best for his club. The titles and the trophies that followed at Rangers proved that.

Graeme was appointed Liverpool manager in April 1991. Kenny later revealed in his autobiography that while he thought Graeme was the best man for the job, if Liverpool had waited until the summer, and asked him, he 'would have gone back. Like a shot.'

The Liverpool board didn't wait until the summer. In all honesty, our former captain was returning to a club that had lost its way. I don't think he quite understood the situation we were in when he first arrived back at Anfield. I'm sure he thought the old guard – players like me, Rushy, Barnesy, Bruce, Ronnie Whelan and Ray Houghton – still had the same sort of control over the dressing room that he had when he was a player. That was no longer the case and I think it surprised him. What he actually inherited was a team on the decline. So it was his job to resurrect some life back into the place. And that meant he had to freshen up the squad.

Souness adopted the same system that he'd successfully used at Rangers; bring in big-name players who, he hoped, would immediately make the team better. Unfortunately for Graeme, the players he signed – despite being the obvious targets at the time – didn't meet or live up to the standards that he knew Liverpool required.

He was looking for attitude, ability, consistency and leadership – players who would make a difference straight away. But the guys he signed didn't have the impact they should have had and because of that some of them suffered a lack of confidence. And with several players already at the club, including me, not at their best, it was a combination that meant Liverpool failed to reach the level our new boss thought we could reach.

Souness was also blamed by some on the outside for trying to implement change too quickly, but all he was doing was simply bringing the club into the 21st century with new methods, some of which were ahead of their time. Granted, the introduction of Phil Boersma to the coaching staff didn't work because he didn't really mesh with Ronnie and Roy, but the problem wasn't the methods. The problem was that the squad he had, including me, wasn't playing to its full potential. We weren't at our best anymore.

Of course there was a difference between Souness and Dalglish – Graeme tried to rule with an iron fist and that didn't suit everyone – but he was doing what he thought was best for the club. This game is all about players. Forget the methods. Forget the tactics. Forget the sport scientists. Forget all that other stuff. It always has been and always will be about the guys who pull on the jersey on a matchday. The main reason Graeme Souness didn't succeed at Liverpool was, ultimately, because his players weren't good enough. There were other reasons, and he's since admitted that he took the wrong approach when dealing with players and was too hard on everyone, but I'm old school and being treated that way when I first joined Liverpool helped mould me into the player I would then become. As far as I'm concerned, he was a victim of circumstance. Football had started to change when Souness took over, but more importantly footballers had started to change.

On a positive note, he did introduce two of Liverpool's greatest players in the modern era into the first team – Robbie Fowler and Steve McManaman. Robbie was one of the most naturally gifted finishers I have ever witnessed. I was lucky enough to see Jimmy Greaves, and when I think of Robbie Fowler I also think of Greavsie. It was frightening how easy they both made it look. Robbie deserves his place as a Liverpool legend along with Macca, who carried the team on many occasions during his time there. Nobody could keep up with Macca in pre-season. He could run past players like no other. I think it's unfortunate the way he left to go to Real Madrid in 1999 – I know a lot of fans weren't happy – but Steve McManaman didn't owe Liverpool anything. He was fantastic and was good enough to have played in any Liverpool team in any era.

With my contract due to expire in the summer of 1992, I put pen to paper on a new three-and-a-half year deal in December 1991 – the last contract I would sign as a Liverpool player. I received £3,500 per week in total, which included my basic wage plus a £25,000 signing-on fee paid in instalments. Bonuses were on top. Although I might have been a long way from being the highest paid player at the club – I believe John Barnes was making £10,000 per week when I left Anfield in 1995 – I was more than happy with what I was earning. It was certainly a heck of a lot more than the £250 per week I was getting when I joined Liverpool in October 1981!

My agent, John Mac, was in charge of the negotiations and while they went smoothly most of the time there was a small bump in the road shortly before the deal was done. We were playing a UEFA Cup tie against Swarovski Tirol in Innsbruck, Austria at the end of November – two goals from Dean Saunders helped secure a 2-0 win in the first leg. The dressing room was buzzing afterwards and Souness told us we could have a couple of beers on the flight home, but no more. I had a couple of beers. Then a couple more. And maybe one or two on top of that. Now Graeme's been around, he knew what was going on and word got back to him that I had more than I should have, but nothing was said at the time.

A meeting had been set up at Anfield to finalise the new contract – the following Monday at 2pm in the manager's office. I arranged to meet John Mac at 1.45pm. We were still sitting there at 2.30pm. We were still sitting there at 3pm. We were still sitting there at 3.30pm. Souness eventually met us at four o'clock.

"I don't need someone who's the captain not following orders and trying to be clever."

The message was clear. I was one hundred per cent wrong in what I did. Three years earlier – before Hillsborough – I would not have behaved like that.

I had the honour of being captain of Liverpool Football Club on 43 occasions, the first of which was in an FA Cup tie at Hull City in February 1989 because Alan Hansen and Ronnie Whelan were both out injured.

To think when I joined the club eight years before that, I wondered if I was good enough to even get in the team, let alone captain it. Pulling on that armband for the first time – and following in the footsteps of legends like Yeats, Smith, Hughes, Thompson, Souness and Hansen – remains one of the proudest moments of my career.

With Ronnie missing a fair chunk of the 1990-91 season, I was fortunate to skipper the team a few more times in his absence, although Glenn Hysén was the preferred choice during most of the second half of the season. Then Graeme Souness took over in April and made me captain for the last five league games.

The armband certainly got passed around in 1991-92. Ronnie started off the season as captain until he damaged his knee in the Merseyside derby at the end of August and was out for seven months. Then I took over as skipper until I injured my hamstring in Auxerre in October and was out for four weeks. Next it was Steve McMahon's turn for a few games until he, too, got hurt and eventually – in December – it landed on the arm of Mark Wright and pretty much stayed there.

Mark was one of England's best players during the World Cup in 1990 and had cost the club £2.5million from Derby County in the summer of 1991, making him the most expensive defender in Britain. Graeme clearly saw him as a ready-made replacement for Alan Hansen. He was brought in to be a leader so to give him the captaincy made sense to me. I've been asked a few times over the years if I felt snubbed by that decision – certainly not. Not for one minute did I think that Graeme was having a go at me. I was on the wrong side of my career. Mark was 28 and in his prime, playing for England and was the most talked about centre-half at the time. It really made sense. I would probably have done the same thing if I'd been in Graeme's shoes.

The announcement that Mark Wright was the new captain of Liverpool was made at training the day before we travelled to play Southampton at the start of December.

I remember Wrighty came to my house that evening – a visit that was both unexpected but also appreciated. There was a knock on the front door just after seven o'clock and he was standing there.

"Look Stevie, as much as I'm happy to be the captain I just don't want you thinking that I don't respect you and I hope you don't hold any grudges."

He didn't need to do that and I thought him coming to the house was very respectful. It didn't hurt because I knew Graeme was right. I knew where I was. I knew where I stood. Might things have been different if I'd stuck to my two-beer limit on the flight back from Austria? I don't think so. The manager's mind was already made up.

When Mark Wright was unavailable I went on to captain Liverpool on another eighteen occasions, doing so for the 43rd and final time against Bolton in an FA Cup tie in January 1993. Less than four years separated the first time I wore the armband – against Hull in February 1989 – and that game at Bolton, yet only one other player, John Barnes, played in both games.

After a settled team for long spells in the mid-Eighties, the turnover of players at Liverpool at the start of the Nineties was frightening as you can see from these two Liverpool line-ups.

1/43: February 18, 1989.
Hull City 2-3 Liverpool.
Grobbelaar, Ablett, Burrows, Nicol(c), Gillespie, Molby, Beardsley, Aldridge, Houghton, Barnes, McMahon.

43/43: January 3, 1993.
Bolton Wanderers 2-2 Liverpool.
Hooper, Marsh, Jones, Nicol(c), Piechnik, Bjørnebye, McManaman, Hutchison, Rush, Barnes, Thomas.

Because of the high turnover of players at the start of the Nineties, it was down to the older boys in the squad to ensure that the social side of things was not being neglected. January 1992 was a fairly quiet month so at Melwood one morning, a few of the lads expressed an interest in going out later that day. We arranged to meet up after training at a bar in Liverpool city centre for a few beers. As usual, one drink became two, two became three and so on but because the piss-up had only been arranged that morning – and we'd come straight from training – none of our wives knew what we were up to.

When I eventually got home about eight o'clock, I found the front door was locked. The back door was locked as well. I could see through the window that Eleanor was sitting at the kitchen table with her friend Allison so I tapped on the window and asked her to let me in. "No chance, you're drunk. Go back to where you came from."

Time for Plan B – gain access to the kitchen by crawling through the dog flap on the back door. Down came the shutter as I was getting down on all fours. Denied once more. I must have stood outside for ten minutes before she shouted to ask if I wanted a cup of tea. Finally, I thought, she was going to let me in. "Hold on a minute," she said. She placed the tea bag in the cup, boiled the kettle, poured the water then brought the cup of tea to the back door. But instead of opening the door, she pulled up the shutter again and handed me the cup of tea through the dog flap. Just as I was about to grab the cup, she poured its contents all over the back step, before proceeding to stand at the window and wave at me.

As funny as my wife thought this was, her friend was morti-fied. Half an hour later, Eleanor finally relented and let me back in the house once she thought I'd sobered up. It certainly brought a new meaning to the Scottish phrase 'yer tea's oot!'

With the title race a straight fight between Manchester United and Leeds United, the FA Cup was our only hope of silverware in 1991-92, Graeme's first full season in charge. Peterborough United had already knocked us out of the League Cup earlier in the season, so we weren't taking anyone lightly, but with Liverpool, Norwich City, Portsmouth and Sunderland making up the semi-final line-up we wouldn't get a better chance to win the FA Cup.

Liverpool versus Portsmouth – we were happy enough with the semi-final draw. A mid-table second division team stood between us and a place at Wembley. We might have been happy to get Pompey but Graeme certainly wasn't amused by the way we played. Goalless after normal time, Darren Anderton gave them the lead with nine minutes of extra-time remaining and we were in the shit.

I partnered Mark Wright at centre-back in that first game at Highbury but with time running out I decided to sacrifice my position and head upfield. I took a short pass from Mike Marsh about 35 yards from goal, weaved (well, kind of…) my way past Warren Aspinall before I was fouled by Andy Awford just outside the box. John Barnes hit the post from the free-kick, the ball bounced a couple of times on the goal line and Ronnie Whelan was quickest to react to score the easiest goal of his life and equalise with just four minutes remaining. Portsmouth had been the better team but somehow we managed to earn a replay.

For the second game at Villa Park we were without Steve McManaman, who'd been stretchered off at Highbury, as well as our boss. A triple heart bypass meant Graeme Souness was forced to watch the game on television from his private ward at the Alexandra Hospital in Cheadle. Kick-off was also delayed by fifteen minutes to allow thousands of fans outside the ground enough time to enter the stadium safely. This happened to a few of our games after Hillsborough – the police simply refused to take any chances.

Darren Anderton had been Portsmouth's danger man in the first match so caretaker boss Ronnie Moran changed things around a little in defence for the replay. David Burrows would normally have been left-back, however he played centre-back that day so that I could move to full-back to look after Anderton. When Darren got going he had pace to burn and was very dangerous, but he was also pretty inexperienced. I'm sure he knew I was vulnerable to pace but he tried to do the same thing over and over again – wanting to go on the outside – so I kept showing him inside. There was no way I was giving him the chance to win a foot race.

We played better in the replay than we'd done in the first game at Highbury (that's not saying much), but we couldn't find a way past the Portsmouth defence or goalkeeper Alan Knight. And we were lucky when, with only five minutes of normal time remaining, Alan McLoughlin's shot hit our bar. With no goals in extra-time, and for the first time ever, an FA Cup semi-final would be decided on penalties.

The spot-kicks were taken at the end with the Liverpool supporters behind the goal in the North Stand but I kept well out of the way when the order was being decided. I just hoped the boys would get the job done before I was required, considering that the last competitive penalty I had taken – Rome, 1984 – was still orbiting the atmosphere somewhere between Earth and Mars.

We scored all three of ours. I remember going up to Dean Saunders and giving him a big hug after his and joking about his run-up, which was so long that it practically started in front of the Holte End up the other end of the park. When Portsmouth's regular taker, John Beresford, missed their fourth penalty it was all over and we were back in an FA Cup final. It was nervous enough for us to be part of, so I hate to imagine how the boss was feeling watching the drama unfold in hospital!

I have to say, though, that I disagree with anyone who doesn't want to decide a game of football with penalty kicks. I've been on the winning end of it as a player and on the losing side as a head coach but my thoughts have never changed. It's part of the game. I've yet to hear one person say they weren't on the edge of their seat during any penalty shoot-out. There's no other or better way to decide a game of football. The only reason you get to a shoot-out is because you can't separate the teams. So why carry on the torture?

The celebrations afterwards were special. Five of our starting eleven that night had never played in an FA Cup final before – Rob Jones, David Burrows, Mark Wright, Dean Saunders and Michael Thomas – so they were ecstatic. We got to face another second division team, Sunderland, in the final. In fact, Aston Villa was the only top-flight team we played in the FA Cup that year – we needed replays to get past Bristol Rovers in round four and Ipswich Town in the fifth round. The old heads – myself, Ronnie, Rushy, Ray and Bruce – knew we'd been fortunate, but sometimes you need a little bit of luck in life.

It was a nice touch by Graeme to allow Ronnie Moran to lead the Liverpool team out in the final at Wembley, and we could all see what it meant to him. The build-up to the game in the media focussed on minnows Sunderland beating mighty Leeds United in 1973 and us losing to Wimbledon four years previously. Would there be another upset? Could the second division side beat the top-flight team and write more FA Cup history?

We were all well aware that an upset was a possibility. The confidence and self-belief of Liverpool teams of old just wasn't there in this particular Liverpool side. But the game itself was a surprise. I have never played in such a one-sided cup final in my whole career. After ten minutes, I remember looking at Jan Molby and he gave me the same look back. We had the same thought – this was too easy. We just passed it around for fun. Sunderland were lucky because the actual ball we used on the day was collecting water. We couldn't move it around as well as we would have liked, otherwise I'm sure we would have scored in that first half. Despite all our possession, it was still goalless when we went in at half-time.

There was no screaming and shouting at the break, no raised voices, just an acknowledgement that if we continued to do what we were doing – and were a bit more clinical in the final third – then the goals would come.

The second half began the way the first half had ended and when Macca set up Michael Thomas for the opening goal two minutes after the restart, we never looked back. Rushy added number two midway through the second half and the trophy was ours.

I've been asked several times over the years what was my greatest achievement in football. Was it the league titles, winning the European Cup in Rome or a specific FA Cup win? Every trophy was just as good as the last one.

Except this one.

I just didn't get the same enjoyment. I didn't get the same fulfilment. It just didn't feel the same as all the other trophies I won at Liverpool. Every other time the team was totally together, in sync, in harmony, but this team wasn't.

I always felt one of Liverpool's greatest strengths – other than having players with great ability – was that the mind of each player was also on the guy standing next to him in a red jersey, accompanied by a willingness to do anything for that teammate. There was also an acute awareness of previous accomplishments by great Liverpool teams of the past. When we used to meet up with the likes of St John and Yeats and Callaghan and Heighway and McDermott there was a sense that we were all one. We may have played in different eras but that feeling was still present.

That same feeling just wasn't there with the 1992 team.

I can't imagine many footballers, when asked to name their favourite away ground, would say Loftus Road. But that's where I scored both my first and last goals for Liverpool.

Goal Number One: *October 1983 – Graeme Souness with the inch-perfect pass and I hit a sweet left-foot shot past Peter Hucker.*

Goal Number Forty-Six: *August 1993 – Nigel Clough's pass was dummied by Rushy and I melted a shot past Tony Roberts.*

Nearly ten years separated them but they were pretty similar. Looking back, I suppose I was fortunate to score them both. I was only on the pitch for the first goal because Joe Fagan thought Craig Johnston might get a red card.

And that last goal, my first for eighteen months incidentally, was scored when there was still blood trickling down the side of my head following a collision a couple of minutes earlier. I actually had to get stitches at half-time and didn't even hear the team talk. If that had happened in today's game I wouldn't even have been on the pitch to score.

My last goal for Liverpool SHOULD have been scored a couple of months later, in front of the Kop, but guess which dumpling missed another penalty? It was my testimonial against a Great Britain XI and Eric Nixon was in the opposition goal. He asked me where I was going to put it but I was too busy explaining to him what I was going to do that I didn't focus properly on the spot kick and ended up hitting the post! Trust me to miss a penalty on two of the biggest days of my footballing life.

My testimonial took place on October 10, 1993, at Anfield of course. We tried to get Rangers and Celtic but the police said 'no'. However, Terry Venables agreed to manage a Great Britain select so we set about calling players to see if they wanted to take part. I'm not normally a worrier but I spent most of the time before the game wondering if anybody would bother turning up. You're basically looking for goodwill from players – asking them to come and play for free. I hate asking anybody for anything. What if they phoned on the Friday night and said they couldn't play anymore? Silly things like that kept going through my head. It was actually impossible to fully enjoy the build-up.

It's different these days with testimonials for the likes of Steven Gerrard and Ryan Giggs, where they are guaranteed full houses at Anfield and Old Trafford and are able to give lots of money to charity.

There's a perception that football players are paid exorbitant amounts of money and are financially secure after their careers finish. But that wasn't the case back then. A testimonial was the chance for a player to secure a bit of extra cash for a future that, at the time, could seem uncertain. Yes, we were well paid for what we did, but it certainly wasn't enough money to live off for the rest of your life. The club promising me a testimonial was actually one of the reasons why I stayed another year – a year too long as it turned out.

With players staying at Liverpool for long periods of time, testimonials were commonplace – mine was the third taking place at Anfield in twelve months.

The actual day was fantastic. It was the lead-up to the game that was a complete and utter nightmare. Pre-match there were appearances from some of the Gladiators and the cast of Brookside, then just before kick-off, Gerry Marsden walked on to the pitch and sang You'll Never Walk Alone. It was amazing and I'm not ashamed to admit there was a tear in my eye.

It was actually the first ever testimonial shown live on Sky Sports, and there's a funny story that goes with that. My old pal from Ayr United, Alan McInally, scored what turned out to be the winner, but it wasn't shown on television because I was doing my lap of honour at the time – having just been substituted – and they showed me instead. He was gutted when he found out! The irony is he now works for Sky and I'm sure he'd find it hilarious if it happened to anyone else.

Once again I'd like to thank Terry Venables for being in charge of the Great Britain Select and all the players who turned up for my big day. It killed me to ask them but they all showed up and, for that, I shall always be grateful.

The evening reception was great. We had a piper pipe us in to the dining room at the Holiday Inn in Liverpool and I got to spend time with family and friends and fellow pros. And one of the highlights was seeing a load of my old Ayr United team-mates who had travelled down from Scotland, including two big influences in my early days at Somerset Park – Jim Fleeting and Jim McSherry – as well as my good mate Ian Cashmore who unfortunately passed away in 2014. Rest in peace, pal.

Take a look at this Liverpool line-up that faced Bristol City in an FA Cup third round replay at Anfield in January 1994. It was the last team that Graeme Souness would pick as manager:

Grobbelaar, Jones, Nicol, Harkness, Ruddock, Clough, Barnes, Walters, Redknapp, McManaman, Rush(c).

How the fuck did we lose that game? Okay, maybe the thirty-somethings in the team – Bruce, me, Barnesy and Rushy – had seen better days, but with talented kids like Jamie and Macca in the side we should still have been far too strong for our opponents. So what went wrong?

That's a hard question to answer. There was little urgency in our play that night and the hunger, that will to win was missing. But I think the problems ran deeper than that. I think you have to look beyond this result because it wasn't the first time we'd produced such an inept performance. I actually think the decline had been apparent for a couple of years – starting during the season when we won the FA Cup in 1992, possibly even earlier – and we'd been on a slippery slope for eighteen months or so, which culminated in the departure of Graeme Souness as manager following that defeat to Bristol City.

Playing for Liverpool was a pleasure. Being able to play with great players at Liverpool was a pleasure. And being able to play with players who were also men of real character and substance was a pleasure.

They taught me about football and also helped me grow as a man. There weren't enough players with those attributes in the Liverpool squads I played in from 1992 onwards. There were too many players in those squads who may have had ability but just weren't up to the task – both on and off the field – of following in the footsteps of previous Liverpool greats. Their way was different from our Liverpool Way.

19

Sink Or Swim

*'When we found out neither of us was playing me and
Stan Staunton hitched a lift to the pub, had a few beers
then came back just in time for the final whistle. 'What
did you think of the game?' asked Big Ron...'*

In his autobiography, Robbie Fowler claims that I didn't like
him because I never spoke to him when he first became part of
the Liverpool squad. To say I never liked him is simply not true
and I'm surprised he thought that. My problem was with the
attitude of some of the younger players who, I felt, were cocky
for no apparent reason. A lot of them who had just signed for
Liverpool were full of themselves. I'm old school and that didn't
sit well with me. But if there was one person who I DIDN'T
feel that way about it was Robbie because the boy could play.

He was a little bit reserved on the two occasions he was
part of the first team squad during the second half of season
1992-93 – understandably so – but that soon changed at the
start of the following season. Of course it would do after a goal
in the League Cup at Fulham on his debut then scoring all five

in the second leg at Anfield. He proved himself quickly and was absolutely fantastic.

Roy Evans was the man appointed to replace Graeme Souness as the new manager of Liverpool Football Club. We were out of the FA Cup and found ourselves 21 points behind league leaders Manchester United so it was no surprise when the board chose a safe pair of hands to try and steady the ship and get us back on track. Knowing Evo very well, I had no problem at all with the appointment. At that stage of my career, my only concern was trying to stay in the team. I started nine of the remaining sixteen games that season, but it was unrealistic to expect that I could still play at the highest level on a regular basis for a team like Liverpool at the age of 32. But you don't realise it at the time. You become delusional. You're probably the only one who isn't aware that you can no longer do what you used to be able to do.

I certainly knew I had lost a yard of pace, or at least I thought I had. What I didn't realise was that I had lost two or three yards. Footballers talk about when the legs go but it's actually not just your legs. It's your body strength. It's your balance. And when they all go then there's no way back. You're looking for other ways of convincing yourself that somehow, miraculously, you'll turn up on a Saturday and be who you were back in the good old days. You just think it will happen. It doesn't. But you're the last person to see that and be aware of it.

I went into pre-season in the summer of 1994 – the final year of my contract – with the intention of fighting for a place in the Liverpool team. Roy was fine with that. I started the first three games – wins against Crystal Palace, Arsenal and Southampton – but the arrival of John Scales and Phil Babb at the start of

September meant I slipped down the pecking order. I got back into the team briefly for a couple of matches – including my last ever game for Liverpool at Anfield, a 4-1 win against Sheffield Wednesday, and my final game for the club in a League Cup tie at Burnley – but I knew. And Roy knew as well. We didn't need to have that conversation. We didn't need to talk about anything. I'm actually glad he let me figure it out myself as opposed to him having to say to me that my time was up at Liverpool Football Club. I just wish I had worked it out for myself at least two years previously.

I wore the famous red shirt for the final time in my career on Saturday, January 14. Unfortunately that red shirt was hidden from view because I was also wearing a Liverpool tracksuit top as well after being named as a substitute! And that tracksuit top stayed on throughout the ninety minutes against Ipswich Town at Anfield. Knowing it was my last game for the club it would have been nice to get on at some point but, as luck would have it, Ipswich won at Anfield for the first time in their history so for Evo to bring on a defender when we were chasing the game would not have been the wisest thing to do. Sentimentality only stretches so far and I completely understood.

On Thursday, January 19, 1995 – after 468 games (W255 D123 L90), 451 starts (343 in the league), 46 goals (36 in the league) and 27 Merseyside derbies – I finally walked out of the front door at Anfield thirteen years, two months, three weeks and three days after joining Liverpool Football Club.

When I think back now I realise just how fantastic it was. Looking back and reflecting and understanding it better, I think to myself 'holy shit, we were good, and I wasn't bad either.' I enjoy all those triumphs far more now than I ever did at the

271

time. We were put in a state of mind that success was expected at Liverpool so any euphoria didn't last long. It was a memorable journey with many moments I'll never forget, but it was time to move on. I signed for Notts County the following day.

I had received a phone call from Howard Kendall, the former Everton manager who had just taken over at Notts County. They were in dire straits and, barring a miracle, were going to be relegated to the Second Division, the third tier of English football. "Come and play for us and be my assistant. I'll teach you the ropes."

There weren't many better coaches to learn from than Howard, previously in charge of some of the best Everton teams in recent memory. The timing was perfect. I knew I was coming to the end of my playing career at the top level and had already started thinking about what was next. Coaching was certainly something that interested me, but to leave Liverpool and go to Notts Country meant a rather dramatic drop in wages. I talked it over with Eleanor and we decided that although I could probably earn roughly the same money as I was getting at Anfield by signing for another Premier League team it seemed a better idea, thinking long term, to go to Notts County and learn from someone like Howard while continuing to play football at a lower level.

I wasn't prepared to leave the family behind, or travel a great distance each day to get to work, so we rented out our house in Heswall on the Wirral and moved to rented accommodation in Farndon, about twenty minutes from Nottingham. I pretty much knew when I signed that Notts County would be relegated, as did Howard, but he persuaded me he had the nucleus of a decent team and with one or two signings we'd come straight back up and would be able to hold our own once again. The only reason I went to that club was because of Howard Kendall. Little did I know what I was getting myself into…

Being a player at Liverpool puts you in a bubble. Behind the scenes everything is done properly. But I wasn't at Anfield anymore. I was at Meadow Lane, and I couldn't believe how unhappy the players were at Notts County. A lot of them had the same gripe – they'd been promised certain things when signing that never materialised. I received pretty much the same response from each player when I was introduced to them:

"Why the hell did you come HERE?"

The whole club was negative, everyone was miserable and this was a huge culture shock to me. Howard had managed to instil a little bit of confidence in the squad, by assuring the players that things would get better, but it was apparent to me that nobody wanted to be there.

Despite the general malaise there were one or two positives in the first couple of months after I arrived.

I'd called time on taking penalties a long time ago. Or at least I thought I had. After two goalless draws, a penalty shoot-out would decide whether Notts County or Stoke City would face Ascoli in the final of the Anglo-Italian Cup. They had no idea I had absolutely no interest in taking a spot kick. But it was only my second game for the club. I was the experienced professional and the former Liverpool player – they was just assumed I would be one of the five to take a penalty. I couldn't exactly say no. What message would that send out to the rest of the team?

On the outside I appeared cool and calm. My demeanour was one of confidence. On the inside there was turmoil.

Let's go back to Rome, 1984 for a moment. The only thing going through my head as I walked up to take the first penalty in a European Cup final was where I was going to put the ball and what I would do after I scored. I was only 22 years old and didn't have a care in the world. Now, on a cold Tuesday night in Stoke, and at the age of 33, the only thought in my head was 'shit, I'm going to miss this!' How does that work?

It was, by far, the most nervous I had ever been during my football career. My clear head as a youngster? Gone. My composure? Gone. Twelve yards from goal, potentially the deciding penalty, all that experience behind me yet all of a sudden I felt like a total rookie. This wasn't the European Cup final. This was the fucking Anglo-Italian Cup. I may have looked like the coolest, calmest man inside the Victoria Ground when I rolled the ball into the corner of the net as the goalkeeper dived the other way but that's as far from the truth as you can imagine. The lads went on to beat Ascoli 2-1 in the final at Wembley in March.

At the start of April, just over two months into my role as player/coach, I walked into Howard's office after the home defeat by Barnsley. He looked at me, his eyes welling up, and said, "I'm done. They're getting rid of me." Then there were tears. "I have never been sacked in my life."

Howard said the board wanted to speak to me and I had to go upstairs.

"If they offer you the job then take it."

"I can't take it – you brought me to the club to help you, not replace you."

"Look, just take it."

I went up to the boardroom and was told that Howard had

been relieved of his duties and the board wanted me to take the job until the end of the season. In hindsight, it was probably the best thing that happened to me because it stood me in good stead when I took over as head coach of New England Revolution a few years later. But at the time I wasn't sure I was doing the right thing – I had no idea if I could even do the job. Suddenly I've gone from being their teammate to being their boss – from being responsible for just myself to being responsible for every other player as well. The team kind of picked itself – that wasn't an issue as the squad was limited in numbers – but we only won one more game and were indeed relegated, finishing bottom of the First Division and some fourteen points from safety.

The biggest problem I had was at the end of the season when chairman Derek Pavis told me to get rid of certain players, those on contracts that the club couldn't afford. A manager has to do what a manager has to do – I would have told them to their face – but I wasn't informed of this course of action until after the players had left for the summer. I had to sign letters that had already been written by the board. The letters were then sent to the players who would not be at the club the following season. I was naive and didn't know any better so I signed them all. How bad is that? There was no way I would ever do it that way again. Any player surplus to requirements at any club I was at from that day forward was told directly, by me, and was never subjected to the embarrassment of receiving a letter. I can assure you that I followed through with that. It's the hardest thing to do, telling a professional football player that you no longer require them at the club, but if you're in charge then you have to have the balls to tell them personally.

I signed all those letters thinking I was getting the job of replacing Howard Kendall as manager of Notts County on a permanent basis. But at the start of June the chairman told me that former Shelbourne boss Colin Murphy was going to be introduced as the new manager of the football club. So in the space of six months I'd gone from being a Premier League player at Liverpool, to being a boss in the first division to playing in the third tier of English football. That was a bit of a wake-up call!

In fairness, Colin did all the right things when he came in, seeking me out and explaining that he understood my predicament. He was also full of praise for the job I'd done since taking over from Howard and for the way I had dealt with things properly, despite the tough times, both on and off the park. Years later, when I was offered the Revs job, I remembered Colin's words about doing things properly regardless of the circumstances – an important lesson to learn as a manager and fortunately one I learned at an early stage of my coaching career.

Pre-season at Notts County under Colin Murphy was something I had never experienced before. For the first ten years or so at Liverpool we followed practically the same routine – two weeks at Melwood followed by a couple of weeks on tour then one more week at home. I only knew one way to prepare for a new season – it worked for us so why change? But I wasn't at Liverpool anymore.

When Colin told the squad he was taking us to an army base in Kent for a week I wondered what on earth that had to do with football or preparing for the season ahead. But that week in Kent was fantastic. Getting up at 7am, having some breakfast together, running down the beach in teams of five carrying giant logs, having lunch together, teaming up with the army on the assault course, having dinner together, sleeping in a dorm then being woken in the morning by a sergeant major blowing a trumpet. It was great. I loved it. I may have been 33 years old but this taught me there were other ways, different ways to do things.

In the following few months at Notts County, under Murphy's management, I enjoyed my football again and was playing well in the old third division. But deep down I believed I could still do a job at a higher level. I spoke with my agent, John Mac, and asked him if he thought that would be possible. He told me the only way that might happen was if I was in the best physical shape possible. He suggested I hire a personal trainer to give me a chance of moving back up the divisions and introduced me to a man called Keith Power.

The first thing Keith wanted to do was put me through some tests to find out where I was physically and what I needed to do to help build up my strength and stamina. So I went down to the racetrack at Silverstone with him and he put me through a series of exercises. I was asked to do some pull-ups, which didn't go well, and asked to lift some weights, which didn't go well either.

The final test was on the treadmill. I was connected to a whole host of various monitoring devices, during which time I had to wear an oxygen mask to monitor my oxygen intake. As bad as the previous exercises had gone – I was embarrassed as I failed them both – when I got on that running machine and burned the thing up Keith's face immediately changed. Here was a guy who had really struggled doing pull-ups and lifting weights but was suddenly now running for fun. In fact, I could have run all day.

There was absolutely nothing wrong with my fitness but it was clear that I needed to work on my strength and conditioning so a weekly schedule was drawn up with a routine I had to follow. My diet also changed as well after I had a meeting with a nutritionist and I cut down my daily intake of packets of crisps from double digits to single digits (kidding). She told me to write down everything I was eating and drinking and, after examining the list, noticed that I didn't drink any water. In all the time I was at Liverpool I don't remember ever drinking water. I used to have a few beers at the pub then go home and have a cup of tea but I would never just drink water. That soon changed.

I signed a six-month agreement with Keith, starting at the beginning of the season and lasting until Christmas, with the sole objective being to get me into the best shape possible and hopefully back playing in the top flight, or if not then at least at an improved level. The whole thing cost me £1,100 but it was the best £1,100 I have ever spent. It got me back in the Premier League and also helped me get an increase in wages.

Shortly after he took over as Notts County boss in June 1995 Colin Murphy made me a promise: "I know you can play at a higher level, and you know you can play at a higher level. If a Premier League team comes in for you during your time here then I won't stand in your way."

We were in second place in the old third division when Colin called me into his office one morning at the start of November and told me that David Pleat had phoned him. Sheffield Wednesday wanted to sign me. The boss knew it would harm his team if he let me go, but he kept his word.

"I'd like to thank you for everything you've done for me – you've been fantastic. I said you can go and if things work out with the negotiations then good luck."

I will forever be grateful to Colin for that.

Notts County was a great learning experience for me. Those two months I was in charge gave me an insight into tactics, man-management, contracts and dealing with chairmen. Then working with Keith Power helped re-energise me and gave my playing career a new lease of life. And Colin Murphy not only proved there was an alternative to the Liverpool Way, but he also showed how to keep a promise. At the time it wasn't easy but those nine and a half months I had at the club played a huge part in shaping my thoughts as a coach.

I met David Pleat at a hotel in Sheffield and was offered a two and a half year deal plus a basic weekly wage of £2,500 to sign for Sheffield Wednesday. He could have offered me two packets of crisps and a can of Coke and I would still have put pen to paper – the opportunity to play in the Premier League once again was something I was not going to turn down. I was about to say 'great, that's fine' but before I could reply he said he would also pay me an additional fixed amount if I played a certain number of games per season. We were sitting chatting after everything had been agreed but there was one question I still needed to ask him:

"David, why should players get a bonus for playing a certain amount of games? When I sign for a team I want to play every match, I don't expect a bonus for playing a certain number of games."

At this stage he must have wished he hadn't added the

appearance bonus when we were talking terms! I find it strange when players' contracts contain a bonus for a certain number of appearances. Why should you need an incentive to play? Surely a player should want to take part in every game. It's always been a bugbear of mine that contracts include additional money when reaching a certain number of appearances. Why should a centre forward get extra cash when he scores ten, fifteen, twenty goals? Does a goal bonus make him try harder? If it does then there's clearly a flaw with that player.

David Pleat brought me to the club predominantly for my experience but also because of my versatility. I could play at the back or anywhere across midfield – when I first joined Sheffield Wednesday I played in central midfield, beginning with my debut at Everton in November 1995 alongside Graham Hyde. I'd not played in the Premier League for a year and had forgotten how quick the speed of play was. Fortunately I was as fit as a fiddle but the pace, compared with what I'd been used to at Notts County, was a real eye-opener. My body was probably in the best shape it had been since 1990, yet the pace of play was still frightening.

By the way, playing at Hillsborough on a regular basis didn't faze me. A Liverpool fan asked me that question on Twitter but it certainly wasn't a case of 'oh my God, I'm going to Hillsborough again.' I wasn't apprehensive about going back there because I'd been given another chance to play in the Premier League. It was who I was playing for, not where I was playing, that mattered to me.

I missed a couple of games around the festive period only because I nearly drowned! I was out walking our three dogs near Farndon Pit one freezing cold morning when Lucy, our

Bernese mountain dog, saw a flock of geese and made for them. Now Lucy must have weighed at least ten stones and she fell through the ice into the water below while chasing the geese. I honestly did not know what to do. If I went in after her, I would have fallen through the ice as well but if I didn't go in then I would have to explain to Eleanor why I'd returned home with only two dogs when I left the house with three.

I tried testing the edge of the ice to see just how thick it was – I probably got about ten feet in and it seemed fine. Being slightly more brazen I took another four or five paces, thinking I would be okay, when I, too, fell through the ice. I was twenty-five feet from the edge but still around fifteen feet from Lucy. As soon as I went through it, I just expected to be able to lean on the surrounding ice with my elbows and pull myself out. But it doesn't work that way. It's nowhere near as easy as getting yourself out of a swimming pool. While treading water I took off my big jacket and my shoes, thinking I'd have a better chance of pulling myself up without the additional weight of the clothes.

By this stage Lucy was trying to paddle towards where I was but my focus was solely on me, not her anymore. Once I realised I couldn't lift myself out – even minus the jacket and shoes – I decided to try and break the ice around me to give myself more room for manoeuvre. Two seconds later Sooty, one of our other dogs, jumped in beside me. I shoved her out. She jumped back in. I shoved her out. She jumped back in. Then Lucy arrived. Just what I needed – two dogs splashing around when I'm trying to extricate myself from the ice. Man's best friend indeed!

I then heard another dog barking, but it didn't sound like my other dog Millie so I shouted 'HELP', maybe three times, in the hope that somebody would hear me. Thankfully a woman named Joanne Issott was walking nearby with her dog and when she saw me in the water she quickly came to my rescue. As she helped me climb out, Lucy and Sooty followed me back to dry land. I've got no idea what I would have done if Joanne hadn't been nearby because my own attempts at a rescue mission had failed miserably.

Being out of the water actually felt worse than being in – I felt warmer under the ice than I did when I got out. I had no jacket, no shoes and was standing there drenched and freezing in only my socks, t-shirt and trousers. Joanne gave me her jacket and said she would run home and get her car to give me and the dogs a lift back to my house. Picture the scene. Joanne's driving a small four-door saloon, I'm in the passenger seat freezing and shivering and my three dogs – one of which weighs at least ten stones – are squashed all across the back seat.

From falling through the ice to getting back home probably took an hour or so. When I got to the house I could hardly talk and was shaking uncontrollably because of the cold. My lips and the tips of my fingers were blue so Eleanor ran me a hot shower. But it was too hot. I was trying to get out – she was trying to push me back in. Absolute chaos. Talk about going from one extreme to the other.

The hypothermia was only mild but related 'flu symptoms still caused me to miss a couple of games, including the FA Cup defeat at Charlton. I was able to recover in time to face Liverpool at Hillsborough in mid-January. Now that was a strange feeling, going up against my old team for the first time since leaving Anfield. If I'm being honest I didn't think I would ever play in the top flight again, let alone against Liverpool when I left the club to join Notts County in January 1995.

So this was an unexpected bonus and I made sure I enjoyed every single minute of it. I played in central midfield while Peter Atherton partnered Des Walker in the centre of defence, directly up against Stan Collymore and Robbie Fowler. They did really well to keep them quiet, but then Rushy came on with ten minutes to go and equalised soon after. Bloody typical! But a 1-1 draw against the team in fourth place in the Premier League was still a good result and kept us mid-table.

I suppose I was pretty versatile during my career, backed up by the fact that I managed to play in every single position before I hung up my boots. But being a goalkeeper? Well, that came about in March 1996 when we were playing Nottingham Forest and Chris Woods got hurt towards the end of the first half.

With goalkeepers not automatically among the substitutes back then, Mark Pembridge came on for Chris and I took over between the sticks. That wasn't the initial plan. David Pleat wanted to bring on Chris Waddle and put him in goal.

"Gaffer, why would you give the gloves to the guy who is most likely to either score or create a goal for us?" I said.

We were 1-0 down and he asked me what the alternative was. I told him I would go in goal. He agreed, but within sixty seconds of the restart, Forest striker Paul McGregor scored and we were 2-0 down. The first time I touched the ball was when I picked it out the back of my net!

Fortunately, I wasn't as busy for the rest of the half and I actually really enjoyed it. On one occasion, I came off my line to catch a cross and it stuck between my gloves. The crowd roared and I felt like Peter Shilton. But Bryan Roy scored their third ten minutes from time, we lost 3-1 and Chris Woods's job was safe.

Another story I remember is when we were due to face Peter-borough in a pre-season friendly, and were staying in Brighton at The Grand Hotel. Not wanting to be stuck inside all day, myself and John Sheridan decided to go for a walk after lunch. The initial idea was to come back to the hotel for an afternoon nap before dinner at 7.30pm. The best laid plans…

Neither of us expected to play the following day so we decided on the way back to nip in to a local pub for a couple of pints and a game of pool. We ended up playing doubles against some of the locals. They tried to beat us. Then they tried again. And again. But they couldn't. Eventually they decided to play us for pints to spice things up instead of just playing for fun. By this stage we'd had a couple of drinks and were on a roll – and now that beer was put up as the prize there was no way we were walking away. A queue quickly formed to play us. Winner stays on. People were coming in to the pub, seeing the line to play us and wanted to join in. Every game was worth a pint.

There were a couple of occasions during the afternoon when we thought it was maybe time to go, but because neither of us thought we'd be playing in the friendly at Peterborough the following day we just kept going. And we kept winning. Then I looked at my watch. It was 6.30pm. We'd come into the pub at 2pm. Dinner was at 7.30pm. We must have had ten pints each in four and a half hours. After winning again – we didn't lose once that day – we finally decided to call it a day and got back to the hotel around seven. After a quick, cold shower to try and sober me up I sat beside Shez at dinner, both of us making sure we kept our heads down. Thankfully nobody said a thing.

At check-out the following morning David Pleat told me there was a problem. The hotel manager had informed him there was an additional thirty pounds charge on the club's bill for cleaning because one of his players had left a jobby on the hotel premises.

I sleepwalk. And during one of these nocturnal wanderings, while naked, I somehow managed to get myself outside on the stairwell of the fire escape when the door slammed behind me. That woke me up! I was stranded. Naked and stranded. And I needed a number two. So I let nature take its course. Then I battered on the door to try and attract the attention of someone who would open the door. Fortunately, it wasn't long before one of the hotel cleaners came to my rescue. Not only did she provide me with a route back inside but she also passed me a towel to cover the crown jewels.

"Which room are you in?"

A simple question.

"Um, I don't know"

So she asked for my name then radioed down to reception to get my room number. Where I was standing wasn't even on the same floor! Finally I got back to my room around 7am and wondered if anyone knew what I'd done. It soon became clear at check-out, when Pleaty pulled me aside, that I had been rumbled.

He asked if I had been drinking. I told him I hadn't but that I did sleepwalk. And then I explained what happened. I told him I was as regular as clockwork and had woken up on the stairwell on the fire escape and was desperate to go. I didn't know what else to say. He actually respected me for telling the truth. Even without the beer that could have happened because I've been in those sorts of situations before.

We arrived in Peterborough and Pleaty read out the team – to our surprise both me and Shez were starting. This wasn't what either of us expected.

I had to be replaced after 36 minutes, when my groin gave way, however up until that point I had played really well in the 'Libero' position in a back three. I was spraying balls to teammates left and right, in total contrast to the way a player should have played given the alcohol consumed less than 24 hours earlier. Shez wasn't so fortunate. Five minutes after I sat down next to Pleaty on the bench, the gaffer turned to me and said: "I think there's something wrong with Sheridan today but I don't know what it is." I knew exactly what the problem was…

My first time back at Anfield as a player since leaving the club was December 7, 1996, and I was really nervous in the build-up – far more nervous than I would be before a normal game. We were staying at a hotel near Haydock Racecourse and just before we got on the bus to go to the game David Pleat came up to me in the foyer.

"Do you think we should have a go at Liverpool today?"

"Absolutely not," I replied.

That's what they wanted you to do, have a go at them, and in doing so, leave space they could exploit. Do you know when someone has that mischievous look on their face? Well, that was the look on the face of the boss. We'd only lost four times in fifteen games at the start of the season, we were playing with confidence and were unbeaten in six games so Pleaty really wanted to go for it at Anfield. I told him that opposing managers in the past had gone there with that kind of bravado and it had played right into Liverpool's hands. If you failed to deny them space then they would kill you.

Steve McManaman and Robbie Fowler were the danger men but our captain, Peter Atherton, did a fantastic man-marking job on Macca and we managed to keep Robbie fairly quiet.

It took me ten or fifteen minutes to settle. I spoke to Kenny afterwards – he was watching from the Main Stand – and he told me he thought I looked a little unsettled at the start. That was simply because I had no idea how to react. I really wanted to do something to show the Liverpool fans what it meant to be back at Anfield again, but I didn't want Sheffield Wednesday supporters thinking I didn't care about their club, my club now.

My mind was everywhere except on the match. The thing that helped me focus? That would be when I missed a great chance to open the scoring! Guy Whittingham showed me how it should be done a few minutes later when he scored the only goal of the game and my return to Anfield was a winning one. In fact, we should have had a penalty inside the last ten minutes when I was absolutely wiped out by Neil Ruddock. Maybe it's just as well the spot kick wasn't awarded because if they'd wanted me to take it – in front of the Kop – I would have run in the opposite direction.

I was sitting in the players' lounge after the game having a beer and contemplating what would have happened if I'd scored with that early chance. I imagine I would have celebrated in front of the Sheffield Wednesday fans – it was up the other end from the Kop – but I'm actually glad I didn't have to find out. We won the game 1-0 and that was enough for me.

Although Sheffield Wednesday flirted with relegation in my first season at Hillsborough we finished a very respectable seventh in my second season. The make-up of the dressing room was unlike any other club I've played at. A football team needs a lot of different characters but this squad was full of the same types of characters – almost to a man everybody was a good player, a hard worker and a nice guy. That all changed when Paolo Di Canio arrived from Celtic to join his fellow Italian Benito Carbone. Paolo was certainly a character!

On one occasion, we were playing a League Cup first leg tie at Grimsby in September 1997 – at half-time we were one-nil down. We went back into the changing room and Paolo just lost it. "This team we're playing is shit – we're playing shit – I'm done."

He took all of his gear off and went into the shower, with one final yell of 'I'M NOT PLAYING, I'M DONE' for good measure. But Peter Shreeves, our assistant coach, was a wily old fox. A real football man who knew his stuff. Always calm and collected, he went into the shower and talked Paolo down off the ledge. With a puff of the cheeks and a shrug of his Italian shoulders Di Canio put his gear back on and went back out for the second half. I doubt his mood got any better when we conceded a second goal seven minutes after the restart and went on to lose two-nil.

The following month the first team squad went to Wales on a golf break. The last pair out on the course were Paolo and Benito Carbone. The rest of us were sat on the balcony overlooking the eighteenth with all the members watching the Italians play the final hole. Benny was probably thirty or forty yards left of the green, pin high, but he skulled it thirty yards over the other side of the green, again pin high. He then got in his buggy and took the most direct route to his ball – by driving straight across the green! So many people watching on from the balcony, all with jaws wide open, and not a sound from any of us. You could have heard a pin drop. Things were never dull when Benny and Paolo were together…

My final appearance for Sheffield Wednesday – although I didn't know it at the time – was at Old Trafford at the beginning of November. It was also David Pleat's last game in charge. We were 4-0 down to Manchester United at half-time and I was brought on to shore things up in the second half. Well, I assume that was the plan and Pleaty wasn't expecting me to score five goals. We lost 6-1 and David was sacked two days later.

It wasn't long before Ron Atkinson was appointed as Pleaty's replacement but, having just turned 36, I wasn't in Big Ron's plans and was sent out on loan to West Bromwich Albion. I played nine times in the First Division but returned to Hillsborough early because of injury, thus allowing me to spend the afternoon in the pub with Aston Villa's Stan Staunton – who was also sidelined – on the penultimate weekend of the season.

I knew I was coming to the tail end of my playing career but I was fine with that. I'd pretty much accepted after leaving Liverpool that I wouldn't play at that level again so as far as I was concerned the extra three years, two of which were spent back in the Premier League, were a bonus. But I was still very fit and still convinced I could do a job for someone so when an offer came in from Conference outfit Doncaster Rovers during the summer of 1998 I couldn't resist one last shot at playing.

Contract negotiations consisted of me sitting in the home dugout at Belle Vue with the chairman, John Ryan, and it took all of ten seconds.

"How much are you looking for?"

"About five hundred pounds per week?"

"And how about a signing-on fee, is £10,000 reasonable?"

"Yep, that's good for me."

"Well then, welcome to Doncaster Rovers."

A little different to how contract negotiations are done these days, I would imagine.

I was lucky enough to win the FA Cup three times – in 1986, 1989 and 1992 – but playing for Doncaster Rovers in the first round in November 1998 and winning 1-0 at Southend United was as enjoyable as any other match I ever played in the competition. It meant as much to me as any of those three triumphs – just in a different way. That game was like a cup final to the Doncaster players and supporters. We were a non-league team away from home against a league side. At Liverpool, we used to sit before games and watch the non-league sides playing the big teams, now I was getting to experience what it was like to be part of that.

At the end of the game at Southend, the Doncaster fans ran on to the field to celebrate and it brought back memories for me of all the other cup final triumphs I'd been involved in. Was it the final? No. But for us, a non-league club, it was the next best thing. To experience what that win meant, not just to my teammates on the field but to the fans on the terraces as well, for me that's what football is all about. We all have our levels of success that we're judged by, and there aren't many players who can reach the levels of success that I was lucky to achieve, but for us, winning that day at Southend was the equivalent of reaching the FA Cup final. And I absolutely loved it.

When people asked me why I joined a team in the Conference I told them it was because I just loved playing football. Whether it was Dover away or whoever, when I went out on that pitch I wanted to do well for Doncaster but I also wanted to show people that I still had that professional pride as well as still having something to offer the game of football. Getting enjoyment from the game is just as important, irrespective of the level played at.

I wasn't at Doncaster for long – I made my debut in September 1998 in a two-nil defeat at Hayes in front of 733 hardy spectators and played my last match in a goalless draw at Stevenage in March 1999 – but I enjoyed every single minute of life in the non-leagues. Yes, it was back to basics – we trained in the grounds of the local deaf school on fields that were more akin to growing potatoes on – but we did things the right way. We had lunch together but instead of everyone going their separate ways afterwards we continued to do things as a squad – including playing indoor carpet bowls in the afternoon. It helped having Ian Snodin as boss, his brother Glynn as his assistant and my former Sheffield Wednesday colleague John Sheridan as a teammate. We might not have had the best players in the world but their attitude was excellent and the respect they gave me was very satisfying.

In March 1999, just before my last home game for Doncaster, the chairman presented me with a memento on the pitch. I may have been at the club for less than a year but that gift meant a lot because it showed me that they appreciated everything I'd done.

I guess your CV measures success but actually being a professional footballer – at any level – is an achievement because it's what millions of kids all over the world want to do. That's all I wanted to do when I was growing up. I didn't think I would play for Ayr United, let alone Liverpool, and win trophies and play for my country. But I also loved playing in the Conference and seeing what it meant to my teammates when we got a good result. It's not until you play at that level that you get to appreciate life at both ends of the spectrum.

Unfortunately, there's so much money in the game these days that players who do well simply retire rather than drop down the divisions. But I think they are missing out. It's a way of giving back. And those nine months at Doncaster Rovers certainly gave me a tremendous amount of self-fulfilment. But all good things eventually come to an end.

One day, completely out of the blue, I received an unexpected offer to move to the United States and coach the Boston Bulldogs. It was an opportunity I couldn't possibly turn down. A chance to start a brand new chapter in my life.

20

Reborn In The USA

*'I phoned Kenny Dalglish to tell him that me and the
family were moving to Boston. 'Why would you want to
live in Lincolnshire?' he replied'*

April 15. It just had to be that date, didn't it? Exactly ten years
to the day since Hillsborough and I was sitting in the departure lounge at Heathrow Airport waiting to board a flight to
America. Sitting there, wishing. Wishing I could have been at
the memorial service at Anfield that afternoon. But I was also
thankful. Thankful that me and my family were getting the
chance to start a new life, an opportunity denied to the families
of every single one of the 96 victims. They say time is a great
healer. That may be true in some cases, but the scars from that
day will always remain.

It's funny the way things work in football. Instead of leaving
Liverpool to join Notts County in January 1995, I could just
as easily have ended up as player-manager at Swindon Town
instead. They had also interviewed Steve McMahon and
wanted to invite us both to their game against Luton Town on

the Saturday. So, Macca and me would be sitting together in the directors' box when only one of us could get the job. Talk about uncomfortable. He and I got on great but it would have been embarrassing for both of us. I told them it wasn't a good idea and declined their offer to attend the match. Macca went to the game and got the job. If those in charge at Swindon honestly thought there was nothing wrong with the two of us sitting together then what else might they have been thinking? Probably best that I didn't find out.

The move to the States originated in January 1999 when I was playing for Doncaster Rovers. Nothing was really happening for me in England. I was coming to the end of my playing career and there seemed to be a lack of coaching opportunities. What would happen when I eventually hung up my boots – where would the income come from? Wait and hope or move and work – I had the backing from the family so the decision was a relatively easy one.

My American journey, which would eventually lead to a ten-year coaching career in Major League Soccer, began in the less-than-glamorous surroundings of Victory Field in Framingham, Massachusetts, home of the Boston Bulldogs. It was covered in snow when I first set eyes upon it during a tour of the 'facilities' the month before moving to the States. Maybe that was a blessing in disguise because if I'd seen how poor the playing surface actually was, I might have had second thoughts about taking the job without getting certain guarantees.

Within three months of joining the Bulldogs as their player/ assistant coach, I suddenly found myself in charge when John Kerr left the club in July 1999 to become head coach at Harvard University.

Money was pretty tight at Boston Bulldogs, a semi-profession-
al outfit playing in the second tier in America. If our return
flight after a game was very early the following morning then
we'd save money and not book a hotel. Instead, we used to go
for a night out, have a few beers and stay out late then get the
bus to the airport in the middle of the night. I remember one
occasion when I told the boys the bus would be leaving at two
thirty in the morning.

A rather early breakfast was supplied by a 24-hour Waffle
House restaurant en route to the airport. When we were
finished eating we told the waitresses on duty to sit down and
put their feet up – some of our lads went behind the counter
and the others started washing dishes, all of them enjoying a
sing-song while doing so. We saved the club money, the boys
got an impromptu night out, the Waffle House staff got half an
hour off and, most importantly, we all had a good time.

After a two game spell in charge of New England Revolution
at the end of 1999, when I filled in briefly after head coach
Walter Zenga was relieved of his duties, I returned to coach
the Bulldogs at the start of the following year. But our financial
predicament had worsened and we ended up playing in the D-3
Pro-League, the third tier of football in America.

We managed to win the league in 2001, and I was named
Manager of the Year, but then I was told we were going to have
to drop down ANOTHER division to the Premier Development League – the fourth tier of football in America which may
as well have been the 156th tier for all the attention paid to it.

It felt like the end of the world.

The American Dream was turning into an American nightmare. I sat on the patio in my neighbour Liam's back garden

one night wondering if I would have to move back to the UK. Up until that point it had always been about me and what was best for my career.

Now, for the first time, I had to take into account what was best for Eleanor, Michael and Katy as well.

When we were first considering the offer to come over to the States in 1999, Eleanor suggested we could go over for 'a year or two' and if it didn't work out then we could always come back. But this wasn't the way I wanted it to end. Not like this.

I was never a quitter during my playing days and I wasn't about to start now. A community event was arranged in December 2001 by the Bulldogs and it was supported by local businesses, including New England Revolution, due to a relationship that was in place between the two clubs which saw fringe players from the Revs come to us on loan.

A few weeks after the community event, I received a telephone call out of the blue from New England Revolution General Manager Todd Smith. I'd spent a fair bit of time chatting to Todd about football at the event but didn't think it was my place to ask if there were any opportunities for me at the Revs. Turns out I didn't have to. He wanted me to become assistant coach to Fernando Clavijo. It was an opportunity I just couldn't turn down and meant our life as a family in the States could continue on what I thought would be a more solid foundation.

Two wins in seven games at the start of the 2002 MLS season was not good enough for Revs owners Robert and Jonathan Kraft and it soon became an even bigger career opportunity than I anticipated. Clavijo was sacked in May after a 5-2 loss at Colorado Rapids and I was appointed head coach on an interim basis until the end of that season.

If Fernando was fired after two wins in seven matches how do you think I felt when I went on to lose ten of my first fifteen games in temporary charge?! After the loss at home to Chicago Fire in August, our record was 7-14-1 and with my P-1 working visa expiring at the end of the year I knew if we didn't reach the play-offs then the chances of me continuing with the Revs, and remaining in the country, were slim to none. Time for another trip to the patio in my neighbour Liam's back garden for some thought-gathering…

I knew we had a decent set of players but they just didn't believe in themselves. That was the biggest problem. It was our job – me, my assistant Matt Driver and goalkeeping coach John Murphy – to shift the focus of the players from losing to actually convincing them that we should be winning games. Two wins in the space of five days at the end of August – at Chicago and at home to Colorado – was the catalyst for an upturn in our fortunes. It seemed as though the penny had finally dropped. The players were starting to believe all the good things and all the positives we had been telling them. Those two victories were the turning point, not only for the Revs that season but also for the Nicol family as well.

It's kind of apt that the two teams we beat in the regular season to kickstart our campaign – Chicago and Colorado – were also the two teams we beat in post-season to secure our place in the MLS Cup final, ironically at Gillette Stadium. But the game against LA Galaxy was one of the worst finals I've ever been in involved in, either as a player or a coach. The pitch was as dry as a bone, the windy conditions were a nightmare for both sets of players and it was an awful spectacle for the record crowd of 63,000 at the game.

Galaxy striker Carlos Ruiz scored the golden goal in extra-time with probably the only real chance of the game, beating our offside trap and finishing the one-on-one opportunity past goalkeeper Adin Brown with just seven minutes remaining. As disappointing as it was to lose, just to be in the final was an achievement given where we'd been earlier in the season. The transformation of a squad of players completely lacking confidence and guidance to one that refused to give up and came so close to a fairytale ending was remarkable.

From the depths of despair in August – and the possibility of having to return to the UK – to a gala dinner in November where I was named MLS Manager of the Year, it was some turnaround in such a short space of time. Oh, and I lost the 'interim' tag when I signed a two-year contract and became head coach of New England Revolution on a permanent basis. After so much uncertainty, the Nicol family finally had some much-needed stability. And the next time I found myself sitting on the patio in my neighbour Liam's back garden I wouldn't have to worry about moving back to England!

It's funny the way things can turn around in a short space of time. We were now able to buy a house, and we chose one in Hopkinton, Massachusetts, pretty close to the property we'd been renting. Michael and Katy were settled at school and had made new friends so we didn't want to uproot them again. And I felt good about myself once more.

That feeling when I got the Revs job on a permanent basis was one of relief, similar to when I signed for Sheffield Wednesday – I knew I was capable of doing a job at a decent level again but I just needed someone to believe in me. Home life was good, work was good and the family was settled. Now all

I needed to do was build on what we'd achieved at the Revs during my interim period in charge.

To get players for MLS, we sometimes had to go to places where nobody else goes. The big teams have global scouting networks but we had to be creative. One day an agent told me about a tournament in Niger, Western Africa which consisted of part-time, international professional players.

Unfortunately, our flight from New York was delayed and on arrival we were told that the hotel had given our rooms to someone else. Despite that, the agent invited us to have dinner with the Niger national team who were staying there. There was meat, vegetables and potatoes. The meat looked suspect, I wasn't sure about the vegetables but I figured that to make potatoes you have to boil them and that would get rid of any bacteria. So that's all we had to eat. A giant helping of potatoes was our only meal after a fifteen-hour flight. Next we had to find a bed for the night.

Driving around after midnight with a taxi driver who thought he was Jackie Stewart was somewhat traumatic, but not quite as traumatic as the place we ended up staying at. Me and my assistant at the time, Steve Myles, had to share a room with what seemed like a million bugs crawling and jumping all over the place. We slept in the same double bed – both of us with our trousers tucked into our socks because of the bugs and the covers as far up our bodies as possible without suffocating us.

The first set of games in the tournament took place the following day. There must have been at least 100 scouts from all over the world watching the games – so much for going where no-one else goes! After spotting a centre-back who we thought could help us, we arranged a flight back home the next day.

We drank 20 bottles of beer each that night to help us sleep through the nightmare of the hotel room. The agent appeared the next day and took us to the so-called best hotel in Niger for lunch. It was a buffet with a host of local delicacies. Guess what we had to eat? Spuds. To top it all off, we later offered $200,000 for the big centre-back but the owner of his team wasn't interested at that price. Maybe if we had thrown in 40 bottles of beer, endless potatoes and a two-night stay in a luxury hotel in Niger we may have done a deal!

Two of my most important signings were made at the beginning of 2004. I took 20-year-old Clint Dempsey with the eighth pick of the MLS SuperDraft and added 51-year-old ex-Arsenal striker Paul Mariner as my assistant on a free transfer from Harvard University, where he'd been coaching. I'd been told that Clint had a bit of an attitude problem. He did have an attitude, there's no question about that, but it was an attitude I liked. He was clearly a winner. If things weren't done right, he'd let others know. He was just the type of kid I was looking for.

We'd just finished a pre-season training session on the island of São Miguel in the Azores in March, with Clint once again a standout, when I suggested to Paul that we alter the system 'to get this kid Dempsey into the team.' Clint had just turned 21 but it was clear from the moment he joined us that he was an exceptional talent. He went on to start 23 of 24 matches that season, scored seven goals and was named 2004 MLS Rookie of the Year. It came as no surprise to me whatsoever when Clint went on to achieve bigger and better things in his career.

Taking New England Revolution to four MLS Cup finals is something I look back on with great pride. I look back on losing four MLS Cup finals with great disappointment. As well as 2002, 2005 was also a scrappy affair where we once again lost to LA Galaxy in extra-time. The next two, in 2006 and 2007, were similar – losing to Houston Dynamo each time.

The final in 2006 was played in Frisco, Texas and we lost on penalties after a 1-1 draw. With just seven minutes of extra-time remaining, Taylor Twellman's goal broke the deadlock and looked to have won us our first MLS Cup. But 42 seconds later they equalised before going on to win 4-3 on spot kicks.

They suggested the players celebrated Taylor's goal too much but I totally disagree with that. Absolute nonsense. We lost concentration and that led to the loss of their goal. Brian Mullan tried to cross the ball into our penalty box. It was going well wide of the goal but came off the side of Avery John's face and landed on the head of the one guy in the league you didn't want it to – Brian Ching. Even then, Brian still had to beat Matt Reis, the best goalkeeper in the league. But he did so by putting his header in the only place that Matt wouldn't get to.

Those series of events have absolutely nothing to do with our celebrations after Taylor's goal. The assumption that my players lost concentration still annoys me to this day. Sometimes the soccer gods are simply not with you.

A year later, in 2007, the soccer gods were once again looking elsewhere. This final defeat hurt the most and the loss stuck in my throat more than any other.

We were the dominant side for 75 of the 90 minutes, but Houston took advantage twice when it mattered most. Twellman's goal after twenty minutes put us in the driving seat and it was a lead we held, and were very comfortable with, until the hour mark.

Their equaliser was, at best, fortunate. Joseph Ngwenya completely whiffed at his first shot before scoring at the second attempt, which was only possible because he'd made such a mess of the initial attempt. Admittedly their second goal with a quarter of an hour to go was an incredible header by Dwayne De Rosario, but after that fifteen-minute period we took control of the game again. Our luck was summed up a minute from time when Pat Onstad's leg somehow kept out a shot from Jeff Larentowicz despite the Houston goalkeeper knowing very little about the initial effort.

When the final whistle went I've never felt so disheartened in all my life. But a manager's job doesn't allow for self-pity so the first thing I had to do was console my squad. The players I felt for the most were the men who had been with me at the Revs since the very beginning – my skipper that day, Steve Ralston, as well as Jay Heaps and Taylor Twellman. Also guys like Matt Reis, Shalrie Joseph, Jeff Larentowicz and Pat Noonan who might not have been there at the start but they helped make that core group very special. I was also very lucky to have excellent captains during my time in charge at New England. Joey Franchino was a star and didn't deserve to be on the losing side in the first three MLS Cup finals, while Steve Ralston and Jay Heaps, mentioned above, were two of my greatest allies throughout my tenure with New England Revolution. They were the guys I went to when there was a problem on the field. They were also the men I trusted to help resolve issues off the field. I would have loved to win just one MLS Cup for them in particular.

When I got back home the day after the final in 2007 there was a phone call I had to make – to Robert and Jonathan Kraft.

It was practically the same call I'd made the day after the final in 2005 and also in 2006.

I didn't have to phone them, I just wanted to call. To explain, even though no explanation was necessary and they weren't expecting one. And to apologise, even though no apology was necessary and they weren't expecting one. Of course they were supportive, but that call in 2007 was the hardest one of all given what had happened at RFK Stadium in Washington. I'm not ashamed to admit there were tears in my eyes during that conversation. That was tough. But not as tough as finding out that Robert Kraft had organised a parade through Boston for the team, thinking we were going to win the MLS Cup.

You can talk about success, you can talk about the romantic nature of the game, and you can talk about being so close to glory but Robert Kraft is all about winning. My only regret with the Revs was that I didn't win the one thing he wanted – the MLS Cup. Four times we nearly won it. But four times we failed at the final hurdle. That still hurts.

I'm proud of my record at the Revs – 299 games, 110 wins, 108 draws, 81 losses – but even if I was to get the chance to coach those last two years again – 2010 and 2011 – I reckon I'd still have found it difficult to ensure a different outcome.

When you're a head coach there's never a minute of the day when you're not thinking about your team. But when things aren't going well any problems are just accentuated. I didn't tell the players anything different in those final two years compared with my first eight years in charge – we just didn't have enough guys on the field who were able to follow orders, and that's a scary position for a coach to be in.

We lacked quality in those last two seasons. I failed to fix the issue and that's why, ultimately, I lost my job.

It's a horrible feeling, that of being helpless. You can do the right things and say the right things but if the majority of players on a matchday don't follow instructions properly then even the most-rousing pre-match or half-time speech is a waste of time. In sport, that helpless feeling is usually reserved for those responsible for others. When it's just yourself – as a player – then it's a lot easier to resolve an issue but when you're responsible for a whole squad, and things start to go wrong, it's much harder. You can't suddenly turn things around just by flicking a switch. I felt like I was in a hopeless situation and I wanted to bang my head against a brick wall on many occasions. I did my best to separate my situation at work from my life at home and tried not to take it back to the house with me, but only Eleanor will tell you if I managed to do that.

We had some horrendous injuries during my last few years in charge but I don't want that being used as an excuse. We just weren't very good. That's the truth. Due to our previous success – reaching at least the Conference final every year between 2002 and 2007 – we didn't receive that much allocation money and our draft picks weren't that high, but the biggest problem was the foreign players I brought in were a bust.

I generally went for more experienced guys because the players we had at the time needed a bit of guidance. When you deal in foreign markets hoping to pick up experienced players there's always a question mark about their fitness – why is a player with what looks like a tremendous CV still available – but, in truth, that was the only problem with those guys. In the end, that was my downfall.

It would be easy to try and deflect blame but it's important that I hold my hands up and admit I got it wrong. I was given permission by the Krafts to spend $1million on a foreign player – I even held talks with Luis Figo and Gilberto Silva among others – but I never did find the right one for our club and I wasn't going to just sign someone for the sake of it. Again, maybe that was also a mistake on my part.

2010 was the first season under my tenure that we had failed to at least reach the play-offs so I knew the following year had to be better. During my first eight years at the Revs we drafted really well, but I got very little from the last two drafts that I took part in. Not being able to improve the squad with quality picks, added to the poor foreign signings I made, meant we were always playing with bare bones.

Ultimately, when your team is leading 4-1 at half-time yet you're still not confident of victory then you know there's a problem. That's what happened to us in Philadelphia in September 2011.

I went in at the break, walked straight through the locker room into the coaches' area and shut the door behind me. I said to my assistants – Remy Roy and Steve Myles – that the game was far from over because I knew our defensive players had mistakes in them. The three of us had seen it before, at Real Salt Lake two months earlier when we led 2-1 and 3-2 yet still couldn't hold on for the win against ten men. We were actually lucky to get a 4-4 draw at Philly because we were hanging on at the end.

I was sitting in the coaches' room after the penultimate game of the MLS season on October 15 – having just witnessed our fifth defeat in a row – when there was a knock on the door.

Revs president Sunil Gulati entered and he asked if my heart was still in it. I didn't say yes. I didn't say no. I just told him I'd hate to go out like this because the team was poor. By that stage I was frazzled and on tablets to control my blood pressure. Five league wins all season meant we failed to make the play-offs but I refused to admit to myself that the end was nigh. My stress levels, however, told me otherwise.

When the call came to go and see Robert and Jonathan I knew what it was about. As I walked in to Robert's office we shook hands, they asked me to take a seat and Robert started talking.

After twenty seconds or so I said, "look, we're big boys, I've had a great time here so you don't need to say anything."

From then, the tone changed. "We've loved what you've done here and we're very proud of you," said Robert, "but it's time to move on." I knew I had to move on and they knew I had to move on, but I don't think there's ever been a more amicable parting of ways. Our excellent relationship continues to this day.

I knew when I became an American citizen in 2009 that I was over here for good. The family is all nearby and we love our life Stateside. Of course, I would never rule out the possibility of coming back to Britain one day, and if the right opportunity came about to return to coaching on either side of the pond then I'd certainly listen to what was being offered, but I certainly don't spend any free time I have applying for jobs.

I love my life right now and I enjoy sitting in a television studio at ESPN getting paid to talk about football. It's certainly a lot less stressful than those last couple of years in charge of the Revs!

21

Heart As Big
As Liverpool

*'Playing for Liverpool Football Club shaped my life.
It made me the person I am today'*

It's one of the lines in the famous old song. 'Walk on, walk on, with hope in your heart…' Except this time, I'd almost given up hope. I was still giving the game my full attention because we had to discuss it on ESPN FC – the football show I now appear on each day in my job as an analyst.

Then Philippe Coutinho pulled a goal back. Then Mamadou Sakho pulled another goal back. Then Dejan Lovren scored the winner in stoppage time. Borussia Dortmund, favourites to win the Europa League, had been knocked out of the competition after another amazing comeback by Liverpool.

I should have known better. I should have known not to count my old club out. I played for them enough times to know all about the never-say-die ethos. Yet I still doubted them. 'Typical' said a colleague of mine watching the game with me at ESPN HQ in Bristol, Connecticut when Lovren scored the winner.

That man was Shaka Hislop. The same Shaka Hislop who was just minutes away from winning the FA Cup with West Ham United in 2006, until Steven Gerrard equalised right at the death in Cardiff to send the final to extra time. Yet another amazing comeback by Liverpool.

I should have known better back in 2005 as well. The Champions League final – Liverpool against AC Milan – was the first game I covered for ESPN. At half-time, with the Reds losing 3-0 in Istanbul, I jokingly asked one of the producers in the studio if I could go home there and then so as not to endure any more anguish in the second half.

Nobody expected a comeback, not even the most fervent Liverpool fan, but when Steven Gerrard pulled one back I started to think we had a chance. Then the second goal went in. 'Maybe we can actually do this.' Then we were awarded a penalty. Surely not? Xabi Alonso's spot kick was saved. Typical. But he was first to the rebound, 3-3! Six minutes of absolute mayhem on the pitch. Pandemonium in the studio. Incredible.

When Andriy Shevchenko had that chance late on, it felt like I was watching in slow motion. He seemed certain to score but Jerzy Dudek somehow kept it out. That was the first time I thought it could be our day.

Football may be about ability, guts and soul, but sometimes you need a bit of luck as well. Being a football fan is about never giving up on your team, irrespective of what happens, but I'd given up hope against AC Milan, West Ham United and against Borussia Dortmund. I'll never learn. It's no fluke by the way, all those comebacks. There's a never-say-die attitude that runs through Liverpool Football Club from top to bottom and, of course, a great team spirit helps as well…

In early 2006, Kenny was helping to organise a repeat of the 1986 FA Cup final – Liverpool against Everton – with all the proceeds from the game at the beginning of May going to the Marina Dalglish Appeal. He called me to tell me about the plans and as soon as I got off the phone with him I booked my flight over from Boston. The Revs had a home game against Chicago Fire on the same day as I was due to fly – April 30 – but I was able to travel overnight and arrive in Manchester on the morning of the game at Anfield. Nothing would have prevented me from being there.

As soon as the Liverpool players walked into that home dressing room at Anfield, we automatically went to the same spot we used to sit. It was uncanny. More than ten years had passed since I was last in there but nothing had really changed, apart from the waist sizes of a few of us! It was like going back in time with all the banter and piss-taking. Then we got out on to the field and did the exact same stuff we used to do. And the Everton boys said the exact same thing happened to them. We'd turned back the clock and everything had fallen straight back into place.

After the game – which Liverpool won 1-0 thanks to a goal by John Durnin in the 90th minute – I remember having a conversation with Jamie Carragher. I have no idea why the subject came up but we were wondering if the England players from 1966 privately hoped that, in their lifetime, they'd be the only Englishmen to win the World Cup. Keep the Old Boys on that pedestal, if you like, with their achievements unmatched for as long as they live. Would they really want the new breed replicating something only they had done? I'm sure the Boys of '66 would always give their backing publicly to the England players playing today at major tournaments – Jamie and me were just wondering if they would have the same opinion in private.

At Liverpool we were the complete opposite. We wanted those players who followed us at Anfield to carrying on winning and keep the club exactly where it was. No envy or jealousy at the money being earned these days and the lavish lifestyles being led. None of that. I think former Liverpool players simply want the team to be the best it can be both on and off the field and all the other stuff is immaterial. It's never been a selfish place, Anfield, and I hope it never will be.

When I left New England Revolution in 2011 the opportunity to continue working in television made total sense – a natural progression. My home in Hopkinton, Massachusetts was less than two hours from ESPN headquarters in Bristol, Connecticut and it was an easy commute. Sitting on a couch in front of a television camera is also a lot less stressful than being a head coach – and blood pressure tablets are not required!

Every pundit is different. I think I am both objective and subjective but most of all I am honest with myself. When it comes down to it I am not frightened to tell it like it is, no matter what it is. I try to provide an honest perspective from a player's point of view, a coach's point of view and a fan's point of view.

People say I'm biased towards Liverpool but I don't agree with that. Am I a Liverpool fan? Absolutely. Do I want them to do well? Absolutely. But when the team is not doing well I'll never shirk the issue. I'm speaking from the heart, especially when talking about all things Liverpool, and I'm always honest about things that happen at Anfield. It would be very easy to put on my red blinkers and say everything done at and done by

Liverpool is the best ever. But people quickly see through that kind of false cheerleading. When I was playing I did my job. When I was coaching I did my job. And now, as an analyst, I'm doing my job to the standard I think it should be done, and if some people don't like what I say, then tough.

It's more than twenty years since I last played for Liverpool Football Club. I played in great Liverpool teams and I played in sub-par Liverpool teams, and by that I mean those that didn't live up to the expectations of previous Liverpool teams. I know what's required so when I see it, I say it. Some might not like it, but I'd like to think I know what I'm talking about. I know the standards that were set at Liverpool before I went there and during my time there, so if I don't see those standards being met now then I'm not frightened to say something.

I have no problem with some of the modern analysts on TV – guys like Gary Neville or Jamie Carragher – educating viewers as to why things happen. I understand there are younger fans coming through who maybe don't relate to me because I played in the Eighties so I think it's important they can relate to guys they've seen playing like Gary or Jamie, and if the analysts are helping to educate at the same time then great. I'm just not a fan of this over-analytical stuff. When we lose the ball what should we do? Well, if you're in a position to close it down then that's what you should do. It's not anything new so please don't tell me this is something that nobody has ever done before.

Some people try and reinvent the wheel when it comes to analysis. Football has always been the same. Get a good shape. Close the ball down. Win it back quickly. Move it quickly. Take care of it.

These are things that haven't changed in a century.

If there's another thing that really annoys me in today's game it's this snobbery of having to pass the ball from the goalkeeper all the way through to the centre forward. Total football and trying to score the perfect goal. I can assure you that if any team ever tried to do that against a front two of Rush and Dalglish and a midfield of Nicol, McMahon, Whelan and Houghton then we simply wouldn't allow it to happen, and that's why we were so successful. Every player understood what he had to do. We used to love it when the opposition goalkeeper rolled it out to the full-back or the centre-half because that allowed us to squeeze the life out of our opponents. We were out of the blocks like Usain Bolt because if we didn't do that then Ronnie Moran would squeeze the life out of us when we got back to the dressing room. Football is a simple game. Shove your complicated tactics up your arse.

It sounds crazy but I watch more Liverpool games now, living in the States, than I did when I stayed in England. That's because every single match is shown live on American television. The popularity of the sport over here has exploded in recent years. But it wasn't always that way. When I first came over here in 1999 it was practically impossible to keep up-to-date with football back home. Not every household had access to the internet, so the only way to get the scores – unless you wanted to wait a week for someone to send you over a newspaper – was to spend a fortune on trans-Atlantic phone calls.

So, now that I'm able to watch them every week, how does present-day Liverpool compare with Liverpool back in my day? Well, the team that came so close to winning the Premier League in 2013-14 took me back to 1987-88 – it was like watching the team I played in. I don't think there's a game from that season that epitomised Liverpool Football Club more than the 5-1 thumping of Arsenal in February 2014.

Four-nil up against the Gunners at half-time – THAT'S how Liverpool should play at Anfield, squeezing the life out of the opposition, not giving them an extra second on the ball and just going for the throat. I remember watching the game on television and thinking to myself that's what the team I played for did as well. It was the way they went about their business. Number one, they worked hard and got after it straight from kick off. And when opportunities came they killed the opposition – totally merciless, and the crowd loved it. Then you add individual talent. John Barnes provided that for us in 1987-88 and Philippe Coutinho played the role of the modern day Barnesy in 2013-14. A joy to watch.

That 5-1 win against Arsenal was the first of eleven consecutive league victories for Brendan Rodgers' men – reminiscent of the eleven wins and a draw that led us to the league title in 1986.

When you're on a run like that it's not so much about tactics; it's about always having that hunger, that desire to win and with that comes momentum. When you're in the zone it makes no difference what any opposition team puts in front of you – whether they bunker in or they come at you – because when you get a taste of meat then you can't wait to go hunting. It's like an unstoppable force. You get on the field and you know you're not going to lose.

I'm sure that's how the Liverpool team in the second half of season 2013-14 felt as well. We were able to sustain that for four or five years in the Eighties simply because of our mental toughness. Unfortunately, somewhere down the line, the team of 2013-14 lost that towards the end of the campaign but what an effort they put in.

Mental toughness is losing the league on the final day of the season in 1989 yet still going out the following year and winning the title, despite having more deficiencies and not playing as well as the team of twelve months earlier. Football is about form, consistency, scoring goals and winning, but it's also about adversity and how to react properly when things aren't going well. We may have lost the league to Arsenal at Anfield but the best teams always react the right way. And that's what we did. That's why the best teams are the best teams. When they take one right in the bollocks they get straight back up and make sure they don't take it again.

Playing for Liverpool Football Club shaped my life. It made me the person I am today, it got me to America and it opened doors that otherwise would have remained shut. It also taught me about hard work, it taught me to be humble and it taught me to maximise my ability.

After leaving Anfield not everyone I played with shared those views. I tried to help some of the lads at Notts County, but it quickly became apparent not all of them had the best attitude. Certain players felt entitled. If things didn't go their way then it wasn't their fault. Not being able to accept blame or culpability was a big problem.

When I became a coach I told my players they were entitled to nothing, they had to earn everything by using their ability. It didn't matter to me if they might not have had the tools to reach the very top. As long as they realised their potential then I was happy.

Wind-ups, taking the piss and having a laugh are just as much a part of my life now at ESPN as they were at Liverpool back in the day. And I wouldn't change that for the world. If you can't have a bit of fun and enjoy yourself then what's the point? We don't have a choice when it comes to growing older but we most certainly do when it comes to growing up.

I had plenty of fun during my career but never lost my head, I always knew what was important. People took the piss out of me but you know what, I laughed along and I gave as good as I got.

I have some regrets but they never got me down for too long. Would I change anything? Yeah, of course I would. I'd have scored my penalty in Rome; got my head to the ball before Lawrie Sanchez at Wembley in 1988 and stopped Michael Thomas scoring in 1989. I'd have won a World Cup and an MLS final too. But does it bother me? Does it keep me awake at night? Does it matter? No.

I'm massively proud of what I achieved in the game. League titles, FA Cups, a European Cup, playing in every position on the field as a professional, representing my country, working with some true legends of the game – it's been great. But the buzz of winning only lasts so long. Lift the trophy, get your picture taken, have a few beers, a bus tour around the city if you're lucky then move on. That was the Liverpool Way. It was My Way too. Maybe that's the secret of success, not just in football but in life as well.

I'm happy where I am now. I'm lucky to have a wonderful family, good friends and people I enjoy working with. I love my job. Talking about football? It doesn't get much better than that. Apart from playing of course.

I'm the pundit now, I'm the fan. I'm not Chico, or Nico, in the dressing room enjoying the banter with Kenny and the lads, I'm in the studio giving my opinion or in the pub debating the game with a pint – and a packet or two of cheese and onion crisps, of course. Or I'm on Twitter, enjoying the company of fans around the world, reacting to the latest story. Things have certainly changed.

When I first kicked the ball through the Co-op window as a starry eyed young lad in Troon, I never imagined I'd be talking to you now as a former international footballer and US citizen. There will always be adventures in life, who knows what's coming next. Go with it. You might end up having fun and enjoying it, just like I have.

Epilogue

Tell Me It's True

'At the end of the storm, there's a golden sky...'

When the alarm went off at ten o'clock this morning I rolled over and picked my phone up from the bedside cabinet. I silenced the alarm then entered two words into Google – 'Hillsborough verdict' – and the first thing I saw was a picture of the families outside the court in Warrington. They were smiling. Seeing them smile made me smile. My day was off to the best possible start.

Today represents an end and a beginning. For all the families and what they've been through, that long fight for justice – far, far too long – their perseverance has finally paid off. For 27 years, to wake up and mainly think about one thing all day before going to bed and trying to sleep... For them now to finally have that weight lifted off their shoulders is absolutely fantastic. The families can start living a normal life now, the life they should have been leading in the first place.

It was the verdict I expected. That the 96 people who died following the tragedy at Hillsborough were unlawfully killed. That bullshit verdict of accidental death at the original inquest had finally been overturned.

It might have been the verdict I expected but until it was actually confirmed, until I was able to read it in black and white and until I was able to see those families with smiles on their faces outside the court, I took nothing for granted. It was impossible to take anything for granted after all those years of the police and the Government burying key evidence. But once it was taken out of their hands, and put in the hands of real people – the jurors – then in my mind there was never really going to be any other outcome. The evidence was so over-whelming – the fact the police and the Government even tried to put up a fight is utterly embarrassing.

The mistake that they made was picking on the wrong city. Liverpool and its people have two things that really stand out – they have passion and they have a heart the size of a lion, so when you're taking that on you better be ready for a fight. I think there's a vital life lesson to be learned here – your ordinary person on the street has to fight for what they believe is right because if you don't fight, if you just give up, then the rest of the world will look at you in a different way. The rest of the world was told that Liverpool fans and Liverpudlians were cowards, scoundrels and thugs. Liverpool fans and Liver-pudlians had to fight for 27 years to prove that wasn't the case. That's the message today – when you believe in something you better fight for it. And don't give in. Don't ever give in.

Everybody knows the truth now. That's the biggest thing I take from today. People have spoken to me about Hillsborough for years and years and when I talked to some of them I felt as though I had to stick up for Liverpudlians. I felt like we were in the minority. Minds were already made up because people had read, and believed, the lies in The S*n all those years ago.

Changing the opinion of somebody who has already made his or her mind up is very difficult. They read what they want to read. They hear what they want to hear. They believe what they want to believe. Now I don't have to say a word or stick up for anybody because it's there in black and white. It's there for all to see and it's fantastic because, forever and a day, nobody can point the finger at anybody apart from politicians and the police. Everybody knows the truth now. No more justification required.

I wasn't scheduled to work today but when the news broke that the jury had reached its verdict then I was asked to come in. I was quite emotional at first when appearing on ESPN's current affairs show Outside The Lines – talking about Hillsborough is always hard – but being able to explain the importance of today's verdict to a nationwide audience in America was extremely cathartic.

It's still easy to get angry at the cover-up, the deceit and the lies. And the anger came back earlier this evening when I watched ESPN and saw the re-airing of its wonderful Hillsborough documentary, directed by Daniel Gordon.

I saw it for the first time in New York in 2014 when I was invited to the premiere, and that's when I felt a mixture of emotions. I was extremely pleased with the content because for the first time the truth was going to be on show to a much wider audience. On the other hand, and as I explained to journalists in a question and answer session afterwards, I was also angry at the end of the film because the truth was on show for all to see but had not yet been accepted by the general public. That was so frustrating.

The documentary is still an extremely difficult watch. The lack of human decency displayed by the police authorities and the level of corruption is staggering. How can grown men stand there and lie? Can you tell me? As for fabricating evidence – wow. Why on earth would a police officer make allegations to a local news agency, which then led to The S*n reporting that fans were looting and picking the pockets of dead people at Hillsborough? Why on earth would you do that? I mean, really. Whether it's the coroner, the chief superintendent, the sergeants, the constables, you name it, they were all told to toe the party line. Fortunately not all of them did and some of the information that was passed on was instrumental in helping with the enquiry. It's unfair to tarnish the reputation of every policeman and policewoman involved in the disaster because the info provided by those who did the right thing and acted properly was invaluable. For too long, members of the self-preservation society got away with it. Not any more because the truth has finally been told.

Anger at everything that happened at Hillsborough – and in the days, weeks and months that followed – is completely understandable. But today should not be about anger. It's about the vindication of everybody from Liverpool involved in and affected by the tragedy. It's about finally getting the opportunity to restore the reputation of a city, and the people of a city, that was tarnished by cover-ups, deceit, lies and mistruths. And, most importantly, it's about truth and justice after all those years. It's also a great big *fuck you* to those who questioned why the families were still fighting for justice, those who had already made their minds up that Liverpool fans were responsible for what happened that day in Sheffield.

I was 27 years old when I played for Liverpool in that FA Cup semi-final at Hillsborough. I'm now 54. For exactly half my life those families have been campaigning for truth and justice. Just think about that for a second. Think about what they've been through. Think about all the times they've been kicked in the teeth. To lose somebody, and then to have it thrown in your face that it was their fault, think about how that would feel. Imagine a family member of yours had been in the Leppings Lane end of the ground that day and you were then told that their death was their own fault, how would you feel? Sadly, and tragically, there are 96 families who know exactly what that feels like.

The way the families have gone about their quest for justice, without ranting and raving and by keeping to the facts is absolutely incredible. They've acted and behaved with the utmost dignity. I don't know if I would have been as patient had my son Michael or daughter Katy been involved. The number of times those families suffered setbacks over the years but never waivered, never lost hope, surely it would have been easy to lose the plot but they didn't.

Liverpool Football Club and the rest of the city can take a lot of credit as well because I'm sure the support we gave to the families helped to make a difference and ensured they, at no point, felt alone. Knowing they weren't alone, I hope, was a big help to them.

Does today's verdict allow for closure? I'm not sure closure is the right word. The one thing the families wanted the world to know – their goal right from the very start – was that the death of their family members was not their fault, as had been claimed. That's certainly what I was always hoping for. That people would know that the deaths of loved ones was caused by poor policing and not by fans. Whether the stadium had flaws in it or not, if the police had done their job properly then it wouldn't have happened.

Prior to September 2012, and the publication of the Hillsborough Independent Panel's report, I must confess I never thought that the families would get justice. But with the help of people like Andy Burnham and Maria Eagle, who called for all documents relating to the disaster to be published, and Theresa May, who accepted the Independent Panel's report and ordered a new criminal enquiry into the tragedy, we've now got what we hoped for all along.

It's now midnight, fourteen hours since my alarm went off at ten o'clock this morning, and I'm on Twitter doing my best to respond to all the messages I've received today. I've also just seen the front page of the first edition of tomorrow's S*n.

Not one single mention of Hillsborough, of the appeal, of the verdict or of the families. To do such a thing is an absolute disgrace and yet another slap in the face to the city of Liverpool and its people. This was the perfect opportunity for the newspaper to say sorry properly, to apologise on behalf of a previous administration and to admit they were wrong. But the fact they haven't even bothered to mention it on the front page tells you that nothing has changed. It may be 27 years since the tragedy, but quite frankly it could be another 127 years and the people of Liverpool still won't buy that rag.

My abiding memory of today's events will be the families and friends singing You'll Never Walk Alone on the steps outside the courtroom in Warrington.

Too often during these last 27 years our anthem has been accompanied by tears, from the time a choral arrangement of the song was played at the first Hillsborough Memorial Service at Liverpool's Anglican Cathedral two weeks after the tragedy to the final Memorial Service at Anfield just eleven days ago. You don't know how happy it makes me feel to see smiles on faces again when that song is being sung.

Today's verdict means the whole world now knows what really happened at Hillsborough on Saturday April 15, 1989, and nobody can point the finger of blame at the Liverpool fans or families ever again. That's because, at long last, justice has prevailed.

One last tweet then time for bed.

Stephen Nicol @SteveNicol61 · Apr 26
I hope all lpool fans and families sleep well tonight for the first time in 27 yrs. They deserve it. We will remember them all for ever

↩   ♻ 86   ♥ 267   •••

Index